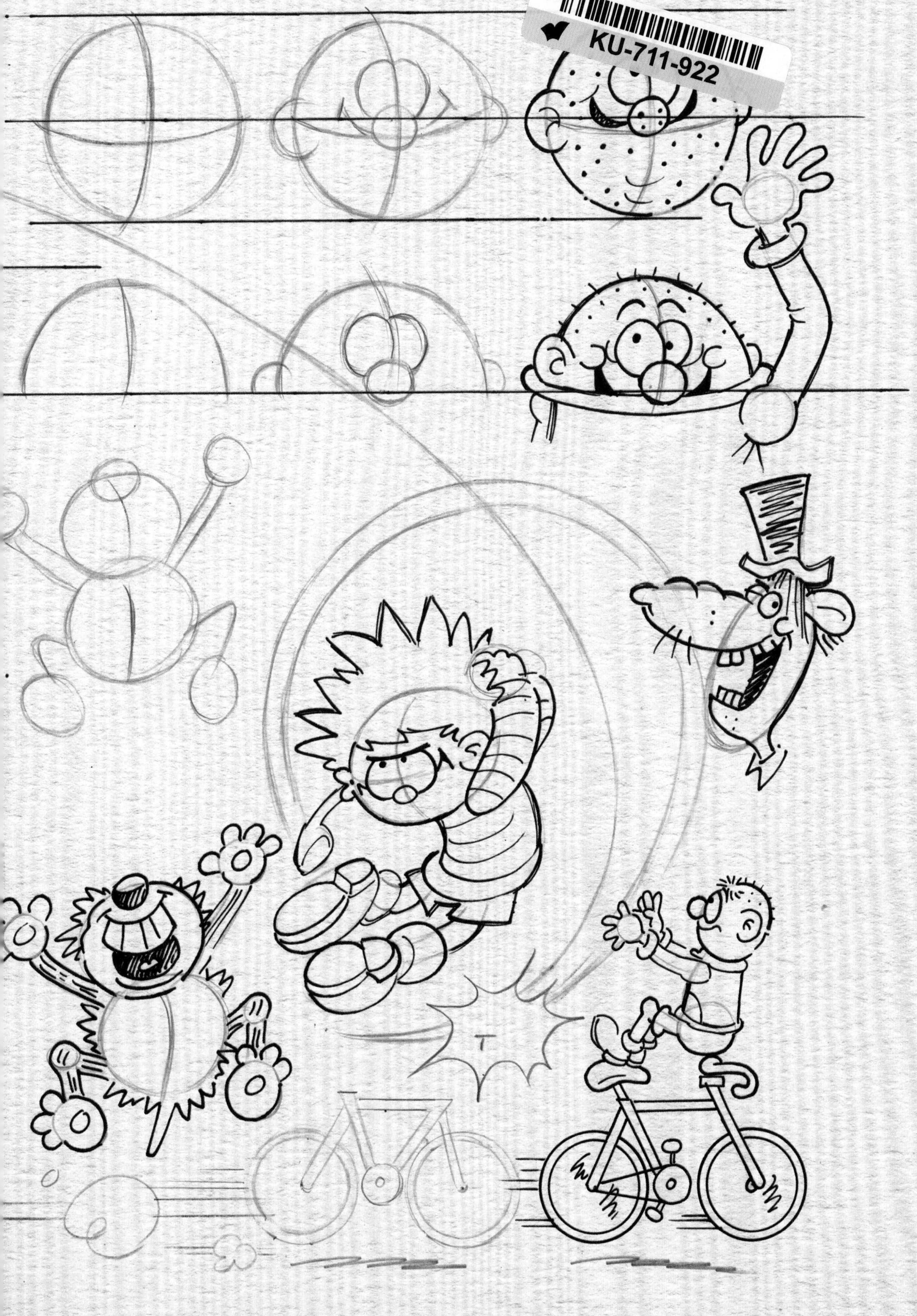

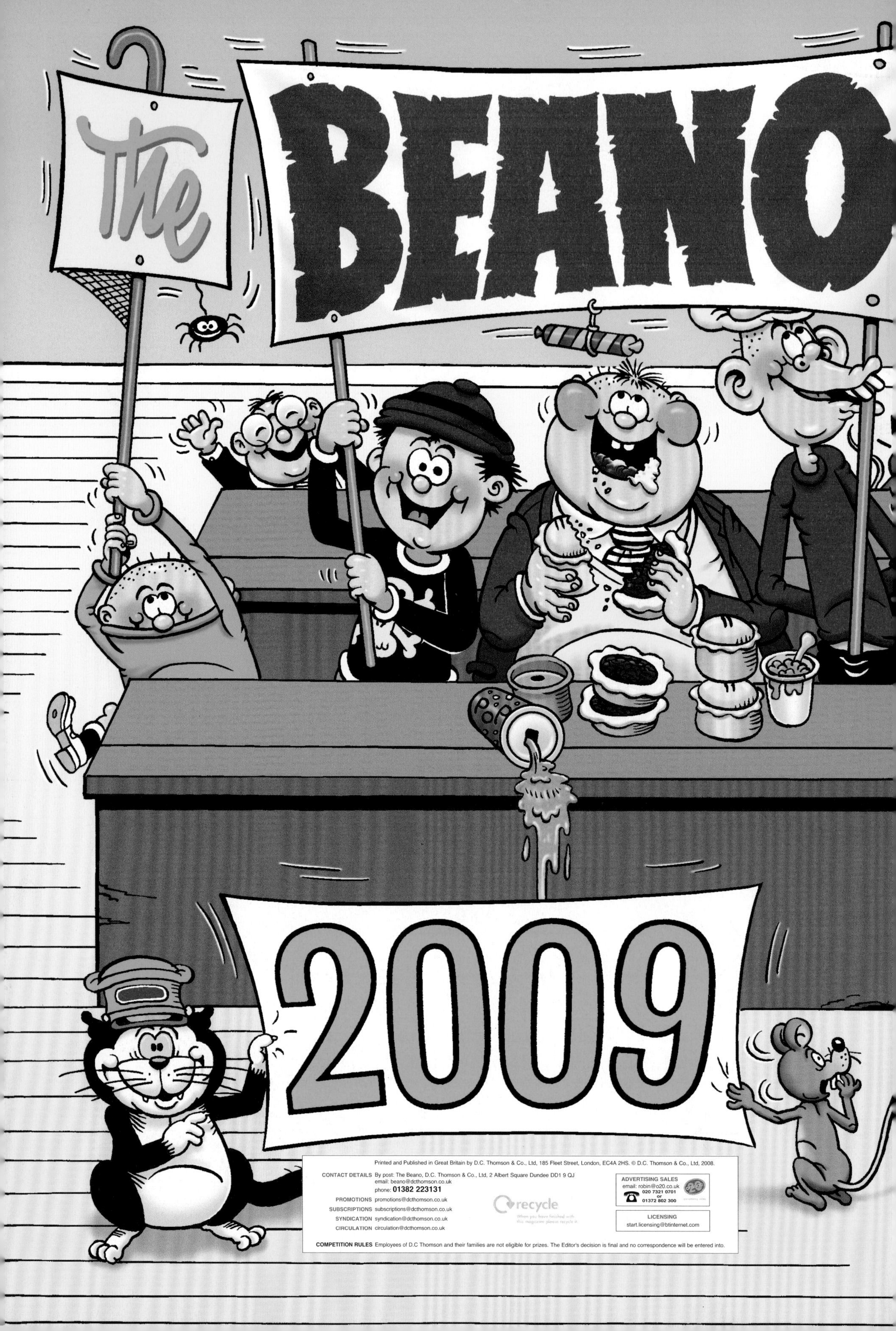
The
BEANO
2009
POP

Printed and Published in Great Britain by D.C. Thomson & Co., Ltd, 185 Fleet Street, London, EC4A 2HS.

CONTACT DETAILS By post: The Beano, D.C. Thomson & Co., Ltd, 2 Albert Square Dundee DD1 9 QJ
email: beano@dcthomson.co.uk
phone: **01382 223131**

PROMOTIONS promotions@dcthomson.co.uk

SUBSCRIPTIONS subscriptions@dcthomson.co.uk

SYNDICATION syndication@dcthomson.co.uk

CIRCULATION circulation@dcthomson.co.uk

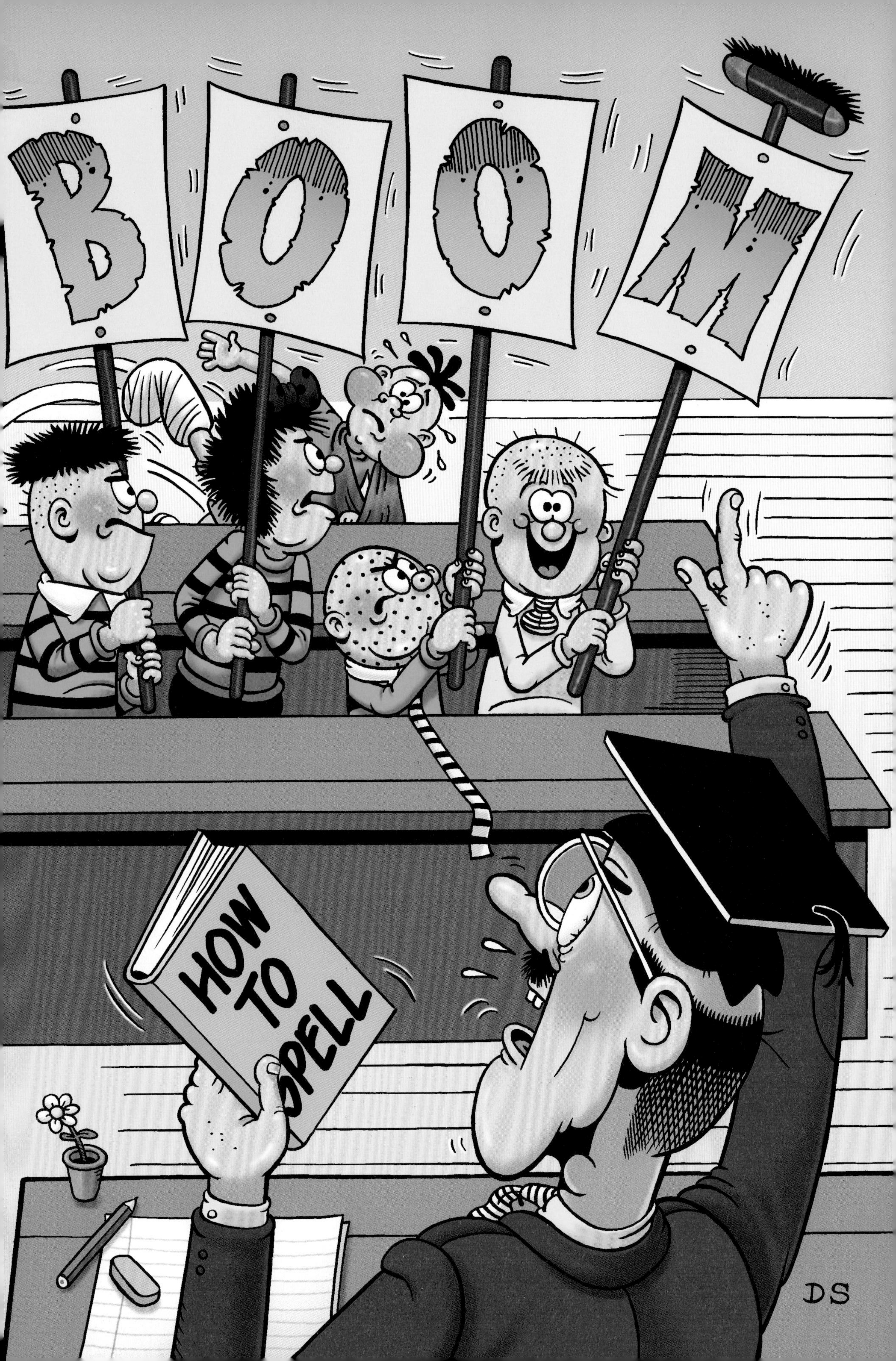
BOOM
HOW TO SPELL
DS

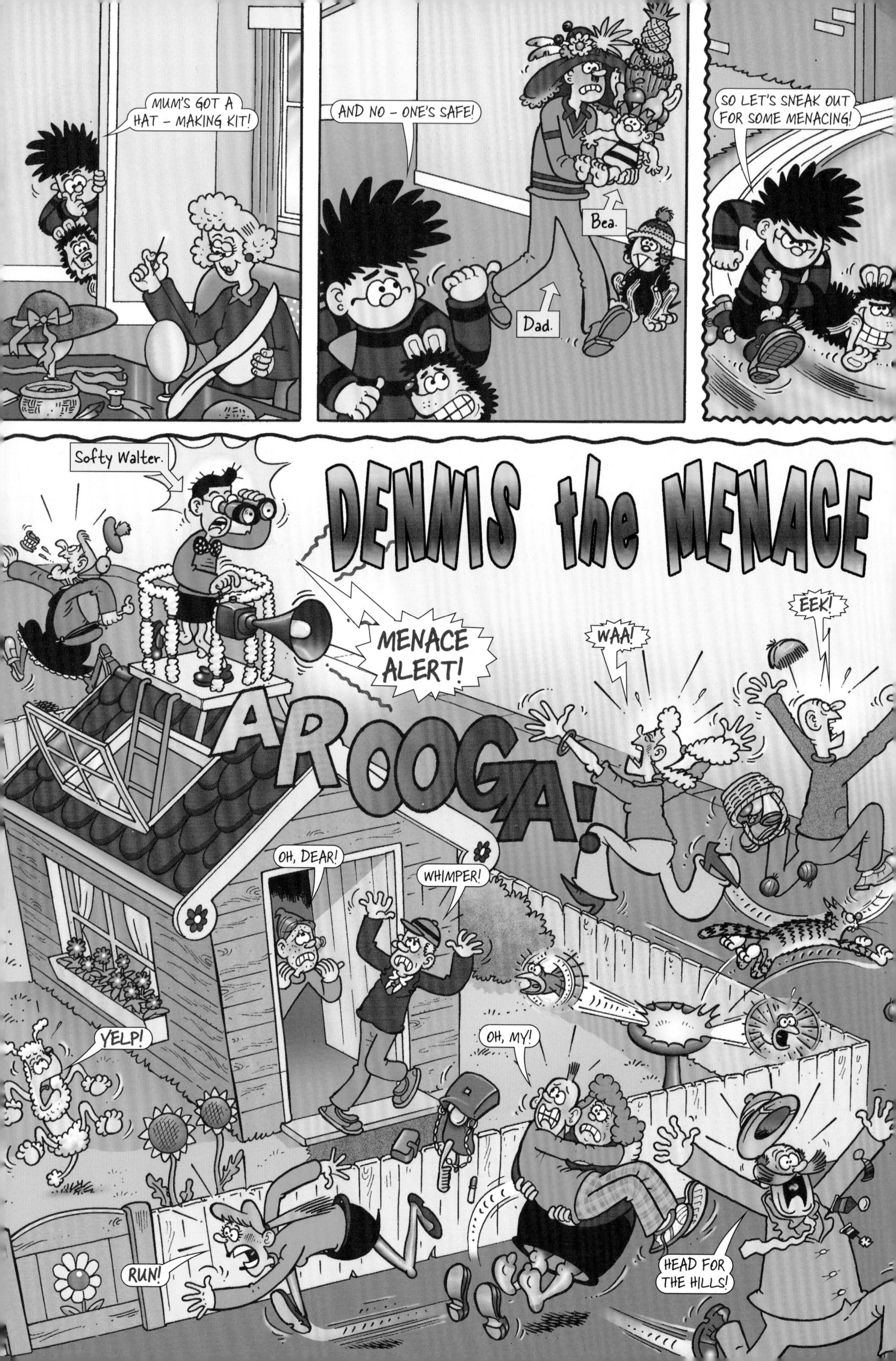
MUM'S GOT A HAT - MAKING KIT!
AND NO - ONE'S SAFE!
Bea.
Dad.
SO LET'S SNEAK OUT FOR SOME MENACING!
Softy Walter.
DENNIS the MENACE
MENACE ALERT!
AROOGA!
WAA!
EEK!
OH, DEAR!
WHIMPER!
YELP!
OH, MY!
RUN!
HEAD FOR THE HILLS!

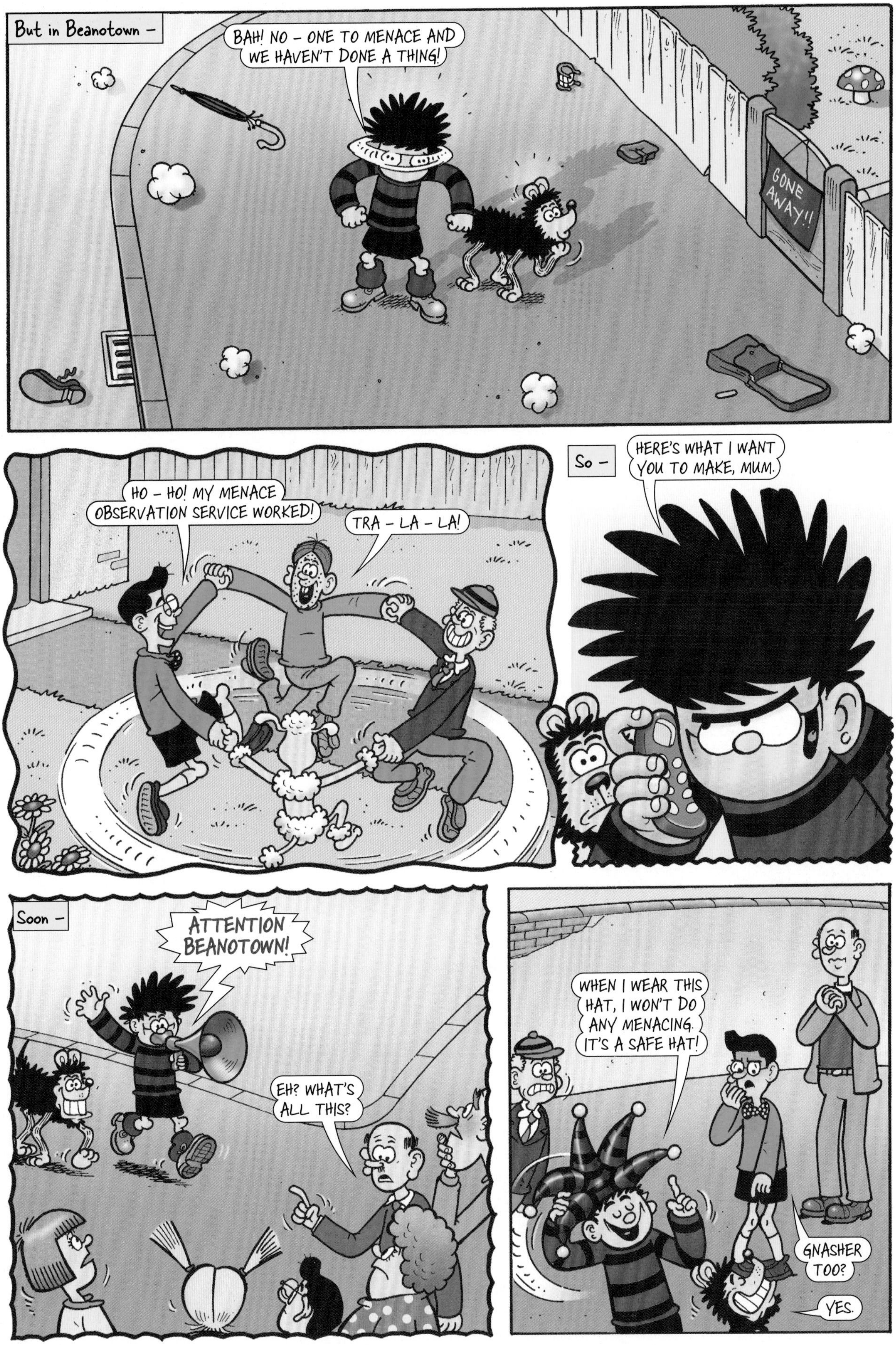

But in Beanotown –
BAH! NO – ONE TO MENACE AND WE HAVEN'T DONE A THING!
GONE AWAY!!
HO – HO! MY MENACE OBSERVATION SERVICE WORKED!
TRA – LA – LA!
So –
HERE'S WHAT I WANT YOU TO MAKE, MUM.
Soon –
ATTENTION BEANOTOWN!
EH? WHAT'S ALL THIS?
WHEN I WEAR THIS HAT, I WON'T DO ANY MENACING. IT'S A SAFE HAT!
GNASHER TOO?
YES.

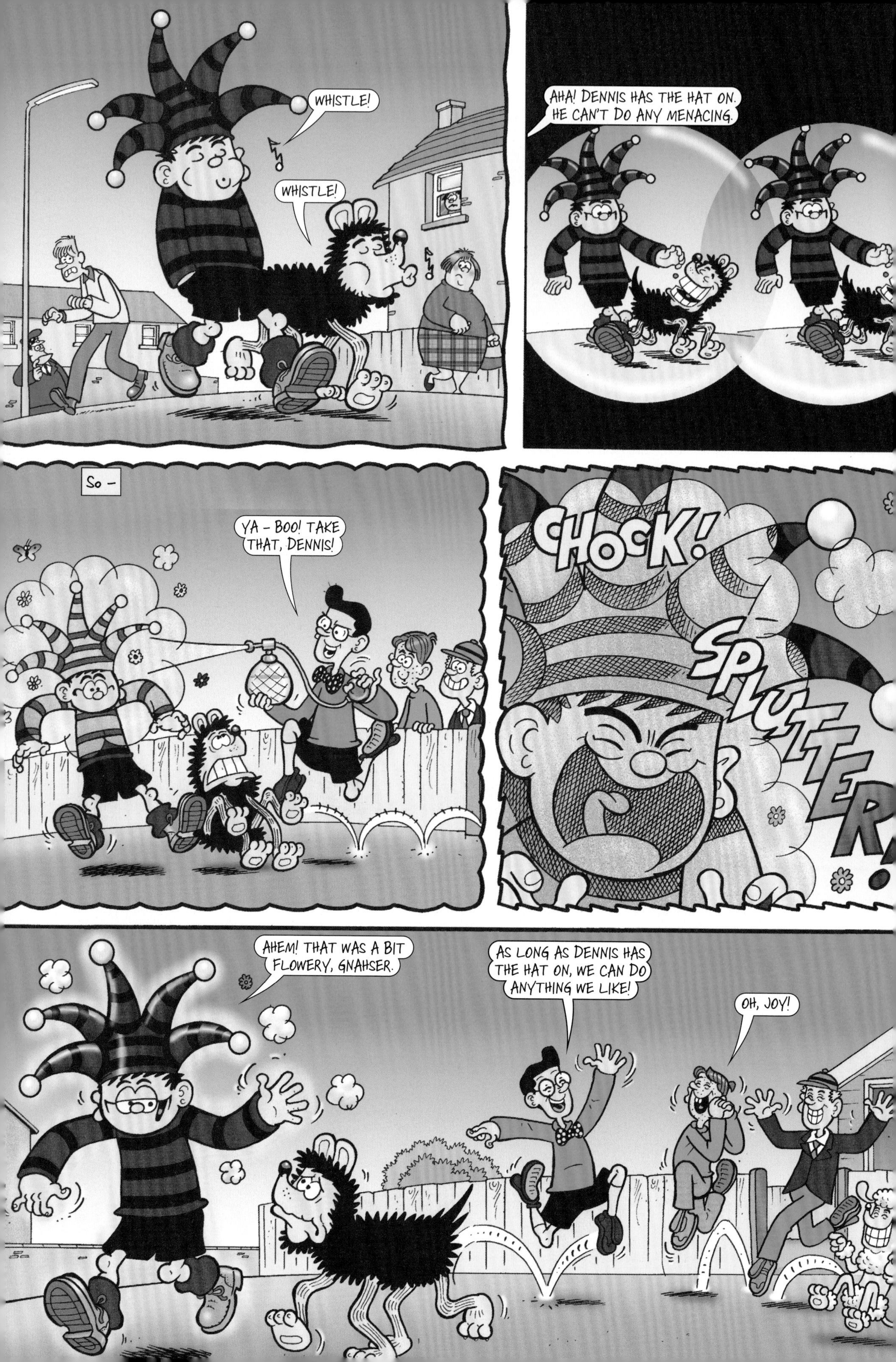
WHISTLE!
WHISTLE!
AHA! DENNIS HAS THE HAT ON. HE CAN'T DO ANY MENACING.
So –
YA – BOO! TAKE THAT, DENNIS!
CHOCK!
SPLUTTER!
AHEM! THAT WAS A BIT FLOWERY, GNAHSER.
AS LONG AS DENNIS HAS THE HAT ON, WE CAN DO ANYTHING WE LIKE!
OH, JOY!

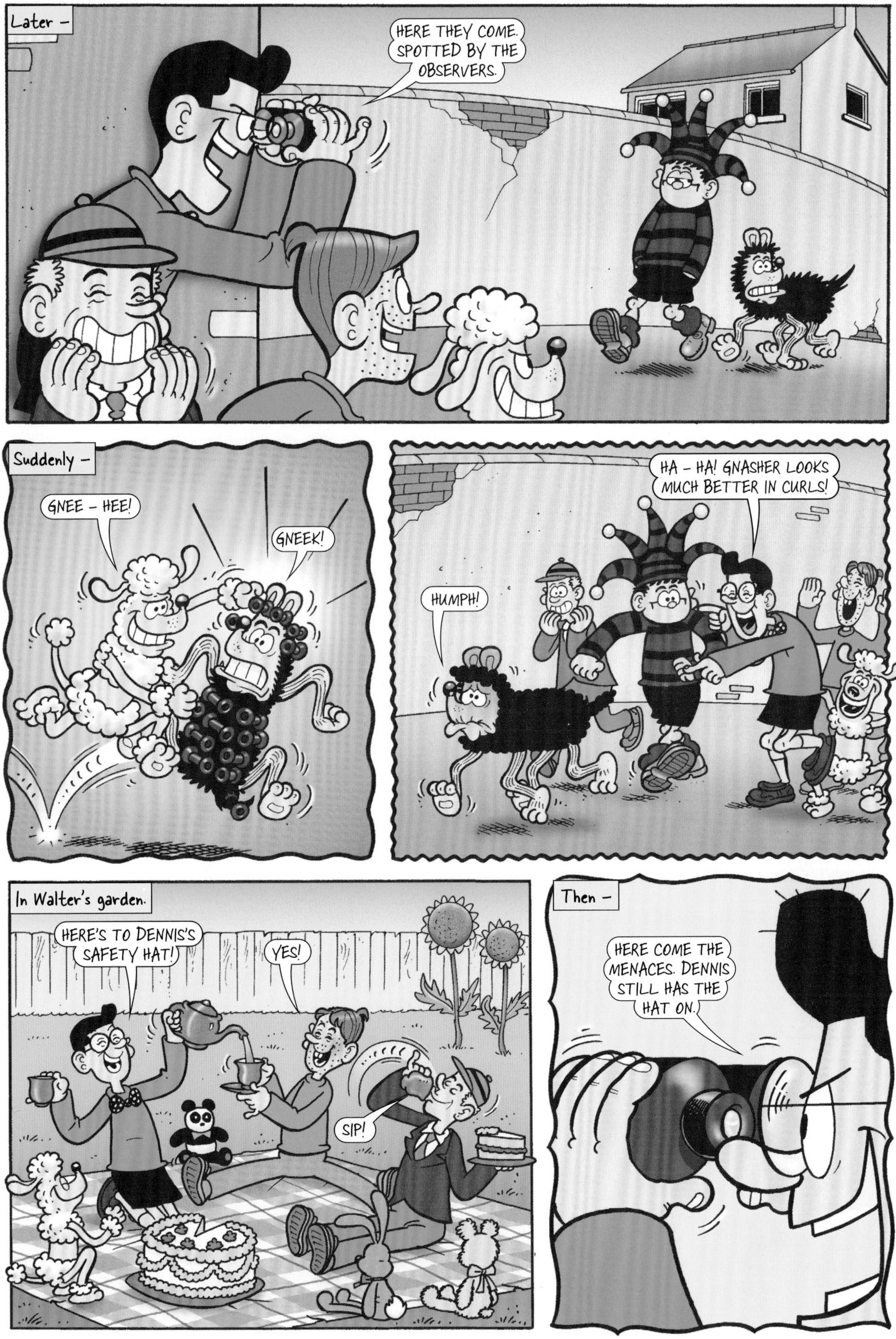

Later –
HERE THEY COME. SPOTTED BY THE OBSERVERS.
Suddenly –
GNEE – HEE!
GNEEK!
HA – HA! GNASHER LOOKS MUCH BETTER IN CURLS!
HUMPH!
In Walter's garden.
HERE'S TO DENNIS'S SAFETY HAT!
YES!
SIP!
Then –
HERE COME THE MENACES. DENNIS STILL HAS THE HAT ON.

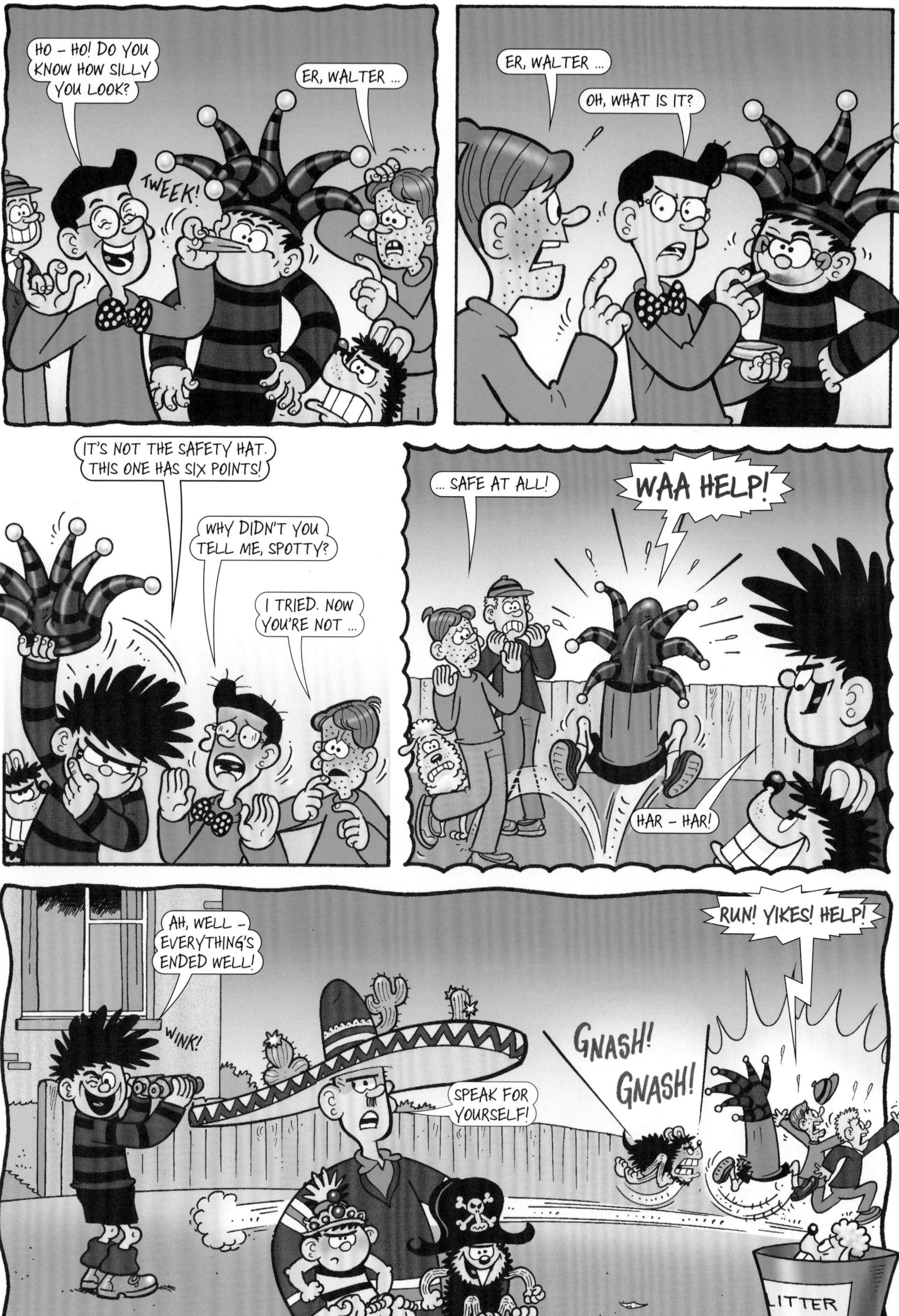
HO – HO! DO YOU KNOW HOW SILLY YOU LOOK?
TWEEK!
ER, WALTER ...
ER, WALTER ...
OH, WHAT IS IT?
IT'S NOT THE SAFETY HAT. THIS ONE HAS SIX POINTS!
WHY DIDN'T YOU TELL ME, SPOTTY?
I TRIED. NOW YOU'RE NOT ...
... SAFE AT ALL!
WAA HELP!
HAR – HAR!
AH, WELL – EVERYTHING'S ENDED WELL!
WINK!
SPEAK FOR YOURSELF!
GNASH!
GNASH!
RUN! YIKES! HELP!
LITTER

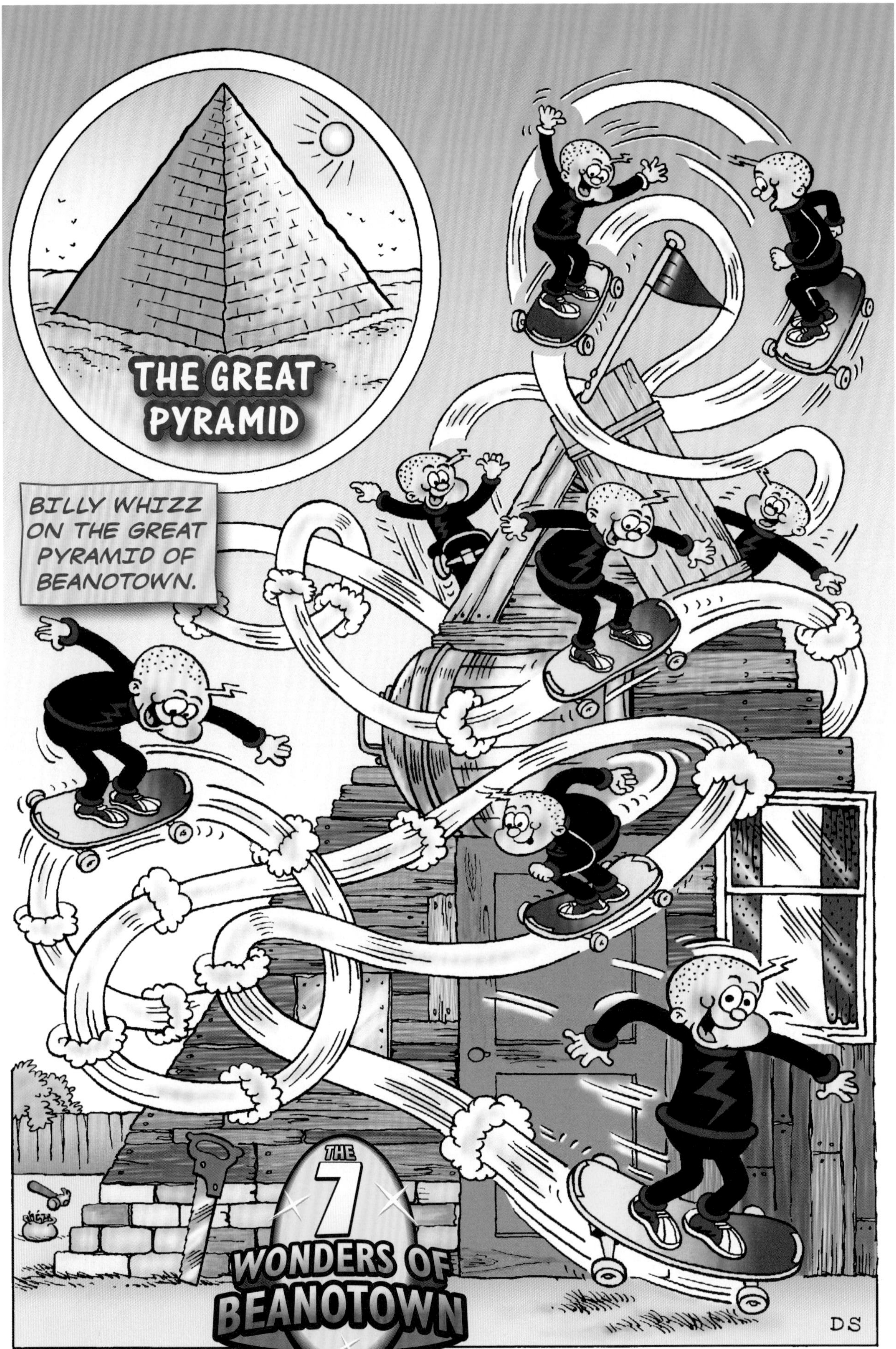
THE GREAT PYRAMID
BILLY WHIZZ ON THE GREAT PYRAMID OF BEANOTOWN.
THE 7 WONDERS OF BEANOTOWN
DS

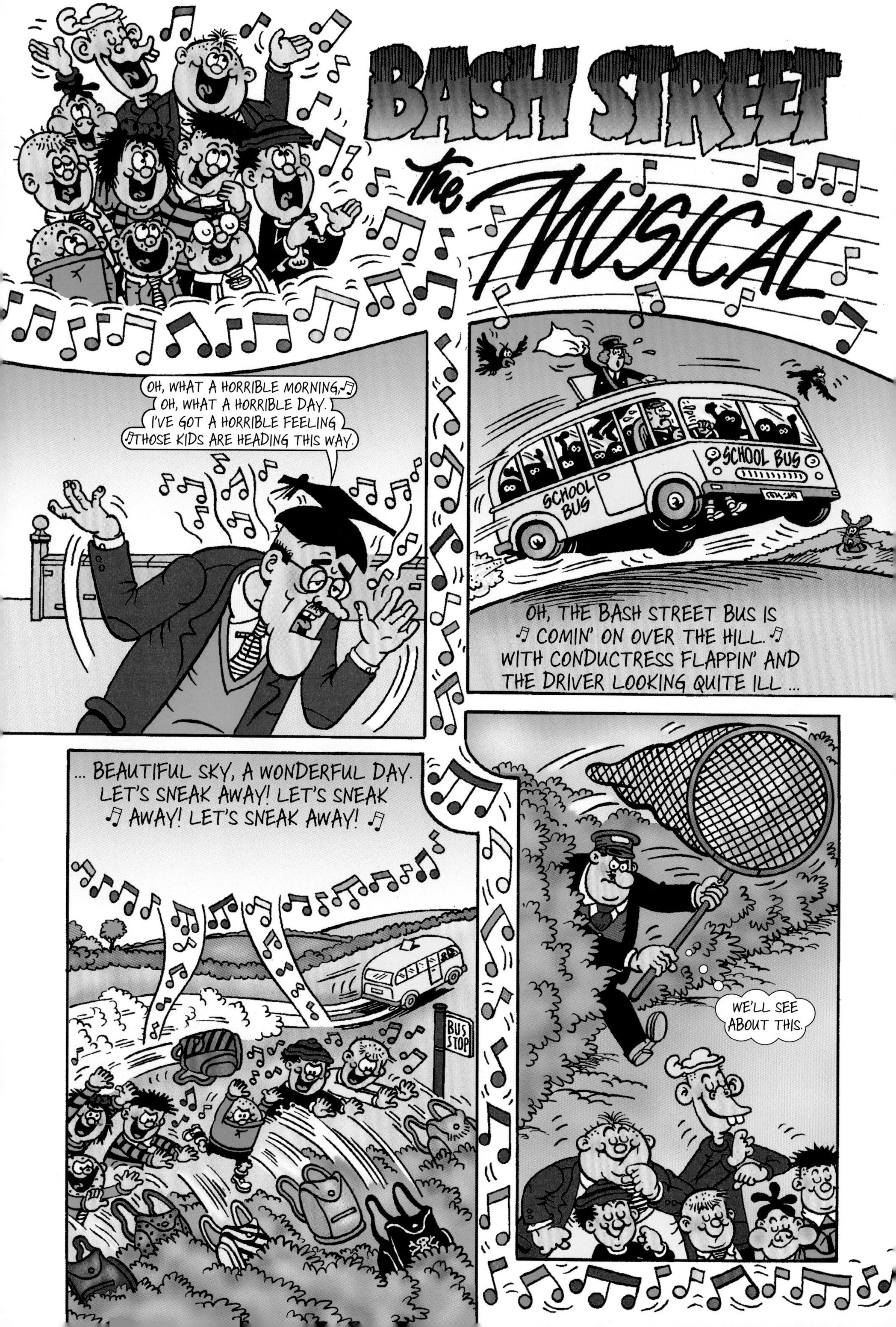
BASH STREET
The MUSICAL
OH, WHAT A HORRIBLE MORNING, ♫ OH, WHAT A HORRIBLE DAY. I'VE GOT A HORRIBLE FEELING ♫THOSE KIDS ARE HEADING THIS WAY.
SCHOOL BUS
SCHOOL BUS
OH, THE BASH STREET BUS IS ♫ COMIN' ON OVER THE HILL. ♫ WITH CONDUCTRESS FLAPPIN' AND THE DRIVER LOOKING QUITE ILL ...
... BEAUTIFUL SKY, A WONDERFUL DAY. LET'S SNEAK AWAY! LET'S SNEAK ♫ AWAY! LET'S SNEAK AWAY! ♫
BUS STOP
WE'LL SEE ABOUT THIS.

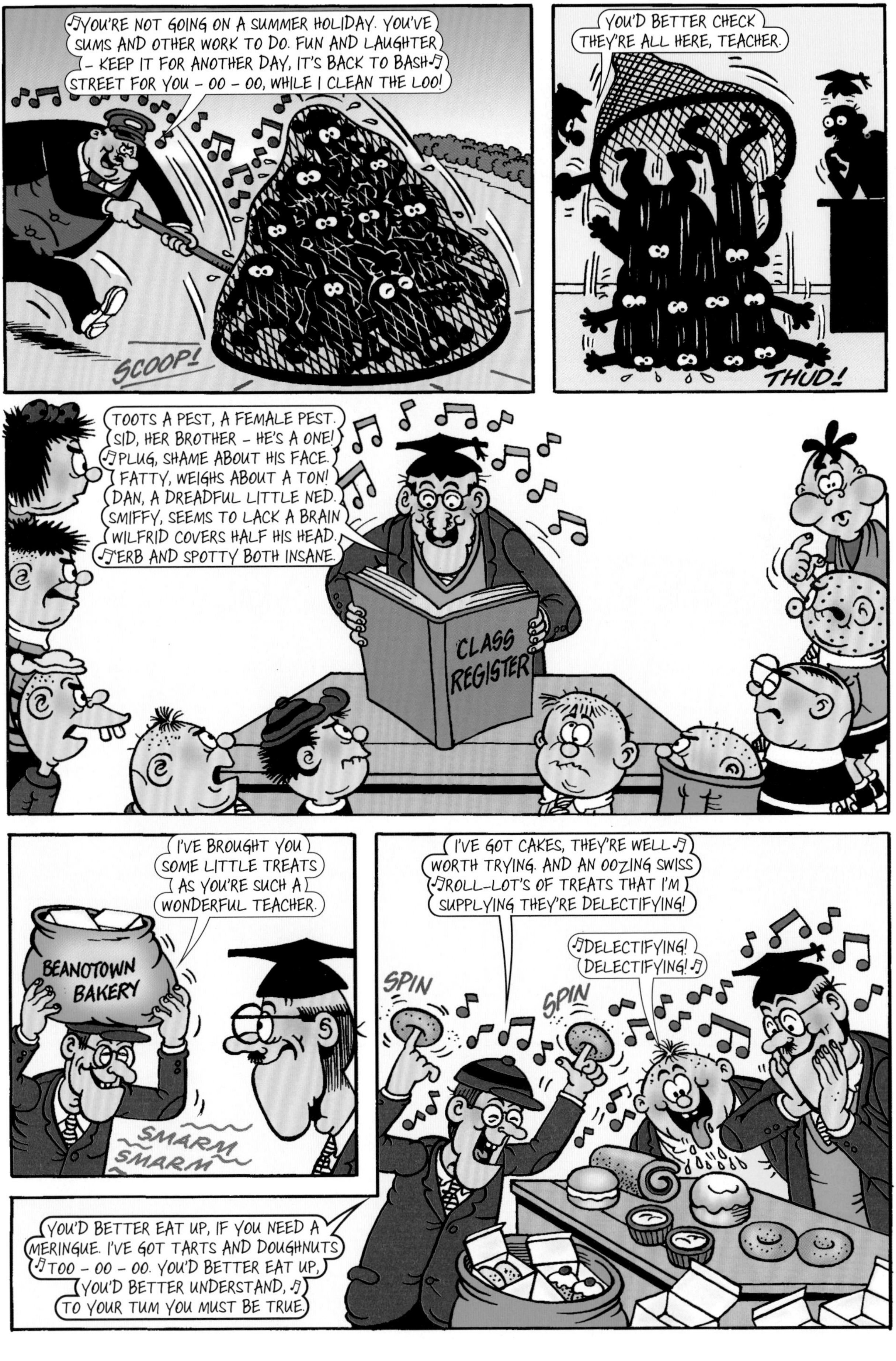
♫YOU'RE NOT GOING ON A SUMMER HOLIDAY. YOU'VE SUMS AND OTHER WORK TO DO. FUN AND LAUGHTER – KEEP IT FOR ANOTHER DAY, IT'S BACK TO BASH♫ STREET FOR YOU – OO – OO, WHILE I CLEAN THE LOO!
SCOOP!
YOU'D BETTER CHECK THEY'RE ALL HERE, TEACHER.
THUD!
TOOTS A PEST, A FEMALE PEST. SID, HER BROTHER – HE'S A ONE! ♫PLUG, SHAME ABOUT HIS FACE. FATTY, WEIGHS ABOUT A TON! DAN, A DREADFUL LITTLE NED. SMIFFY, SEEMS TO LACK A BRAIN WILFRID COVERS HALF HIS HEAD. ♫'ERB AND SPOTTY BOTH INSANE.
CLASS REGISTER
I'VE BROUGHT YOU SOME LITTLE TREATS AS YOU'RE SUCH A WONDERFUL TEACHER.
BEANOTOWN BAKERY
SMARM SMARM
I'VE GOT CAKES, THEY'RE WELL♫ WORTH TRYING. AND AN OOZING SWISS ♫ROLL–LOT'S OF TREATS THAT I'M SUPPLYING THEY'RE DELECTIFYING!
SPIN
SPIN
♫DELECTIFYING! DELECTIFYING!♫
YOU'D BETTER EAT UP, IF YOU NEED A MERINGUE. I'VE GOT TARTS AND DOUGHNUTS ♫TOO – OO – OO. YOU'D BETTER EAT UP, YOU'D BETTER UNDERSTAND, ♫ TO YOUR TUM YOU MUST BE TRUE.

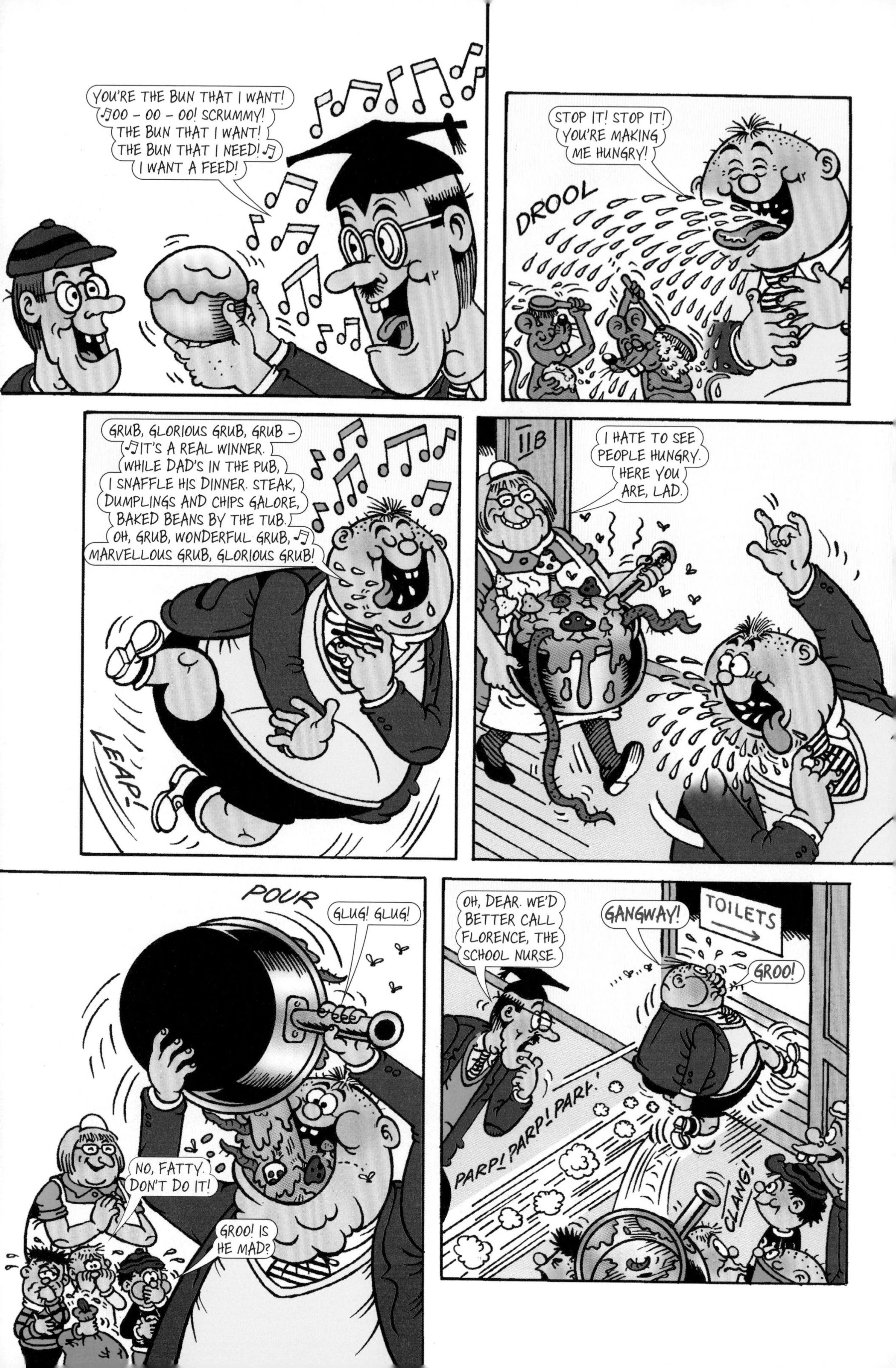
YOU'RE THE BUN THAT I WANT! ♫OO – OO – OO! SCRUMMY! THE BUN THAT I WANT! THE BUN THAT I NEED! ♫ I WANT A FEED!
STOP IT! STOP IT! YOU'RE MAKING ME HUNGRY!
DROOL
GRUB, GLORIOUS GRUB, GRUB – ♫IT'S A REAL WINNER. WHILE DAD'S IN THE PUB, I SNAFFLE HIS DINNER. STEAK, DUMPLINGS AND CHIPS GALORE, BAKED BEANS BY THE TUB. OH, GRUB, WONDERFUL GRUB, ♫ MARVELLOUS GRUB, GLORIOUS GRUB!
LEAP!
IIB
I HATE TO SEE PEOPLE HUNGRY. HERE YOU ARE, LAD.
POUR
GLUG! GLUG!
NO, FATTY. DON'T DO IT!
GROO! IS HE MAD?
OH, DEAR. WE'D BETTER CALL FLORENCE, THE SCHOOL NURSE.
GANGWAY!
TOILETS
GROO!
PARP! PARP! PARP!
CLANG!

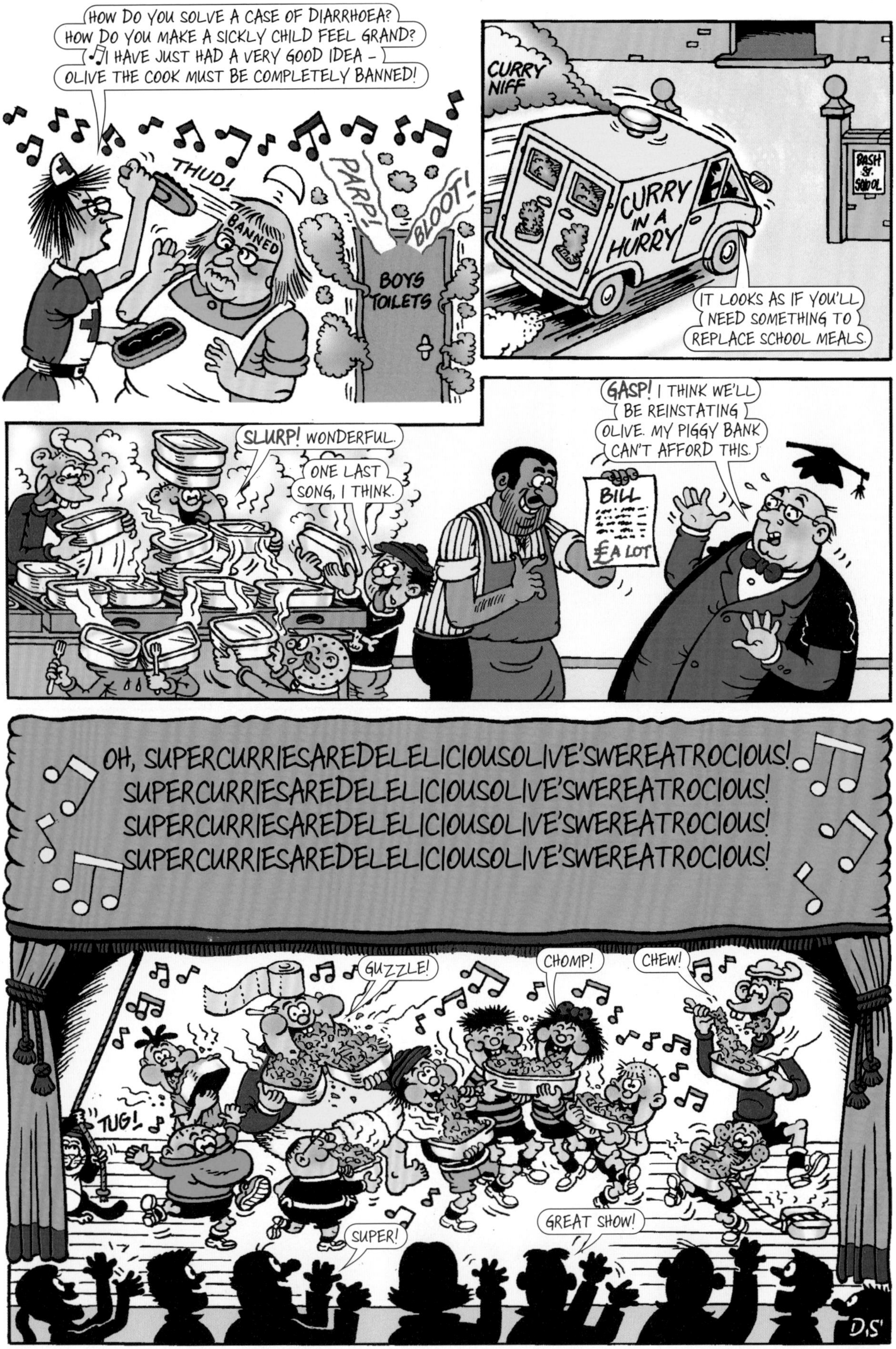
HOW DO YOU SOLVE A CASE OF DIARRHOEA? HOW DO YOU MAKE A SICKLY CHILD FEEL GRAND? I HAVE JUST HAD A VERY GOOD IDEA – OLIVE THE COOK MUST BE COMPLETELY BANNED!
THUD!
BANNED
PARP!
BLOOT!
BOYS TOILETS
CURRY NIFF
CURRY IN A HURRY
BASH ST. SCHOOL
IT LOOKS AS IF YOU'LL NEED SOMETHING TO REPLACE SCHOOL MEALS.
SLURP! WONDERFUL.
ONE LAST SONG, I THINK.
BILL
£A LOT
GASP! I THINK WE'LL BE REINSTATING OLIVE. MY PIGGY BANK CAN'T AFFORD THIS.
OH, SUPERCURRIESAREDELELICIOUSOLIVE'SWEREATROCIOUS!
SUPERCURRIESAREDELELICIOUSOLIVE'SWEREATROCIOUS!
SUPERCURRIESAREDELELICIOUSOLIVE'SWEREATROCIOUS!
SUPERCURRIESAREDELELICIOUSOLIVE'SWEREATROCIOUS!
GUZZLE!
CHOMP!
CHEW!
TUG!
SUPER!
GREAT SHOW!
D.S.

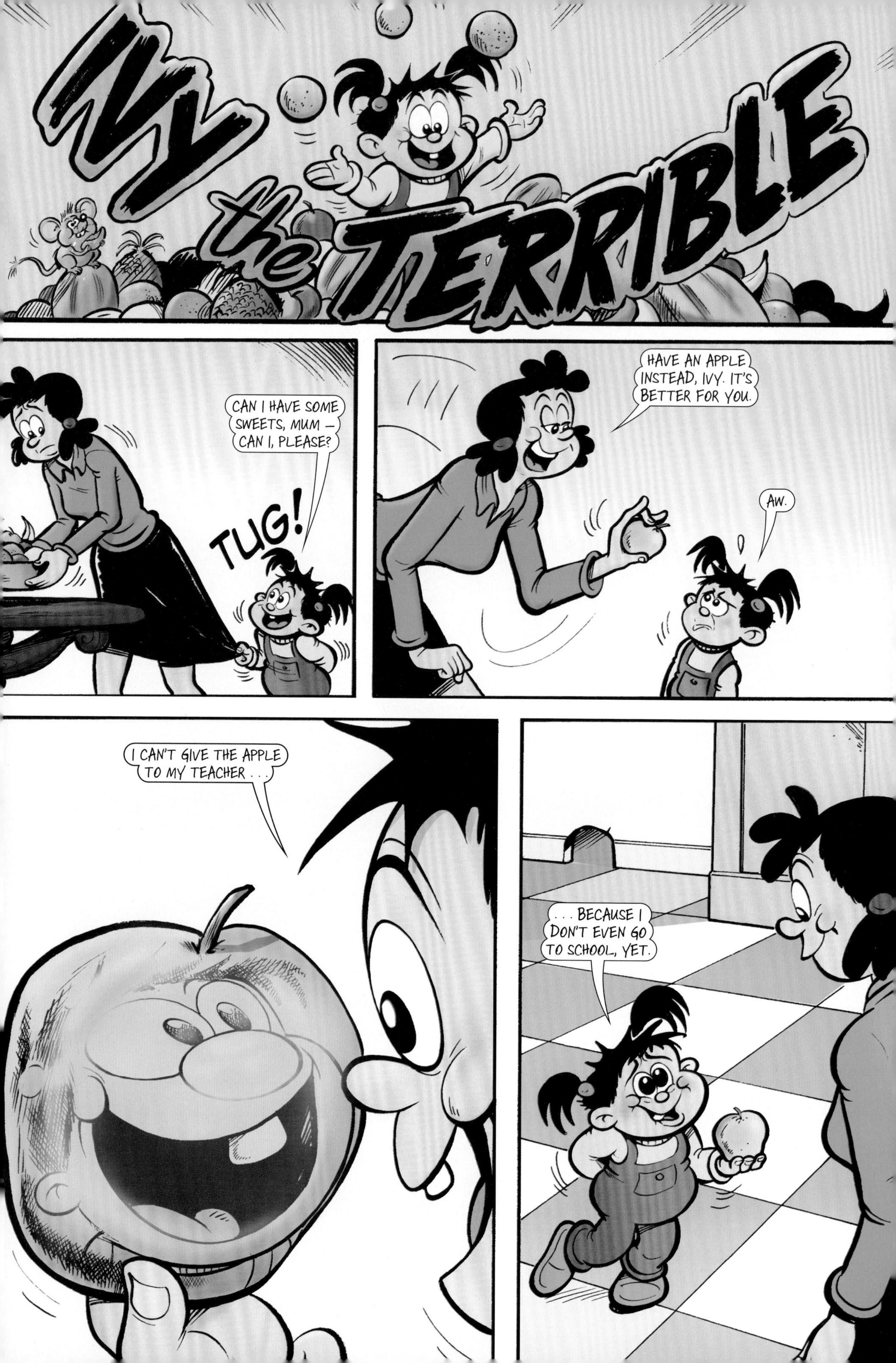
Ivy the TERRIBLE
CAN I HAVE SOME SWEETS, MUM — CAN I, PLEASE?
TUG!
HAVE AN APPLE INSTEAD, IVY. IT'S BETTER FOR YOU.
AW.
I CAN'T GIVE THE APPLE TO MY TEACHER . . .
. . . BECAUSE I DON'T EVEN GO TO SCHOOL, YET.

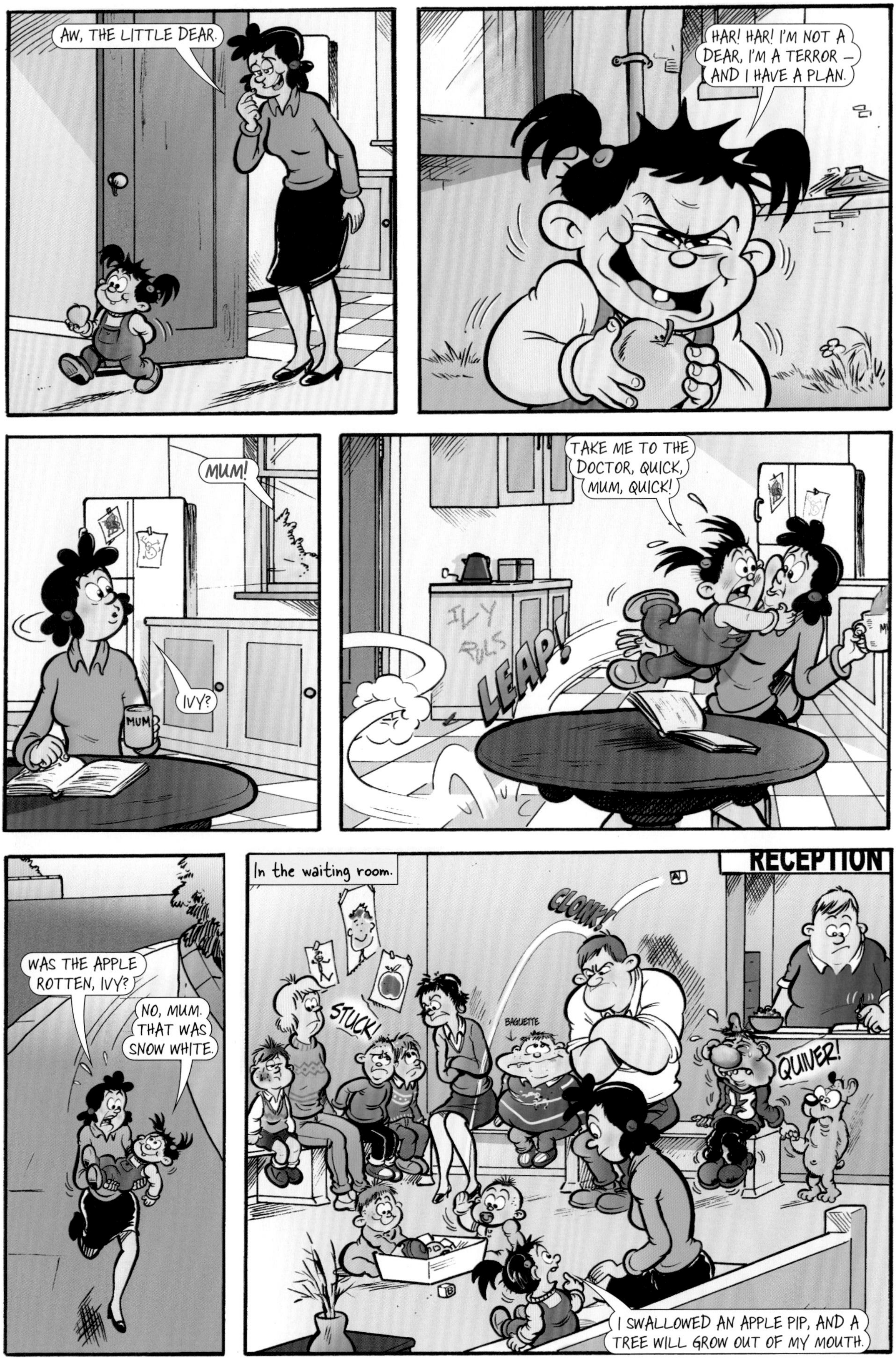
AW, THE LITTLE DEAR.
HAR! HAR! I'M NOT A DEAR, I'M A TERROR — AND I HAVE A PLAN.
MUM!
IVY?
TAKE ME TO THE DOCTOR, QUICK, MUM, QUICK!
IVY RULS
LEAP!
MUM
WAS THE APPLE ROTTEN, IVY?
NO, MUM. THAT WAS SNOW WHITE.
In the waiting room.
RECEPTION
CLONK!
STUCK!
BAGUETTE
QUIVER!
I SWALLOWED AN APPLE PIP, AND A TREE WILL GROW OUT OF MY MOUTH.

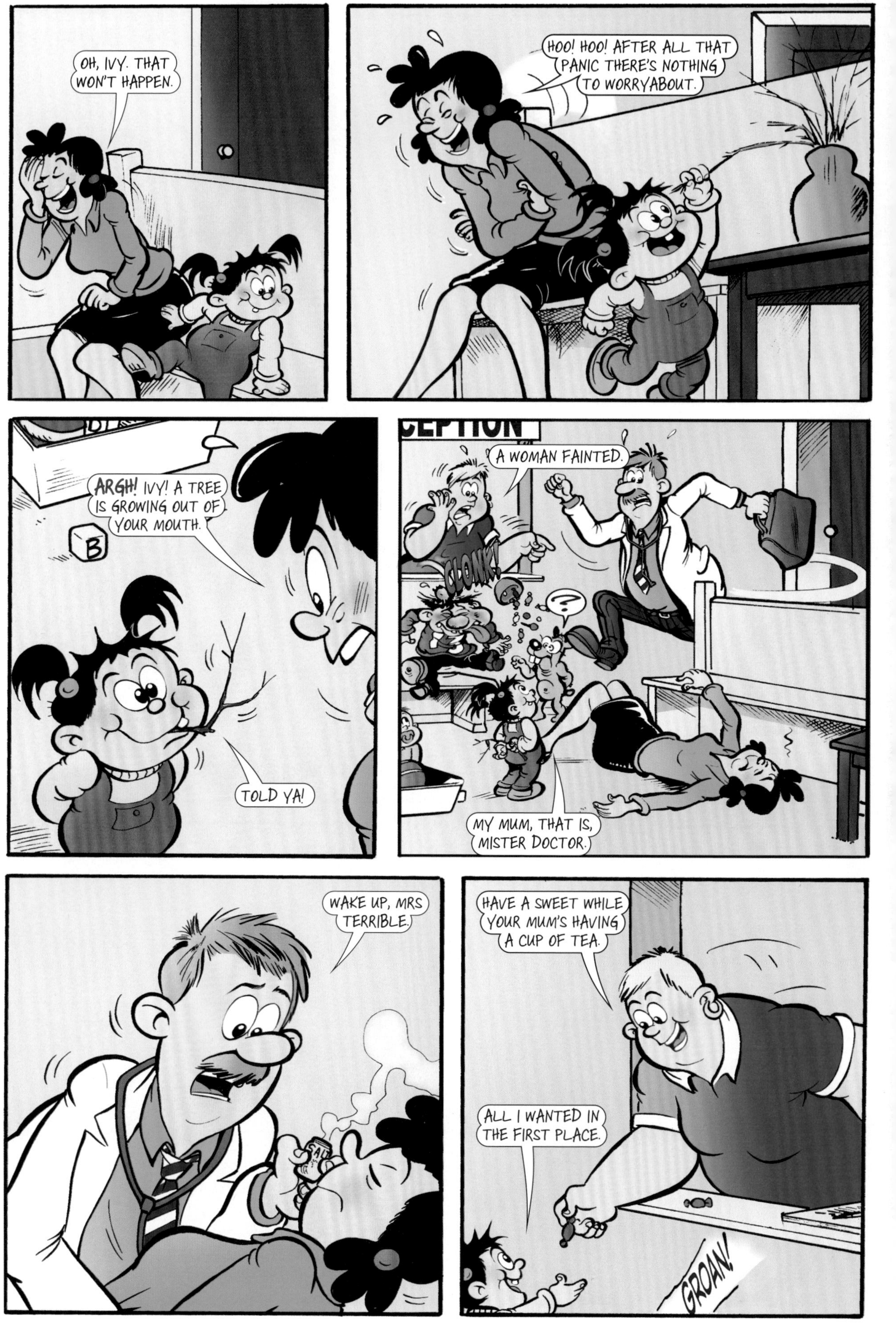
OH, IVY. THAT WON'T HAPPEN.
HOO! HOO! AFTER ALL THAT PANIC THERE'S NOTHING TO WORRYABOUT.
ARGH! IVY! A TREE IS GROWING OUT OF YOUR MOUTH.
TOLD YA!
A WOMAN FAINTED.
CLONK!
?
MY MUM, THAT IS, MISTER DOCTOR.
WAKE UP, MRS TERRIBLE.
HAVE A SWEET WHILE YOUR MUM'S HAVING A CUP OF TEA.
ALL I WANTED IN THE FIRST PLACE.
GROAN!

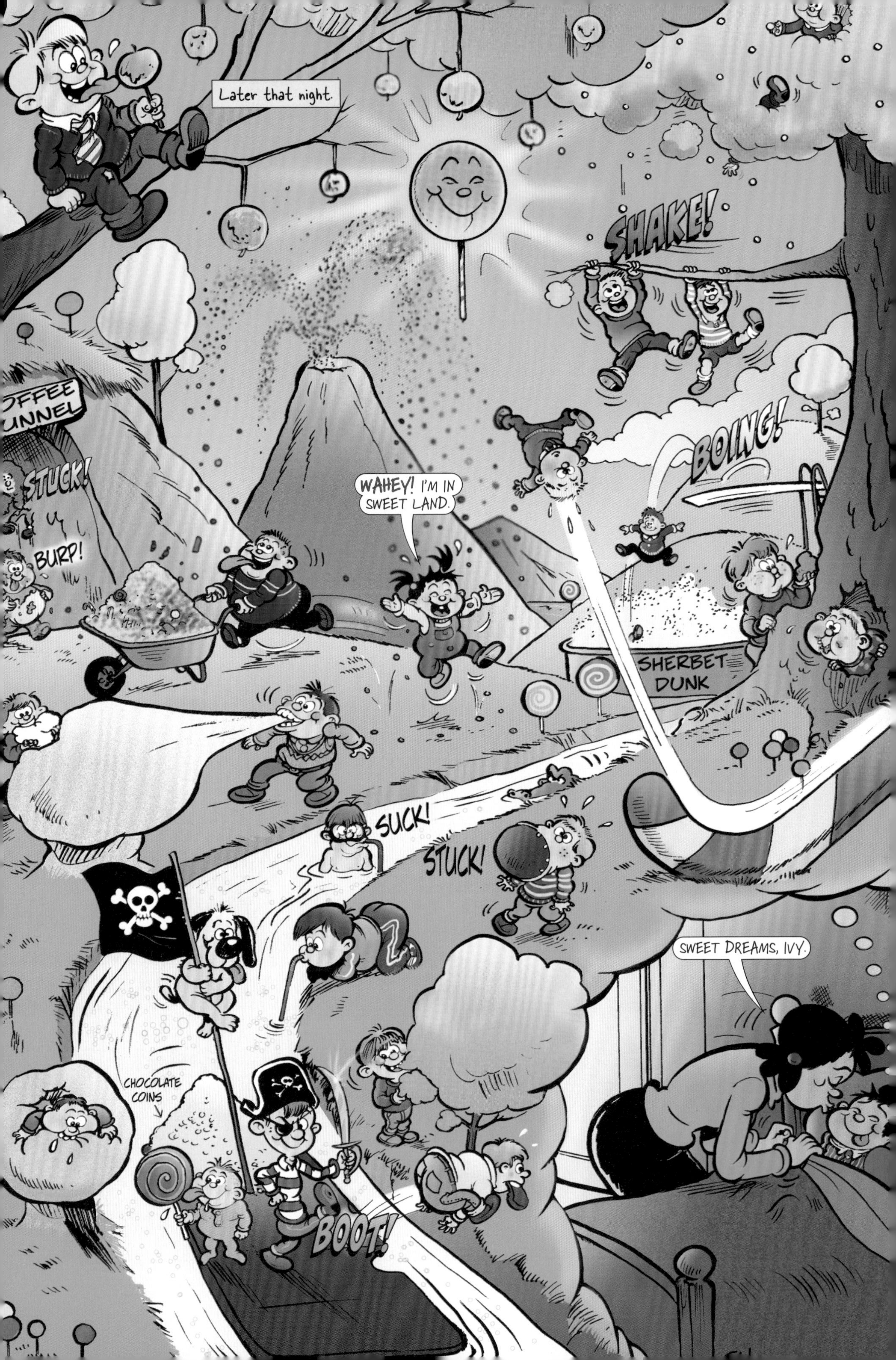

Later that night.
SHAKE!
OFFEE
UNNEL
STUCK!
BURP!
WAHEY! I'M IN SWEET LAND.
BOING!
SHERBET DUNK
SUCK!
STUCK!
SWEET DREAMS, IVY.
CHOCOLATE COINS
BOOT!

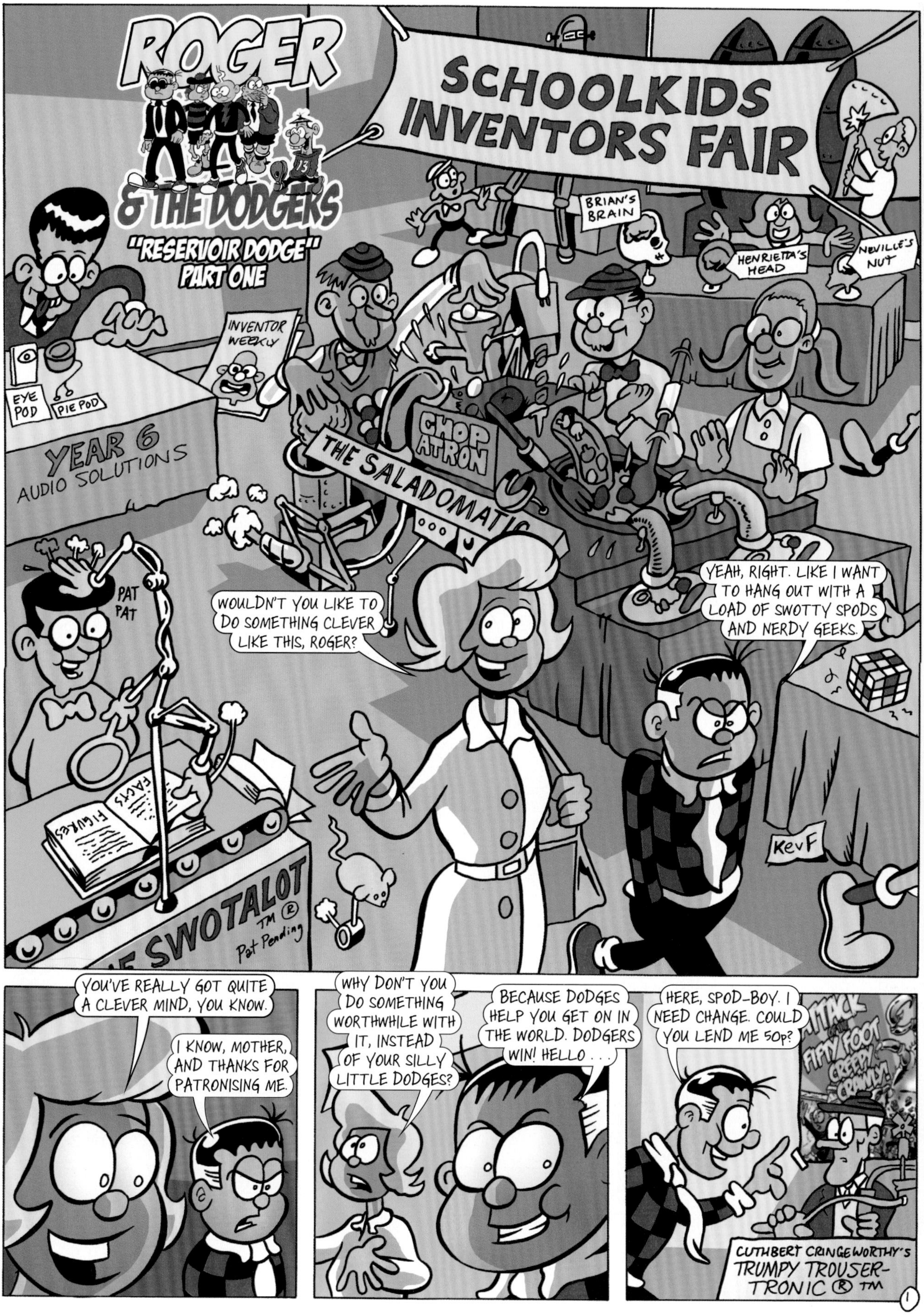
ROGER & THE DODGERS
"RESERVOIR DODGE" PART ONE
SCHOOLKIDS INVENTORS FAIR
BRIAN'S BRAIN
HENRIETTA'S HEAD
NEVILLE'S NUT
INVENTOR WEEKLY
EYE POD
PIE POD
YEAR 6 AUDIO SOLUTIONS
CHOP ATRON
THE SALADOMATIC
PAT PAT
FACTS
FIGURES
THE SWOTALOT TM ® Pat Pending
WOULDN'T YOU LIKE TO DO SOMETHING CLEVER LIKE THIS, ROGER?
YEAH, RIGHT. LIKE I WANT TO HANG OUT WITH A LOAD OF SWOTTY SPODS AND NERDY GEEKS.
KevF
YOU'VE REALLY GOT QUITE A CLEVER MIND, YOU KNOW.
I KNOW, MOTHER, AND THANKS FOR PATRONISING ME.
WHY DON'T YOU DO SOMETHING WORTHWHILE WITH IT, INSTEAD OF YOUR SILLY LITTLE DODGES?
BECAUSE DODGES HELP YOU GET ON IN THE WORLD. DODGERS WIN! HELLO . . .
HERE, SPOD-BOY. I NEED CHANGE. COULD YOU LEND ME 50p?
ATTACK OF THE FIFTY FOOT CREEPY CRAWLY!
CUTHBERT CRINGEWORTHY'S TRUMPY TROUSER-TRONIC ® TM

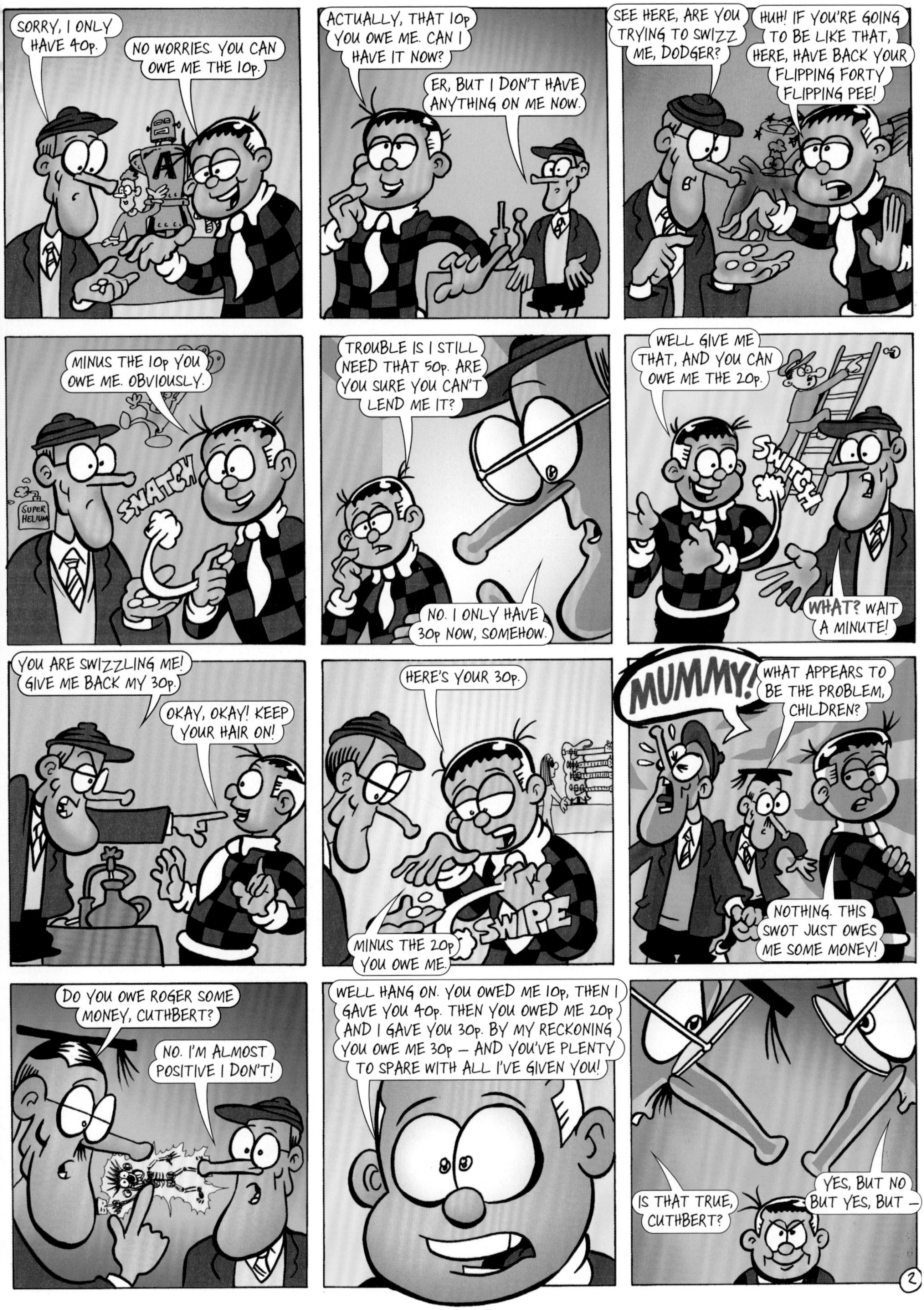
SORRY, I ONLY HAVE 40p.
NO WORRIES. YOU CAN OWE ME THE 10p.
ACTUALLY, THAT 10p YOU OWE ME. CAN I HAVE IT NOW?
ER, BUT I DON'T HAVE ANYTHING ON ME NOW.
SEE HERE, ARE YOU TRYING TO SWIZZ ME, DODGER?
HUH! IF YOU'RE GOING TO BE LIKE THAT, HERE, HAVE BACK YOUR FLIPPING FORTY FLIPPING PEE!
MINUS THE 10p YOU OWE ME. OBVIOUSLY.
SUPER HELIUM
SNATCH
TROUBLE IS I STILL NEED THAT 50p. ARE YOU SURE YOU CAN'T LEND ME IT?
NO. I ONLY HAVE 30p NOW, SOMEHOW.
WELL GIVE ME THAT, AND YOU CAN OWE ME THE 20p.
SWITCH
WHAT? WAIT A MINUTE!
YOU ARE SWIZZLING ME! GIVE ME BACK MY 30p.
OKAY, OKAY! KEEP YOUR HAIR ON!
HERE'S YOUR 30p.
MINUS THE 20p YOU OWE ME.
SWIPE
MUMMY!
WHAT APPEARS TO BE THE PROBLEM, CHILDREN?
NOTHING. THIS SWOT JUST OWES ME SOME MONEY!
DO YOU OWE ROGER SOME MONEY, CUTHBERT?
NO. I'M ALMOST POSITIVE I DON'T!
WELL HANG ON. YOU OWED ME 10p, THEN I GAVE YOU 40p. THEN YOU OWED ME 20p AND I GAVE YOU 30p. BY MY RECKONING YOU OWE ME 30p – AND YOU'VE PLENTY TO SPARE WITH ALL I'VE GIVEN YOU!
IS THAT TRUE, CUTHBERT?
YES, BUT NO BUT YES, BUT –

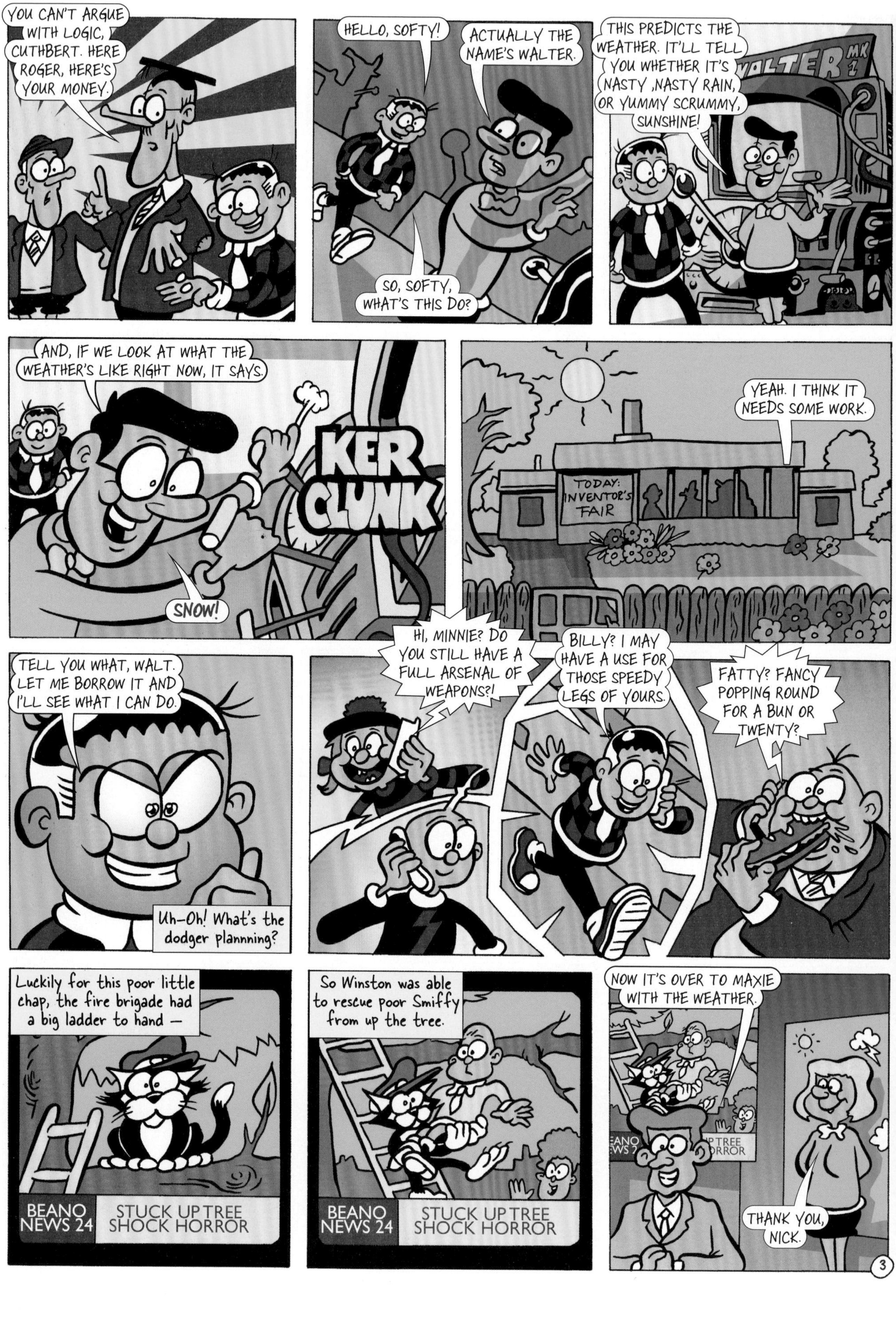

YOU CAN'T ARGUE WITH LOGIC, CUTHBERT. HERE ROGER, HERE'S YOUR MONEY.
HELLO, SOFTY!
ACTUALLY THE NAME'S WALTER.
SO, SOFTY, WHAT'S THIS DO?
THIS PREDICTS THE WEATHER. IT'LL TELL YOU WHETHER IT'S NASTY ,NASTY RAIN, OR YUMMY SCRUMMY, SUNSHINE!
WALTER MK 1
AND, IF WE LOOK AT WHAT THE WEATHER'S LIKE RIGHT NOW, IT SAYS.
KER CLUNK
SNOW!
TODAY: INVENTOR'S FAIR
YEAH. I THINK IT NEEDS SOME WORK.
TELL YOU WHAT, WALT. LET ME BORROW IT AND I'LL SEE WHAT I CAN DO.
Uh-Oh! What's the dodger plannning?
HI, MINNIE? DO YOU STILL HAVE A FULL ARSENAL OF WEAPONS?!
BILLY? I MAY HAVE A USE FOR THOSE SPEEDY LEGS OF YOURS.
FATTY? FANCY POPPING ROUND FOR A BUN OR TWENTY?
Luckily for this poor little chap, the fire brigade had a big ladder to hand –
BEANO NEWS 24
STUCK UP TREE SHOCK HORROR
So Winston was able to rescue poor Smiffy from up the tree.
BEANO NEWS 24
STUCK UP TREE SHOCK HORROR
NOW IT'S OVER TO MAXIE WITH THE WEATHER.
THANK YOU, NICK.

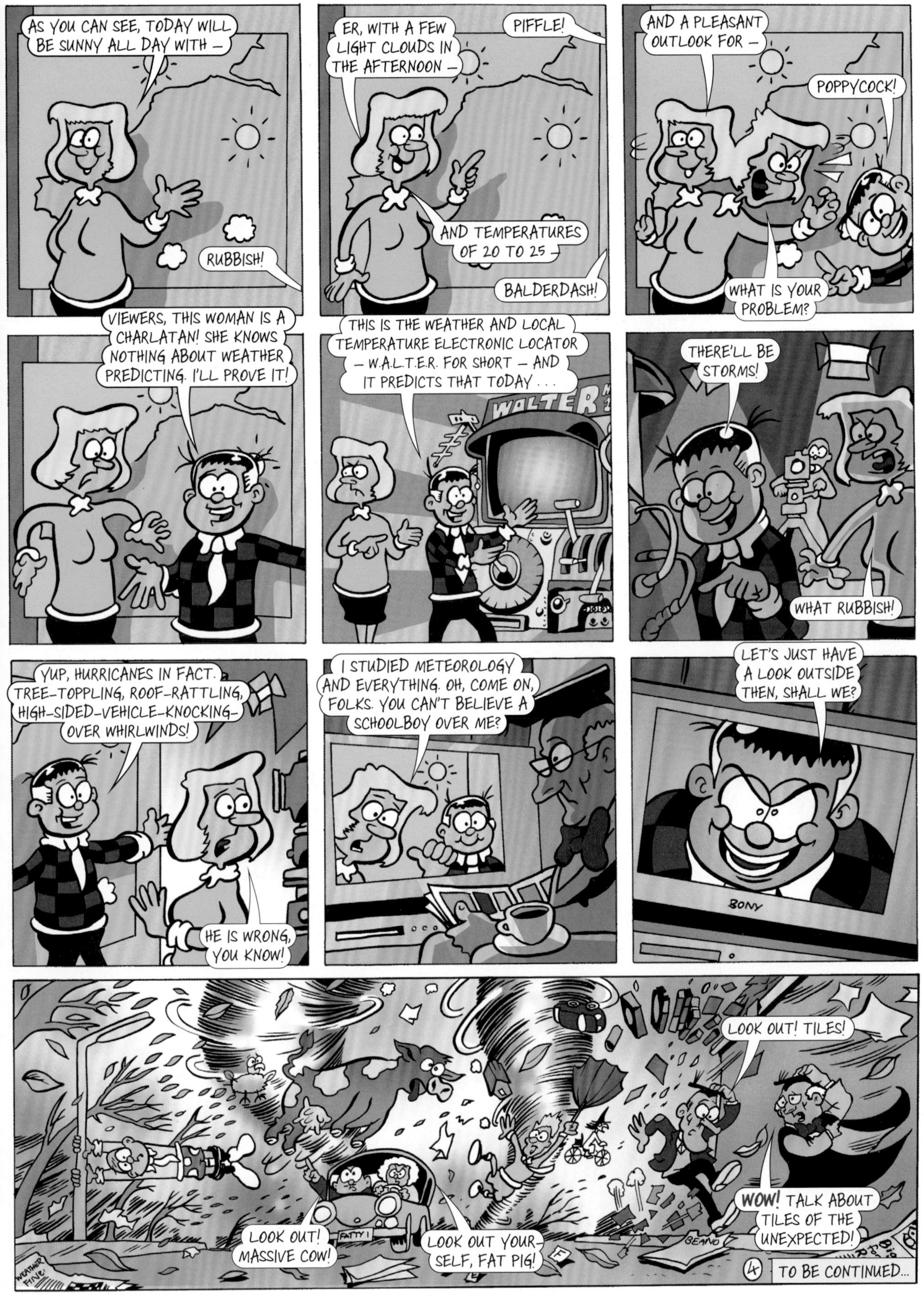
AS YOU CAN SEE, TODAY WILL BE SUNNY ALL DAY WITH –
RUBBISH!
ER, WITH A FEW LIGHT CLOUDS IN THE AFTERNOON –
PIFFLE!
AND TEMPERATURES OF 20 TO 25 –
BALDERDASH!
AND A PLEASANT OUTLOOK FOR –
POPPYCOCK!
WHAT IS YOUR PROBLEM?
VIEWERS, THIS WOMAN IS A CHARLATAN! SHE KNOWS NOTHING ABOUT WEATHER PREDICTING. I'LL PROVE IT!
THIS IS THE WEATHER AND LOCAL TEMPERATURE ELECTRONIC LOCATOR – W.A.L.T.E.R. FOR SHORT – AND IT PREDICTS THAT TODAY . . .
WALTER
THERE'LL BE STORMS!
WHAT RUBBISH!
YUP, HURRICANES IN FACT. TREE-TOPPLING, ROOF-RATTLING, HIGH-SIDED-VEHICLE-KNOCKING-OVER WHIRLWINDS!
HE IS WRONG, YOU KNOW!
I STUDIED METEOROLOGY AND EVERYTHING. OH, COME ON, FOLKS. YOU CAN'T BELIEVE A SCHOOLBOY OVER ME?
LET'S JUST HAVE A LOOK OUTSIDE THEN, SHALL WE?
BONY
LOOK OUT! TILES!
LOOK OUT! MASSIVE COW!
FATTY!
LOOK OUT YOURSELF, FAT PIG!
WOW! TALK ABOUT TILES OF THE UNEXPECTED!
BEANO
4
TO BE CONTINUED...

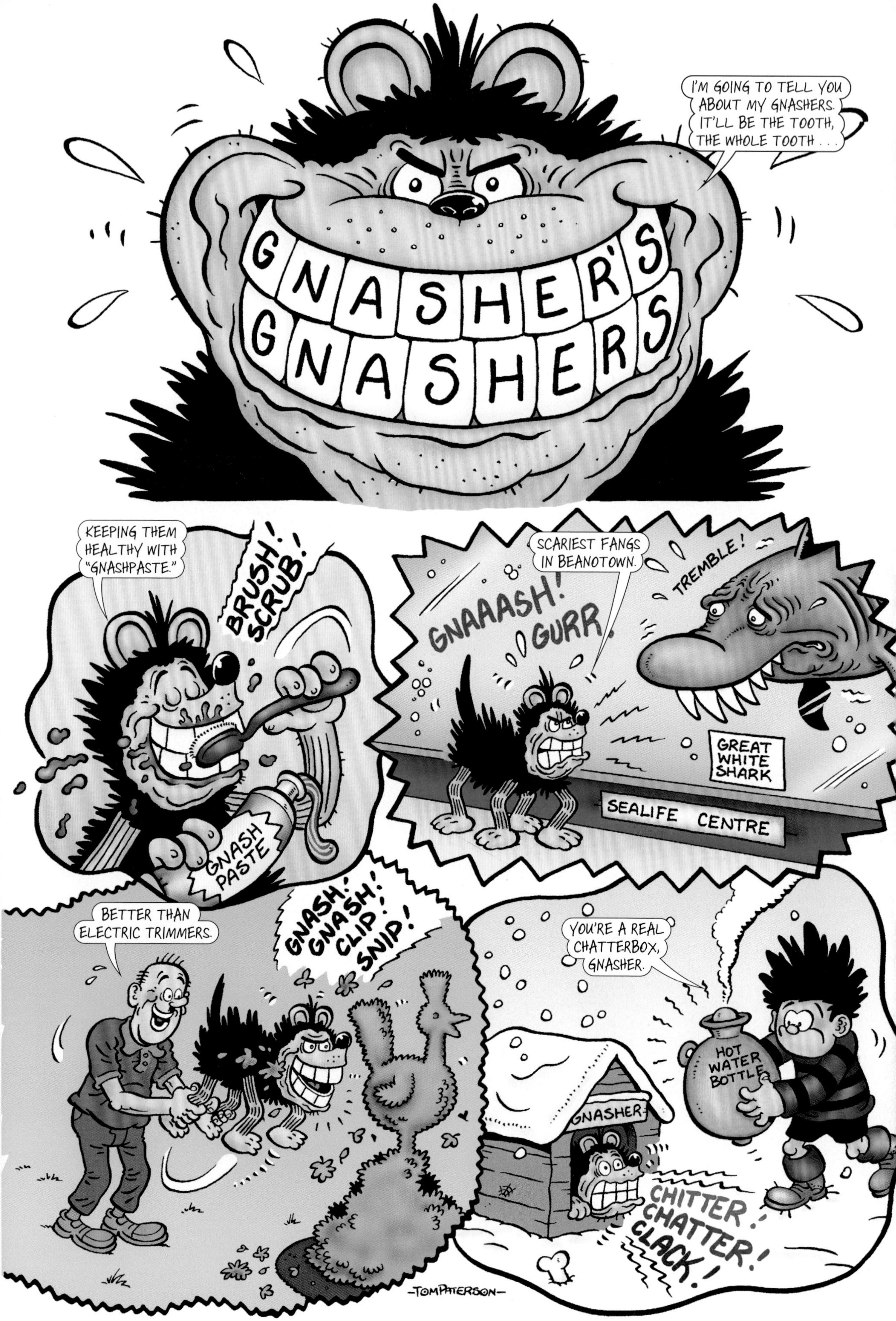
GNASHER'S GNASHERS
I'M GOING TO TELL YOU ABOUT MY GNASHERS. IT'LL BE THE TOOTH, THE WHOLE TOOTH . . .
KEEPING THEM HEALTHY WITH "GNASHPASTE."
BRUSH! SCRUB!
GNASH PASTE
SCARIEST FANGS IN BEANOTOWN.
TREMBLE!
GNAAASH! GURR.
GREAT WHITE SHARK
SEALIFE CENTRE
BETTER THAN ELECTRIC TRIMMERS.
GNASH! GNASH! CLIP! SNIP!
YOU'RE A REAL CHATTERBOX, GNASHER.
HOT WATER BOTTLE
GNASHER
CHITTER! CHATTER! CLACK!
TOM PATERSON

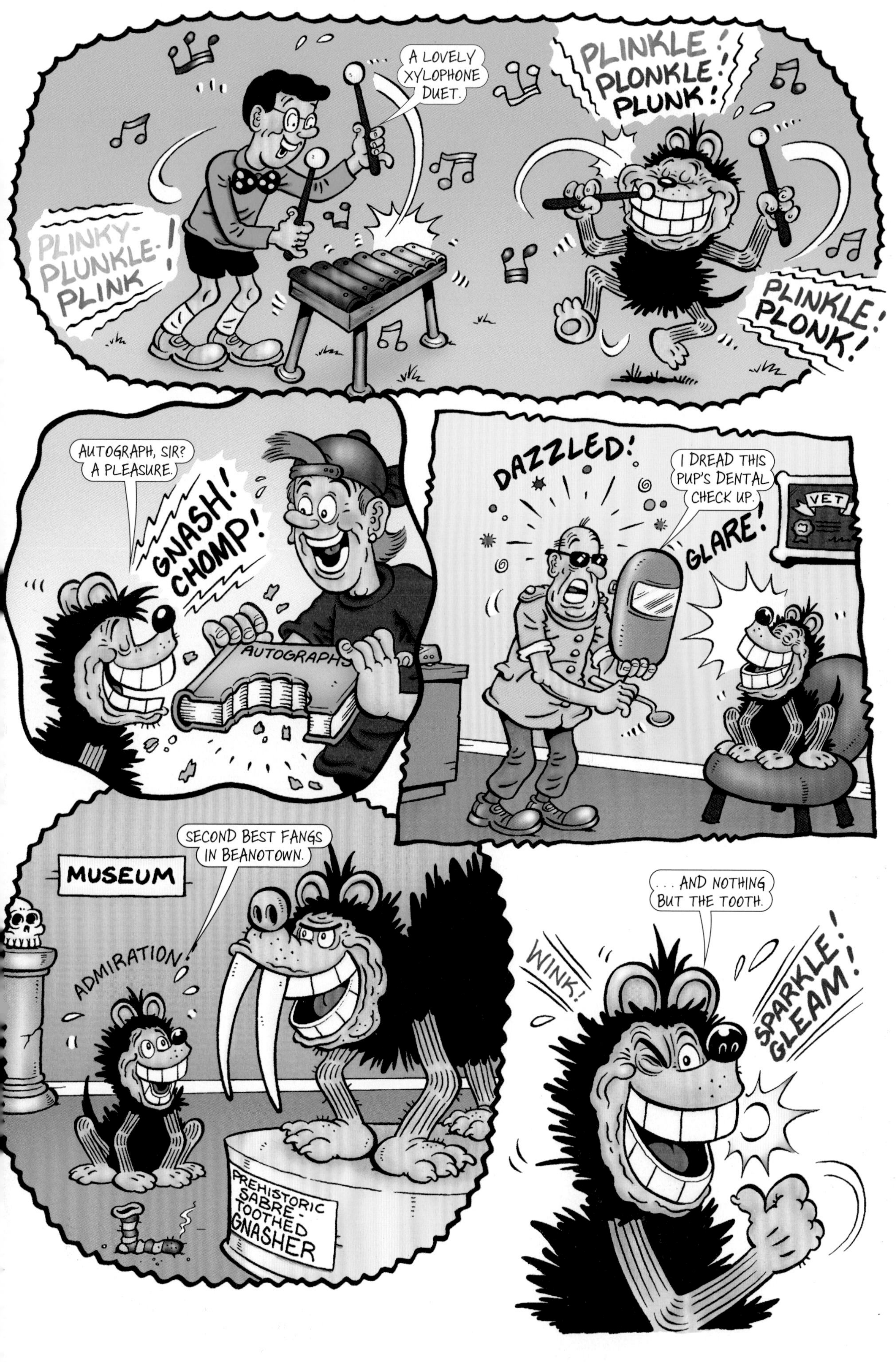
PLINKY-PLUNKLE-PLINK!
A LOVELY XYLOPHONE DUET.
PLINKLE! PLONKLE! PLUNK!
PLINKLE! PLONK!
AUTOGRAPH, SIR? A PLEASURE.
GNASH! CHOMP!
AUTOGRAPHS
DAZZLED!
I DREAD THIS PUP'S DENTAL CHECK UP.
GLARE!
VET
MUSEUM
SECOND BEST FANGS IN BEANOTOWN.
ADMIRATION!
PREHISTORIC SABRE-TOOTHED GNASHER
. . . AND NOTHING BUT THE TOOTH.
WINK!
SPARKLE! GLEAM!

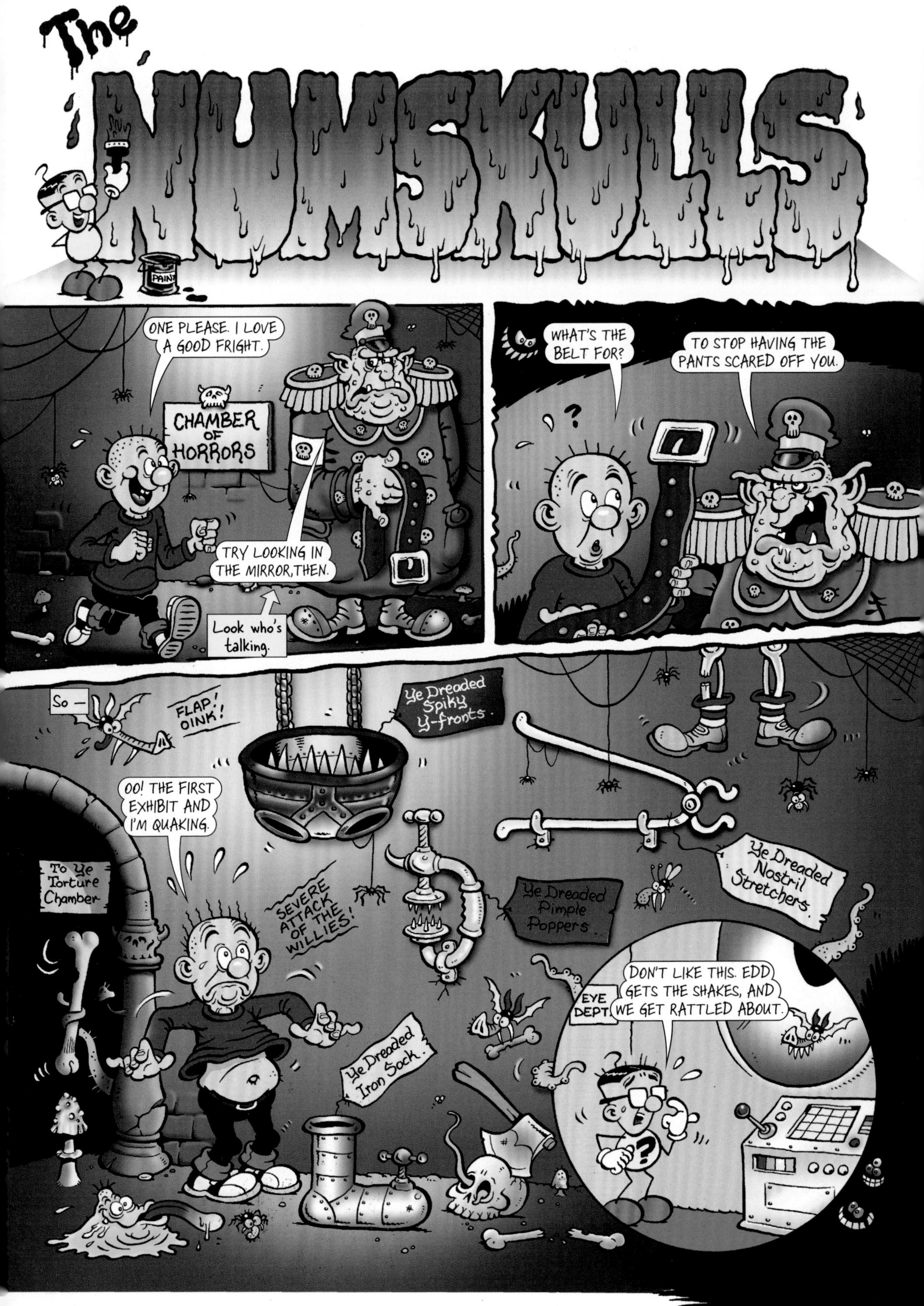

The NUMSKULLS
PAINT
ONE PLEASE. I LOVE A GOOD FRIGHT.
CHAMBER OF HORRORS
TRY LOOKING IN THE MIRROR, THEN.
Look who's talking.
WHAT'S THE BELT FOR?
TO STOP HAVING THE PANTS SCARED OFF YOU.
So —
FLAP! OINK!
Ye Dreaded Spiky Y-fronts.
OO! THE FIRST EXHIBIT AND I'M QUAKING.
To Ye Torture Chamber
SEVERE ATTACK OF THE WILLIES!
Ye Dreaded Pimple Poppers.
Ye Dreaded Nostril Stretchers.
Ye Dreaded Iron Sock.
EYE DEPT.
DON'T LIKE THIS. EDD GETS THE SHAKES, AND WE GET RATTLED ABOUT.

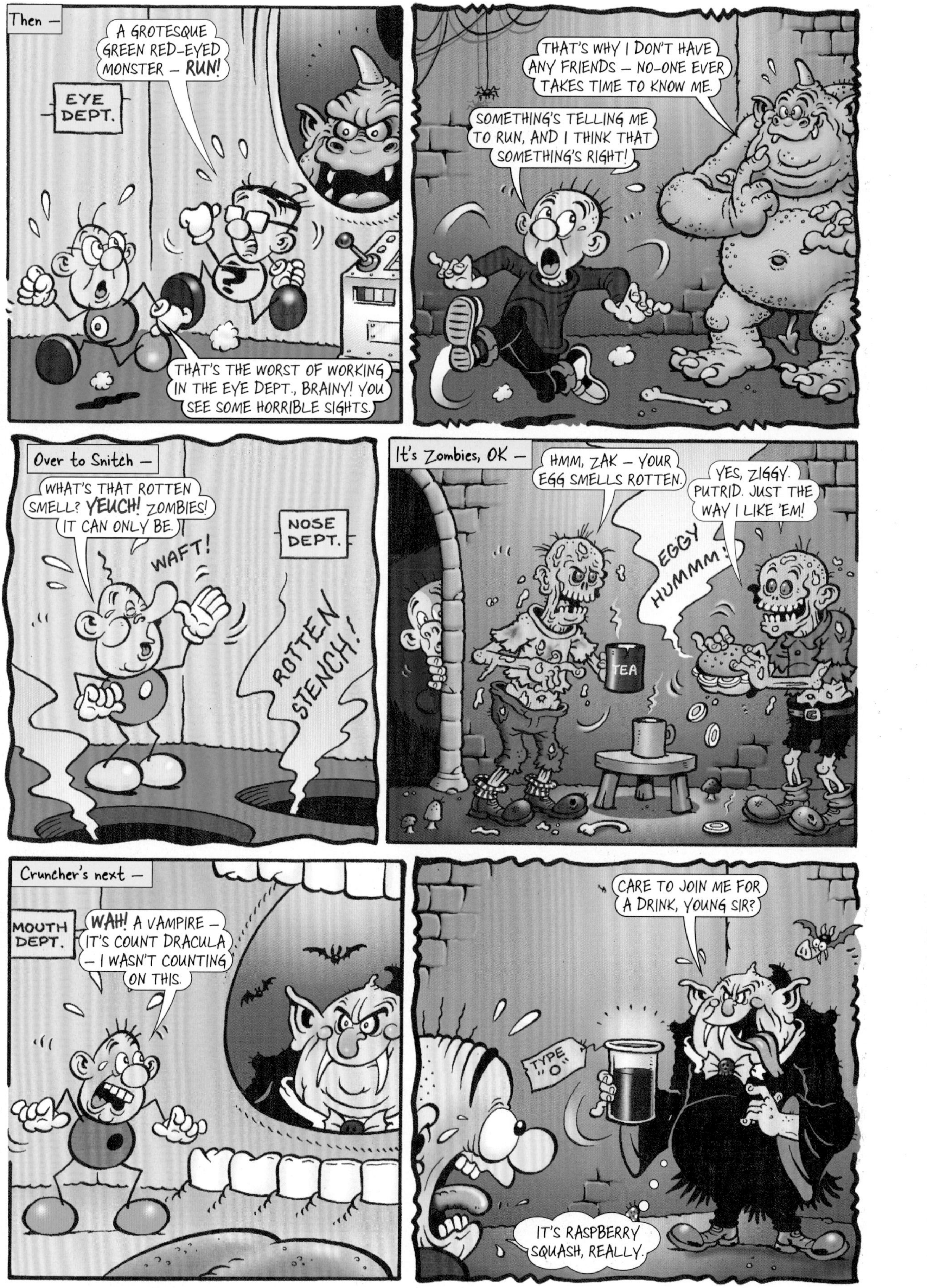
Then –
A GROTESQUE GREEN RED-EYED MONSTER – RUN!
EYE DEPT.
THAT'S THE WORST OF WORKING IN THE EYE DEPT., BRAINY! YOU SEE SOME HORRIBLE SIGHTS.
THAT'S WHY I DON'T HAVE ANY FRIENDS – NO-ONE EVER TAKES TIME TO KNOW ME.
SOMETHING'S TELLING ME TO RUN, AND I THINK THAT SOMETHING'S RIGHT!
Over to Snitch –
WHAT'S THAT ROTTEN SMELL? YEUCH! ZOMBIES! IT CAN ONLY BE.
NOSE DEPT.
WAFT!
ROTTEN STENCH!
It's Zombies, OK –
HMM, ZAK – YOUR EGG SMELLS ROTTEN.
YES, ZIGGY. PUTRID. JUST THE WAY I LIKE 'EM!
EGGY HUMMM!
TEA
Cruncher's next –
MOUTH DEPT.
WAH! A VAMPIRE – IT'S COUNT DRACULA – I WASN'T COUNTING ON THIS.
CARE TO JOIN ME FOR A DRINK, YOUNG SIR?
TYPE O
IT'S RASPBERRY SQUASH, REALLY.

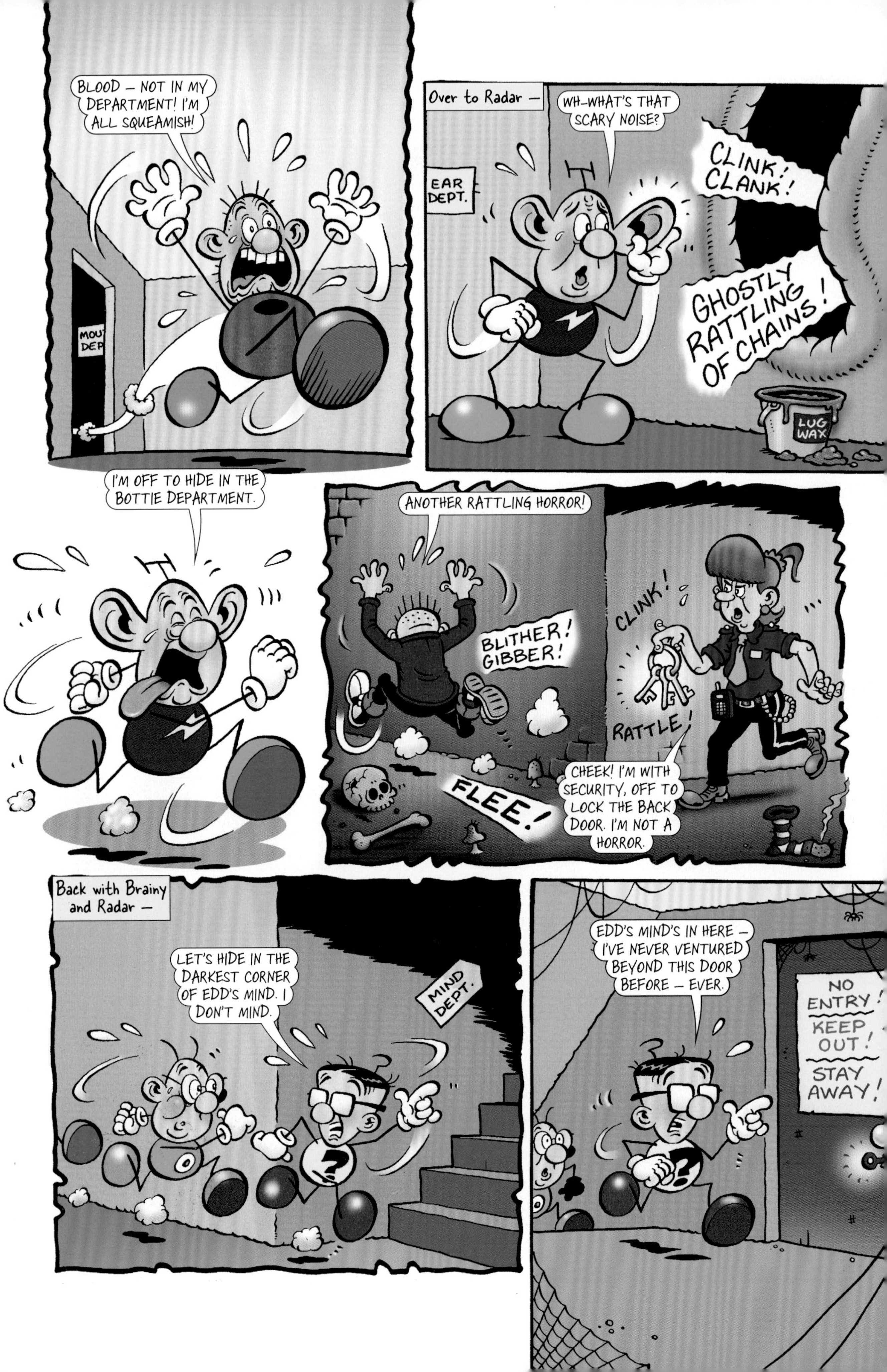
BLOOD – NOT IN MY DEPARTMENT! I'M ALL SQUEAMISH!
Over to Radar –
WH–WHAT'S THAT SCARY NOISE?
EAR DEPT.
CLINK! CLANK!
GHOSTLY RATTLING OF CHAINS!
LUG WAX
I'M OFF TO HIDE IN THE BOTTIE DEPARTMENT.
ANOTHER RATTLING HORROR!
BLITHER! GIBBER!
CLINK!
RATTLE!
FLEE!
CHEEK! I'M WITH SECURITY, OFF TO LOCK THE BACK DOOR. I'M NOT A HORROR.
Back with Brainy and Radar –
LET'S HIDE IN THE DARKEST CORNER OF EDD'S MIND. I DON'T MIND.
MIND DEPT.
EDD'S MIND'S IN HERE – I'VE NEVER VENTURED BEYOND THIS DOOR BEFORE – EVER.
NO ENTRY! KEEP OUT! STAY AWAY!

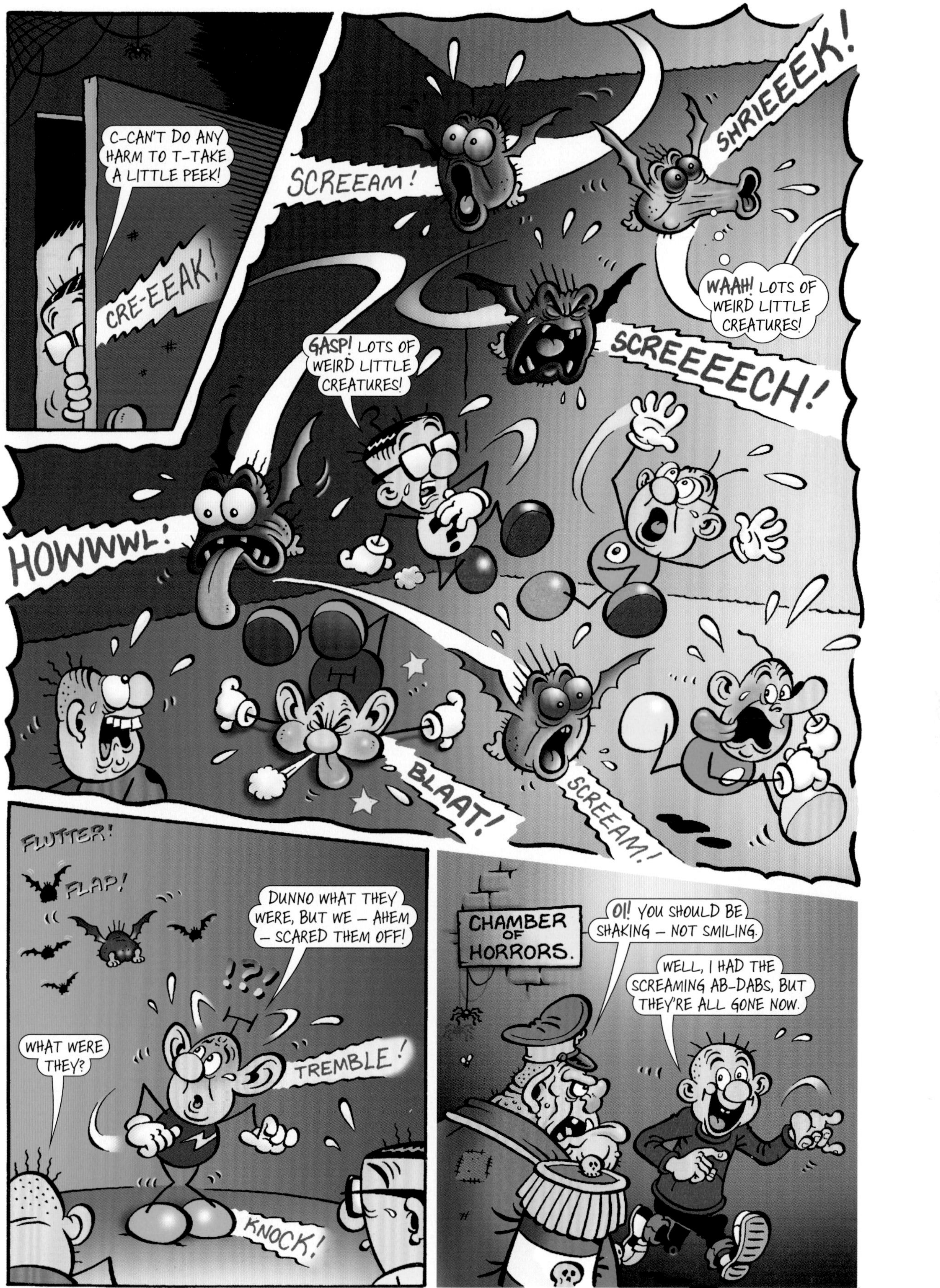

C-CAN'T DO ANY HARM TO T-TAKE A LITTLE PEEK!
CRE-EEAK!
SCREEAM!
SHRIEEEK!
WAAH! LOTS OF WEIRD LITTLE CREATURES!
GASP! LOTS OF WEIRD LITTLE CREATURES!
SCREEEECH!
HOWWWL!
BLAAT!
SCREEAM!
FLUTTER!
FLAP!
DUNNO WHAT THEY WERE, BUT WE – AHEM – SCARED THEM OFF!
!?!
TREMBLE!
WHAT WERE THEY?
KNOCK!
CHAMBER OF HORRORS.
OI! YOU SHOULD BE SHAKING – NOT SMILING.
WELL, I HAD THE SCREAMING AB-DABS, BUT THEY'RE ALL GONE NOW.
-TOM PATERSON-

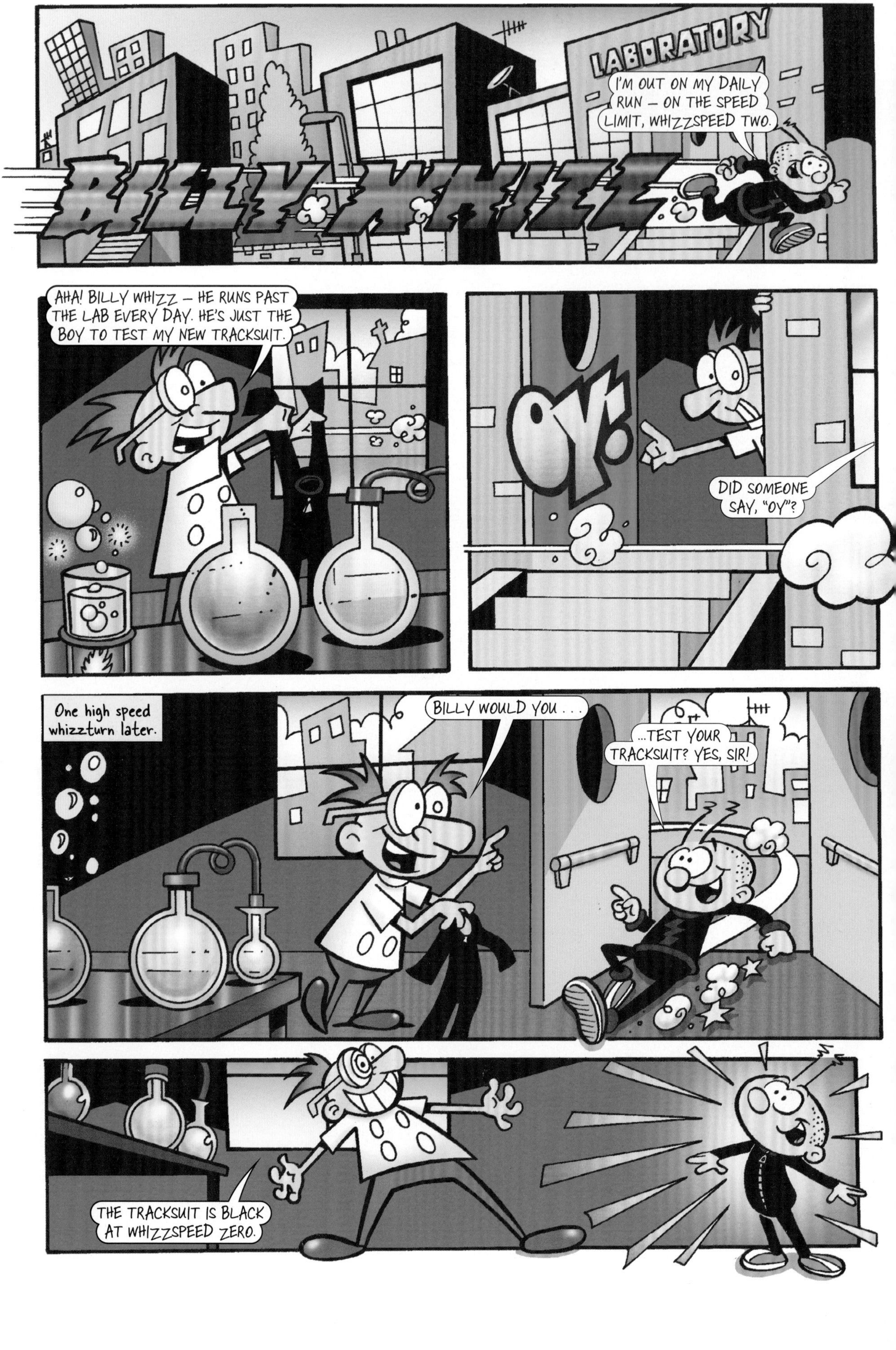
LABORATORY
I'M OUT ON MY DAILY RUN – ON THE SPEED LIMIT, WHIZZSPEED TWO.
AHA! BILLY WHIZZ – HE RUNS PAST THE LAB EVERY DAY. HE'S JUST THE BOY TO TEST MY NEW TRACKSUIT.
OY!
DID SOMEONE SAY, "OY"?
One high speed whizzturn later.
BILLY WOULD YOU . . .
...TEST YOUR TRACKSUIT? YES, SIR!
THE TRACKSUIT IS BLACK AT WHIZZSPEED ZERO.

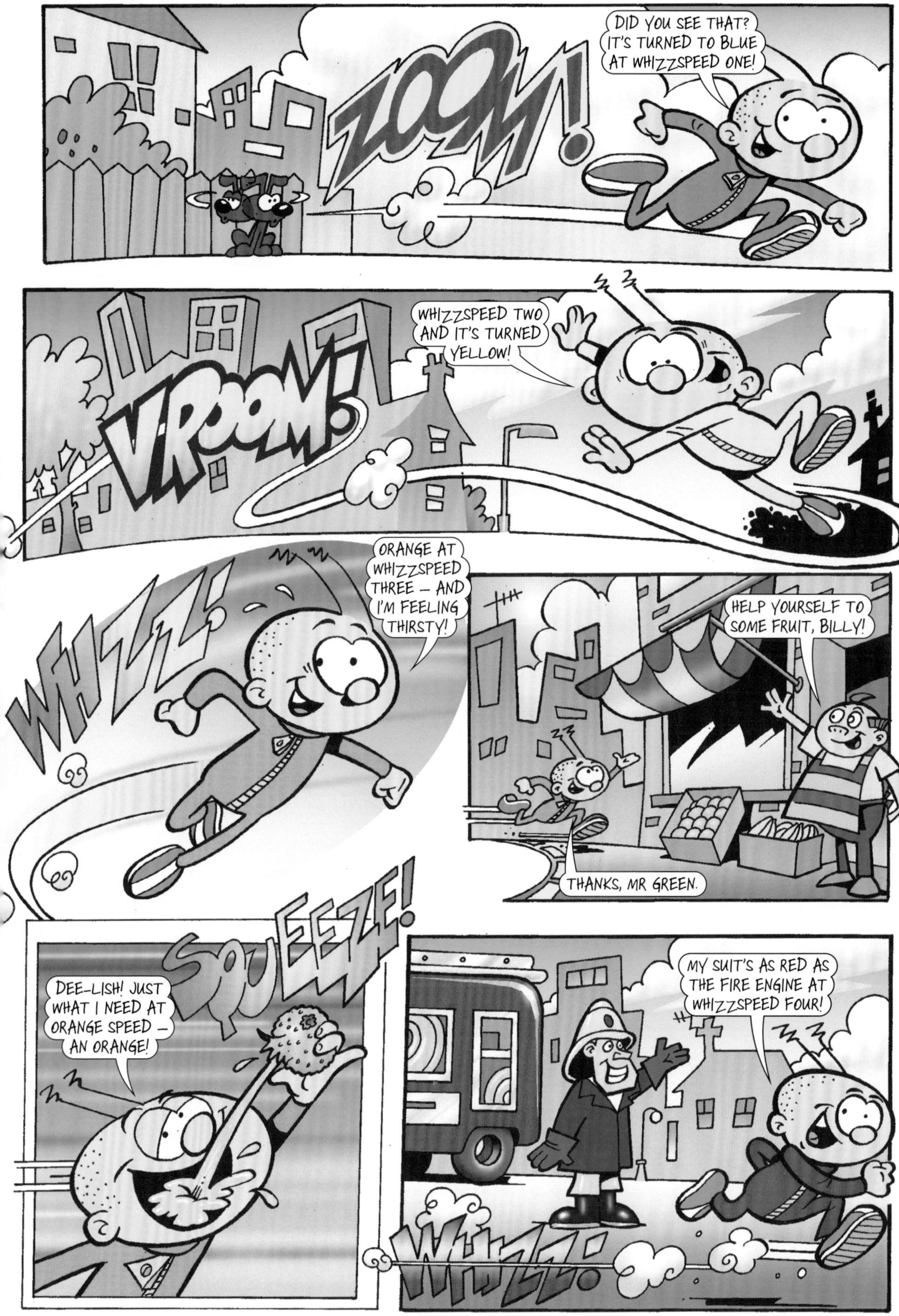
ZOOM!
DID YOU SEE THAT? IT'S TURNED TO BLUE AT WHIZZSPEED ONE!
VROOM!
WHIZZSPEED TWO AND IT'S TURNED YELLOW!
WHIZZ!
ORANGE AT WHIZZSPEED THREE – AND I'M FEELING THIRSTY!
HELP YOURSELF TO SOME FRUIT, BILLY!
THANKS, MR GREEN.
SQUEEZE!
DEE-LISH! JUST WHAT I NEED AT ORANGE SPEED – AN ORANGE!
MY SUIT'S AS RED AS THE FIRE ENGINE AT WHIZZSPEED FOUR!
WHIZZ!

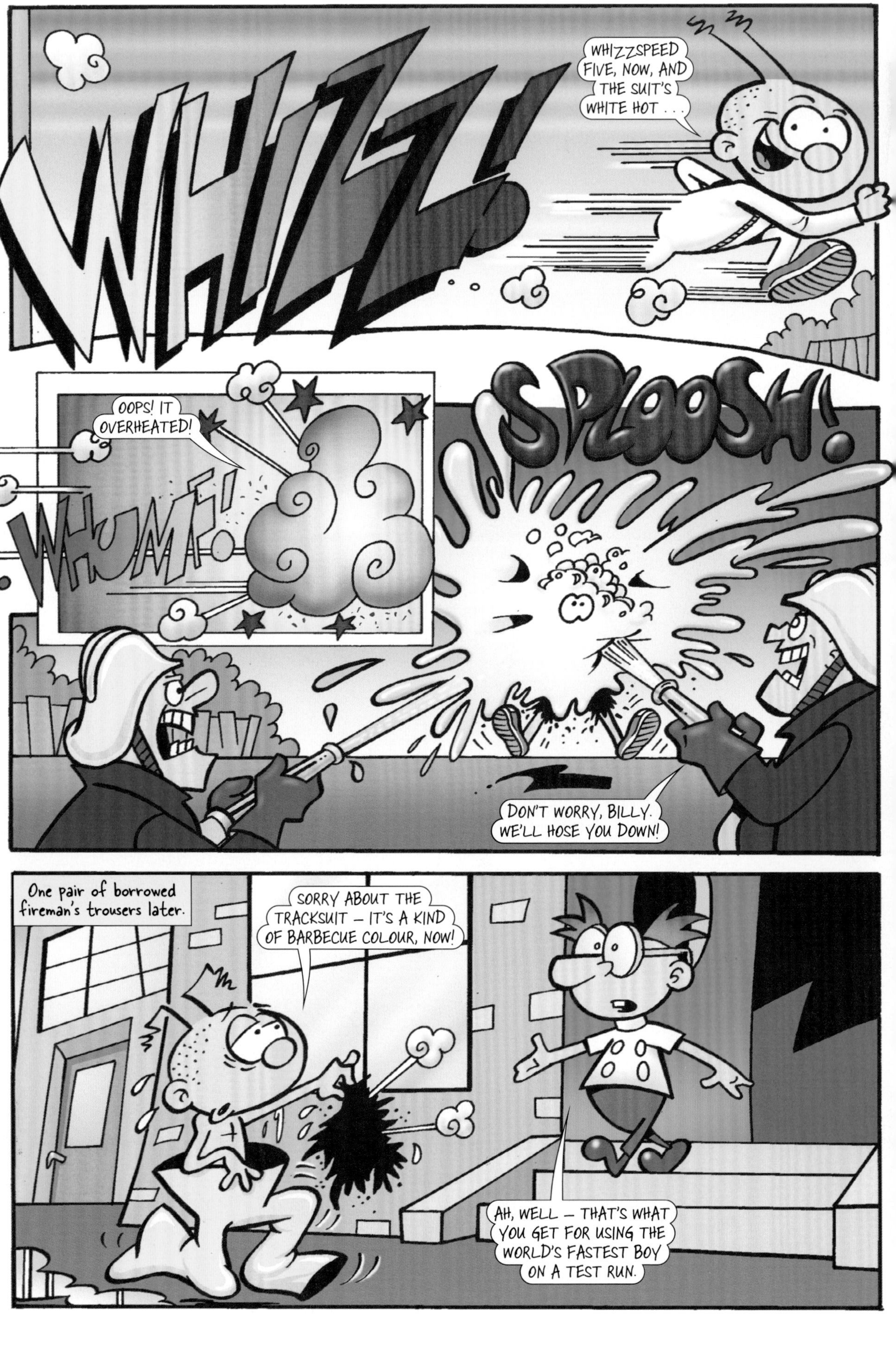
WHIZZ!
WHIZZSPEED FIVE, NOW, AND THE SUIT'S WHITE HOT . . .
OOPS! IT OVERHEATED!
WHUMF!
SPLOOSH!
DON'T WORRY, BILLY. WE'LL HOSE YOU DOWN!
One pair of borrowed fireman's trousers later.
SORRY ABOUT THE TRACKSUIT – IT'S A KIND OF BARBECUE COLOUR, NOW!
AH, WELL – THAT'S WHAT YOU GET FOR USING THE WORLD'S FASTEST BOY ON A TEST RUN.

MINNIE the MINX

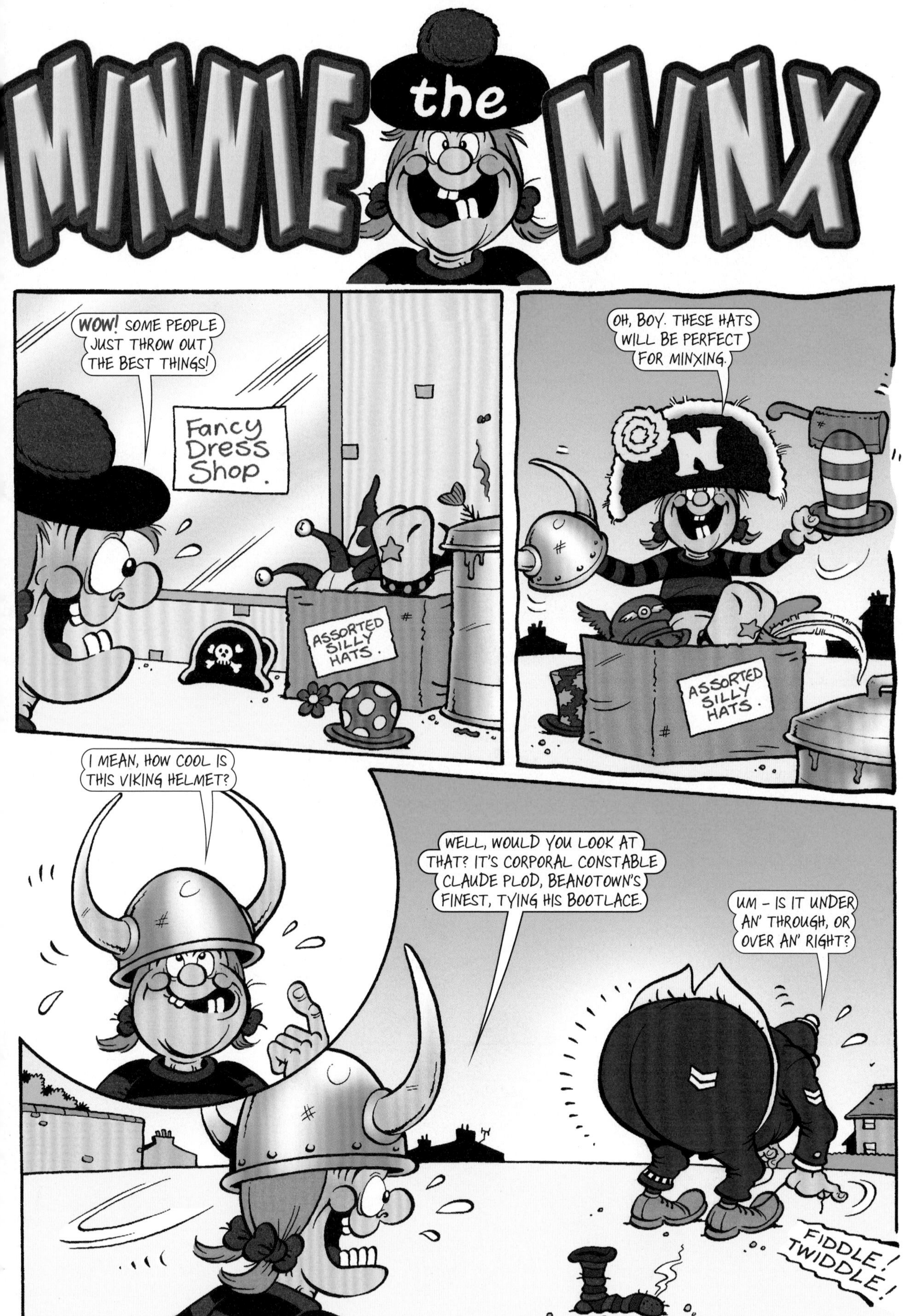

WOW! SOME PEOPLE JUST THROW OUT THE BEST THINGS!
Fancy Dress Shop.
ASSORTED SILLY HATS.
OH, BOY. THESE HATS WILL BE PERFECT FOR MINXING.
ASSORTED SILLY HATS.
I MEAN, HOW COOL IS THIS VIKING HELMET?
WELL, WOULD YOU LOOK AT THAT? IT'S CORPORAL CONSTABLE CLAUDE PLOD, BEANOTOWN'S FINEST, TYING HIS BOOTLACE.
UM – IS IT UNDER AN' THROUGH, OR OVER AN' RIGHT?
FIDDLE! TWIDDLE!

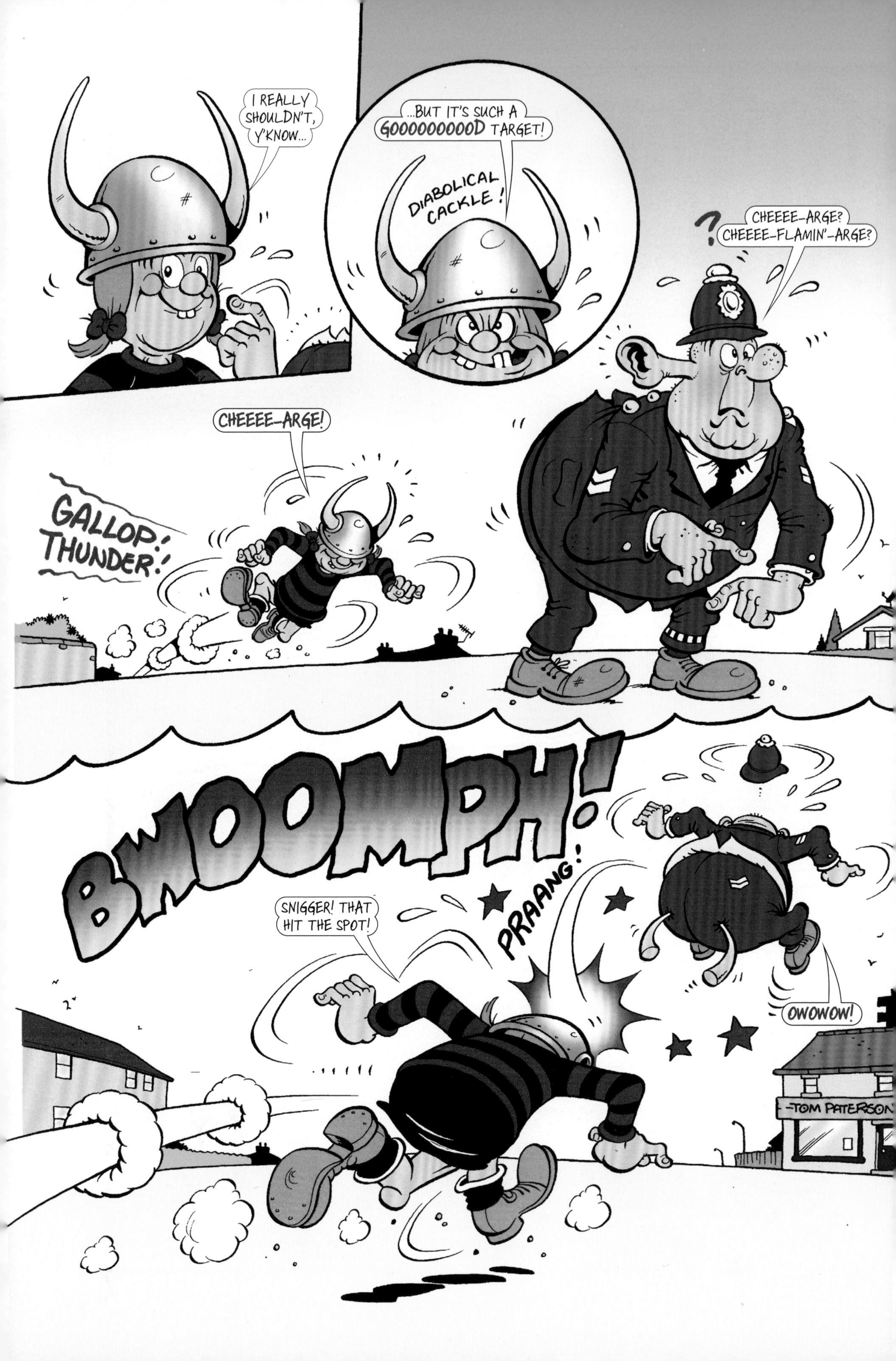
I REALLY SHOULDN'T, Y'KNOW...
...BUT IT'S SUCH A GOOOOOOOOD TARGET!
DIABOLICAL CACKLE!
CHEEEE-ARGE? CHEEEE-FLAMIN'-ARGE?
?
CHEEEE-ARGE!
GALLOP! THUNDER!
BWOOMPH!
PRAANG!
SNIGGER! THAT HIT THE SPOT!
OWOWOW!
-TOM PATERSON

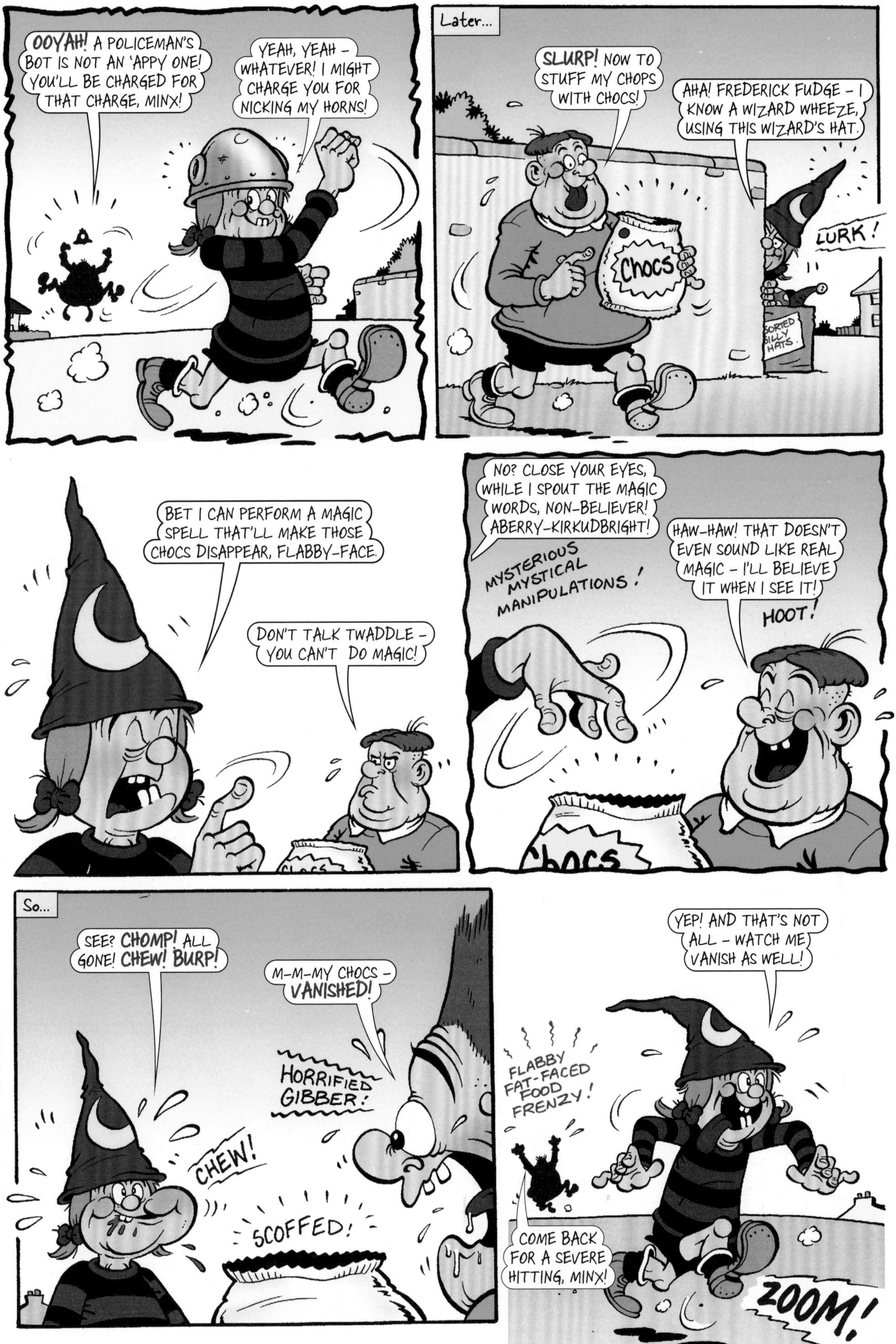
OOYAH! A POLICEMAN'S BOT IS NOT AN 'APPY ONE! YOU'LL BE CHARGED FOR THAT CHARGE, MINX!
YEAH, YEAH – WHATEVER! I MIGHT CHARGE YOU FOR NICKING MY HORNS!
Later...
SLURP! NOW TO STUFF MY CHOPS WITH CHOCS!
AHA! FREDERICK FUDGE – I KNOW A WIZARD WHEEZE, USING THIS WIZARD'S HAT.
Chocs
LURK!
BET I CAN PERFORM A MAGIC SPELL THAT'LL MAKE THOSE CHOCS DISAPPEAR, FLABBY-FACE.
DON'T TALK TWADDLE – YOU CAN'T DO MAGIC!
NO? CLOSE YOUR EYES, WHILE I SPOUT THE MAGIC WORDS, NON-BELIEVER! ABERRY-KIRKUDBRIGHT!
MYSTERIOUS MYSTICAL MANIPULATIONS!
HAW-HAW! THAT DOESN'T EVEN SOUND LIKE REAL MAGIC – I'LL BELIEVE IT WHEN I SEE IT!
HOOT!
So...
SEE? CHOMP! ALL GONE! CHEW! BURP!
M-M-MY CHOCS – VANISHED!
HORRIFIED GIBBER!
CHEW!
SCOFFED!
YEP! AND THAT'S NOT ALL – WATCH ME VANISH AS WELL!
FLABBY FAT-FACED FOOD FRENZY!
COME BACK FOR A SEVERE HITTING, MINX!
ZOOM!

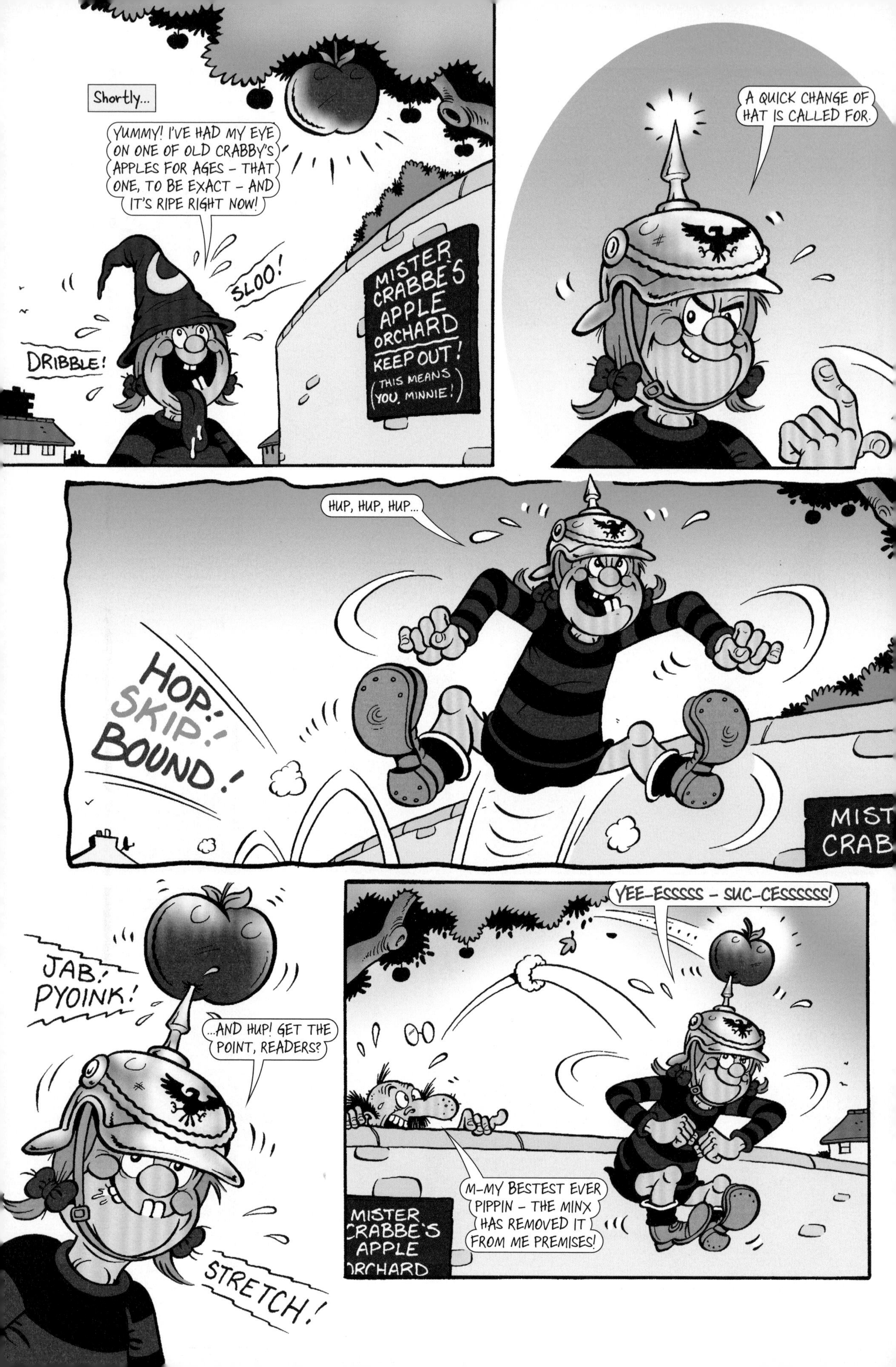
Shortly...
YUMMY! I'VE HAD MY EYE ON ONE OF OLD CRABBY'S APPLES FOR AGES – THAT ONE, TO BE EXACT – AND IT'S RIPE RIGHT NOW!
SLOO!
DRIBBLE!
MISTER CRABBE'S APPLE ORCHARD KEEP OUT! (THIS MEANS YOU, MINNIE!)
A QUICK CHANGE OF HAT IS CALLED FOR.
HUP, HUP, HUP...
HOP! SKIP! BOUND!
MIST CRAB
JAB! PYOINK!
...AND HUP! GET THE POINT, READERS?
STRETCH!
YEE-ESSSSS – SUC-CESSSSSS!
M-MY BESTEST EVER PIPPIN – THE MINX HAS REMOVED IT FROM ME PREMISES!
MISTER CRABBE'S APPLE ORCHARD

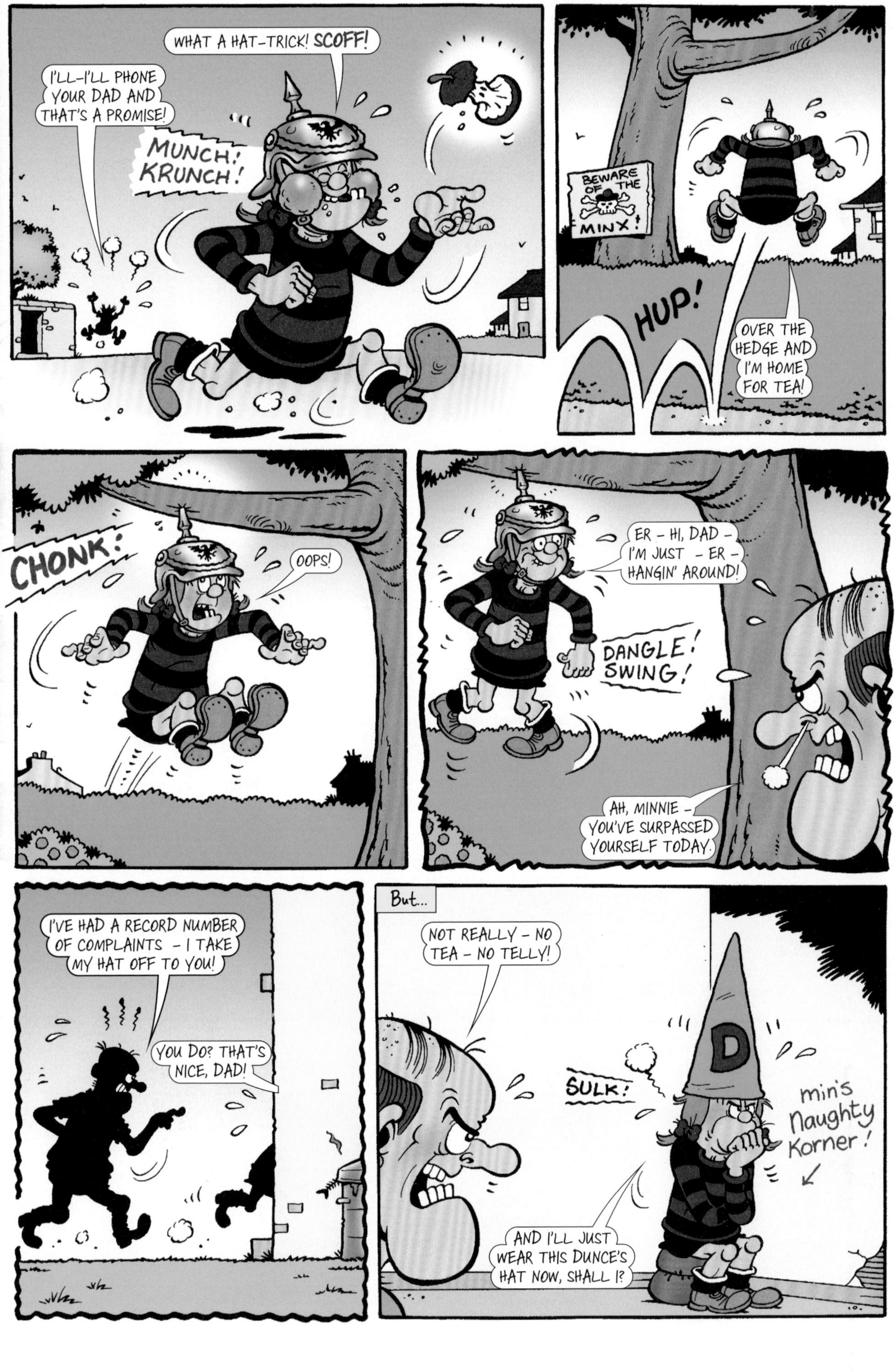
WHAT A HAT-TRICK! SCOFF!
I'LL-I'LL PHONE YOUR DAD AND THAT'S A PROMISE!
MUNCH! KRUNCH!
BEWARE OF THE MINX!
HUP!
OVER THE HEDGE AND I'M HOME FOR TEA!
CHONK!
OOPS!
ER – HI, DAD – I'M JUST – ER – HANGIN' AROUND!
DANGLE! SWING!
AH, MINNIE – YOU'VE SURPASSED YOURSELF TODAY.
I'VE HAD A RECORD NUMBER OF COMPLAINTS – I TAKE MY HAT OFF TO YOU!
YOU DO? THAT'S NICE, DAD!
But...
NOT REALLY – NO TEA – NO TELLY!
SULK!
D
min's Naughty Korner!
AND I'LL JUST WEAR THIS DUNCE'S HAT NOW, SHALL I?

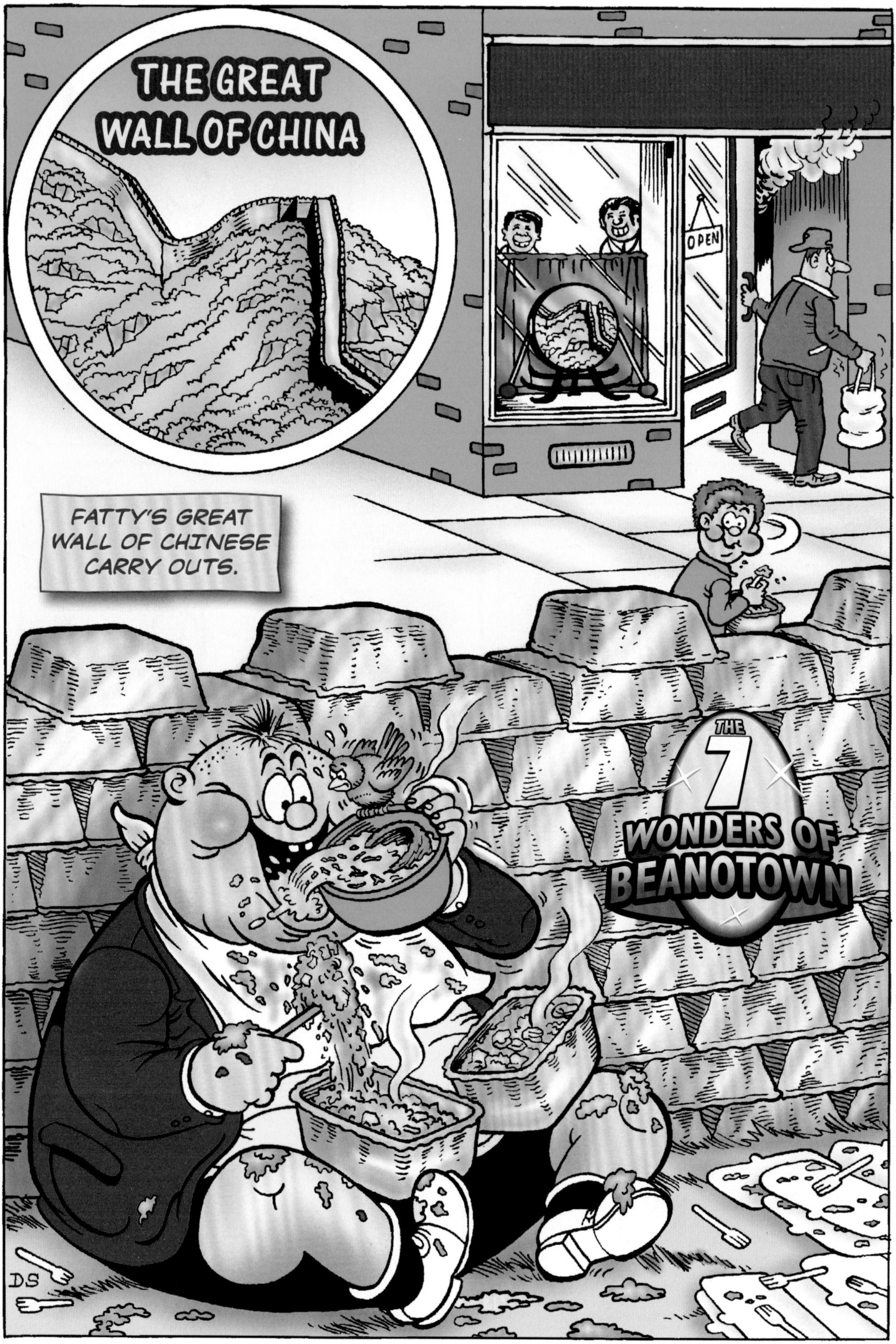
THE GREAT WALL OF CHINA
OPEN
FATTY'S GREAT WALL OF CHINESE CARRY OUTS.
THE 7 WONDERS OF BEANOTOWN
DS

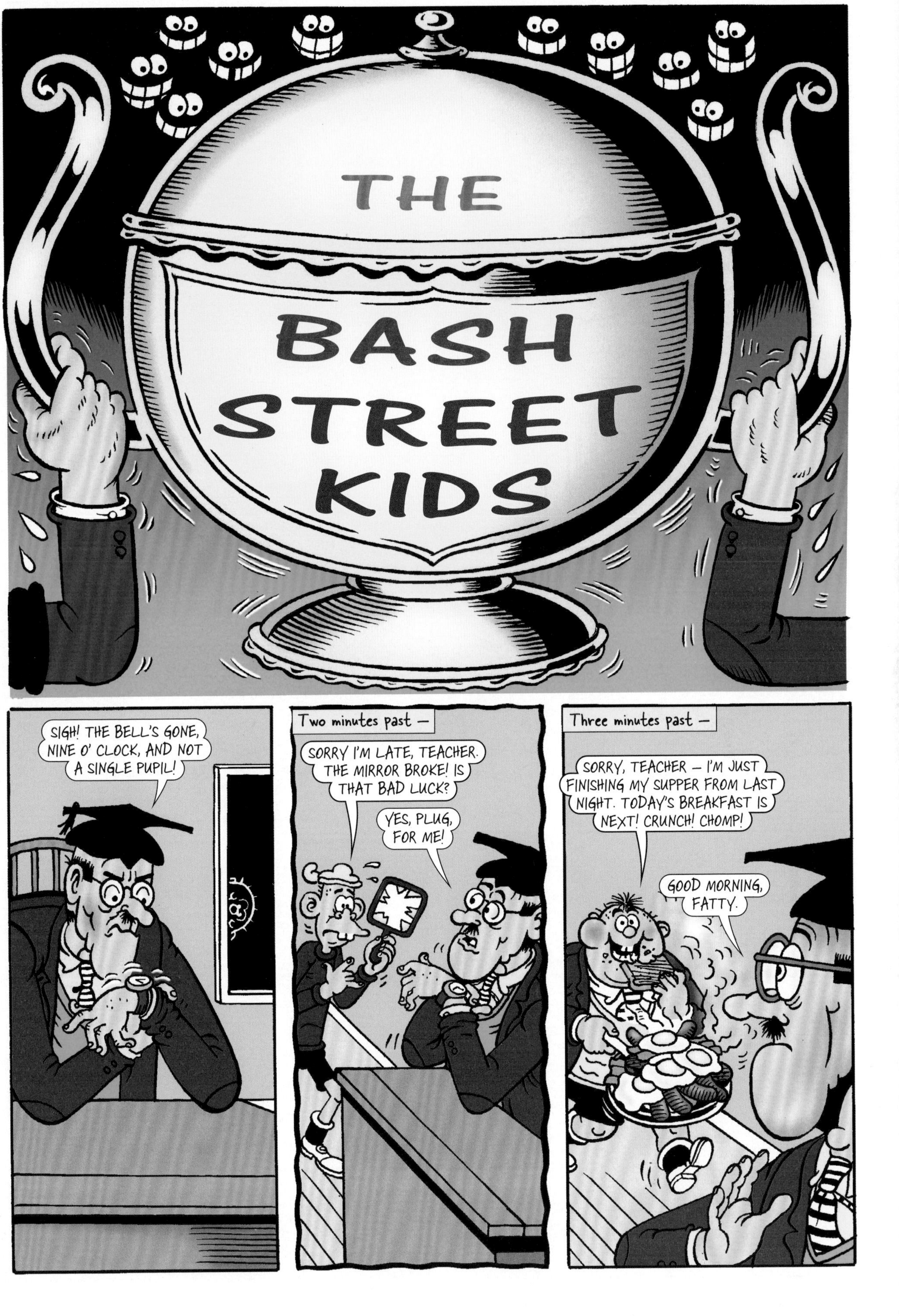
THE
BASH STREET KIDS
SIGH! THE BELL'S GONE, NINE O' CLOCK, AND NOT A SINGLE PUPIL!
Two minutes past —
SORRY I'M LATE, TEACHER. THE MIRROR BROKE! IS THAT BAD LUCK?
YES, PLUG, FOR ME!
Three minutes past —
SORRY, TEACHER — I'M JUST FINISHING MY SUPPER FROM LAST NIGHT. TODAY'S BREAKFAST IS NEXT! CRUNCH! CHOMP!
GOOD MORNING, FATTY.

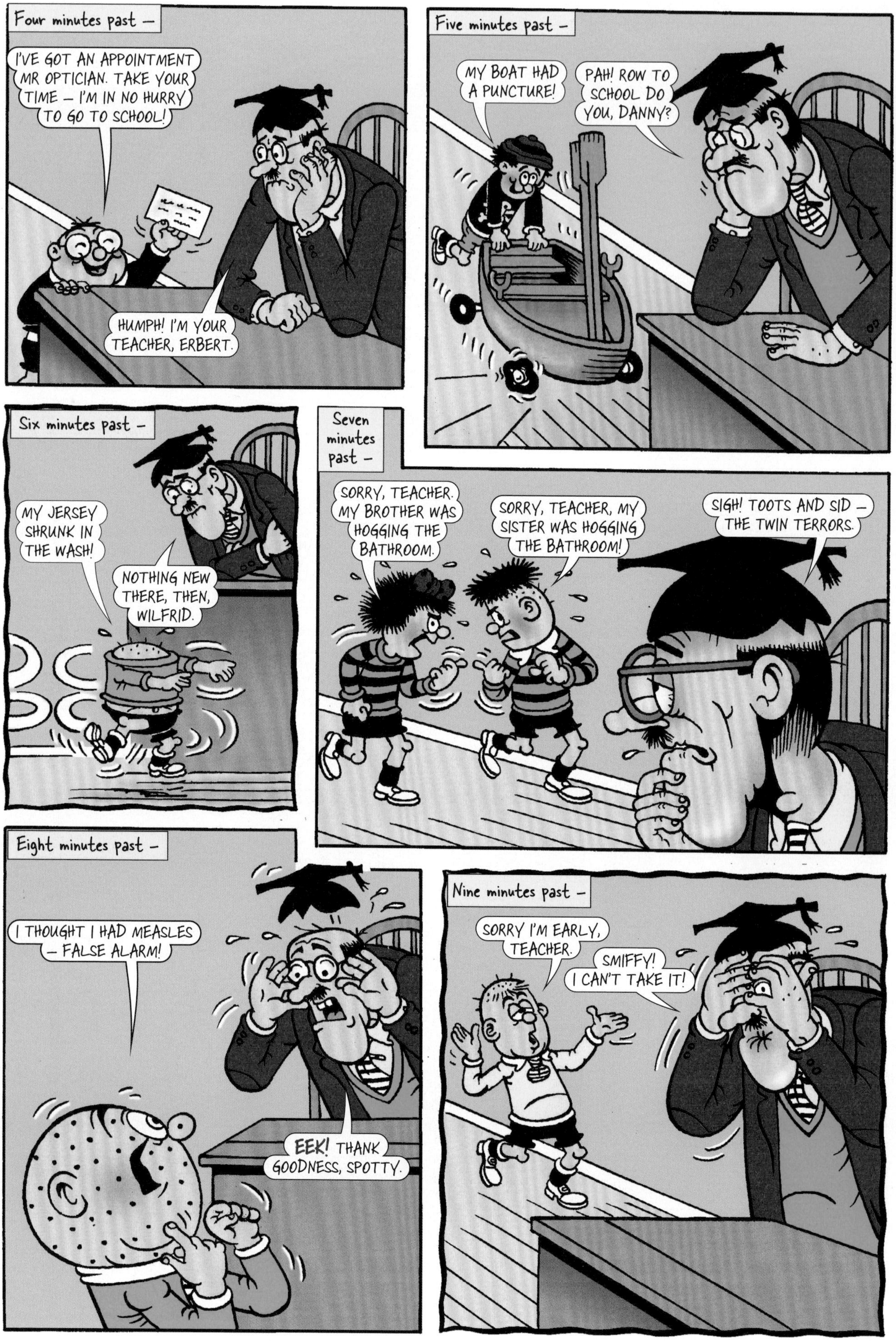
Four minutes past –
I'VE GOT AN APPOINTMENT MR OPTICIAN. TAKE YOUR TIME – I'M IN NO HURRY TO GO TO SCHOOL!
HUMPH! I'M YOUR TEACHER, ERBERT.
Five minutes past –
MY BOAT HAD A PUNCTURE!
PAH! ROW TO SCHOOL DO YOU, DANNY?
Six minutes past –
MY JERSEY SHRUNK IN THE WASH!
NOTHING NEW THERE, THEN, WILFRID.
Seven minutes past –
SORRY, TEACHER. MY BROTHER WAS HOGGING THE BATHROOM.
SORRY, TEACHER, MY SISTER WAS HOGGING THE BATHROOM!
SIGH! TOOTS AND SID – THE TWIN TERRORS.
Eight minutes past –
I THOUGHT I HAD MEASLES – FALSE ALARM!
EEK! THANK GOODNESS, SPOTTY.
Nine minutes past –
SORRY I'M EARLY, TEACHER.
SMIFFY! I CAN'T TAKE IT!

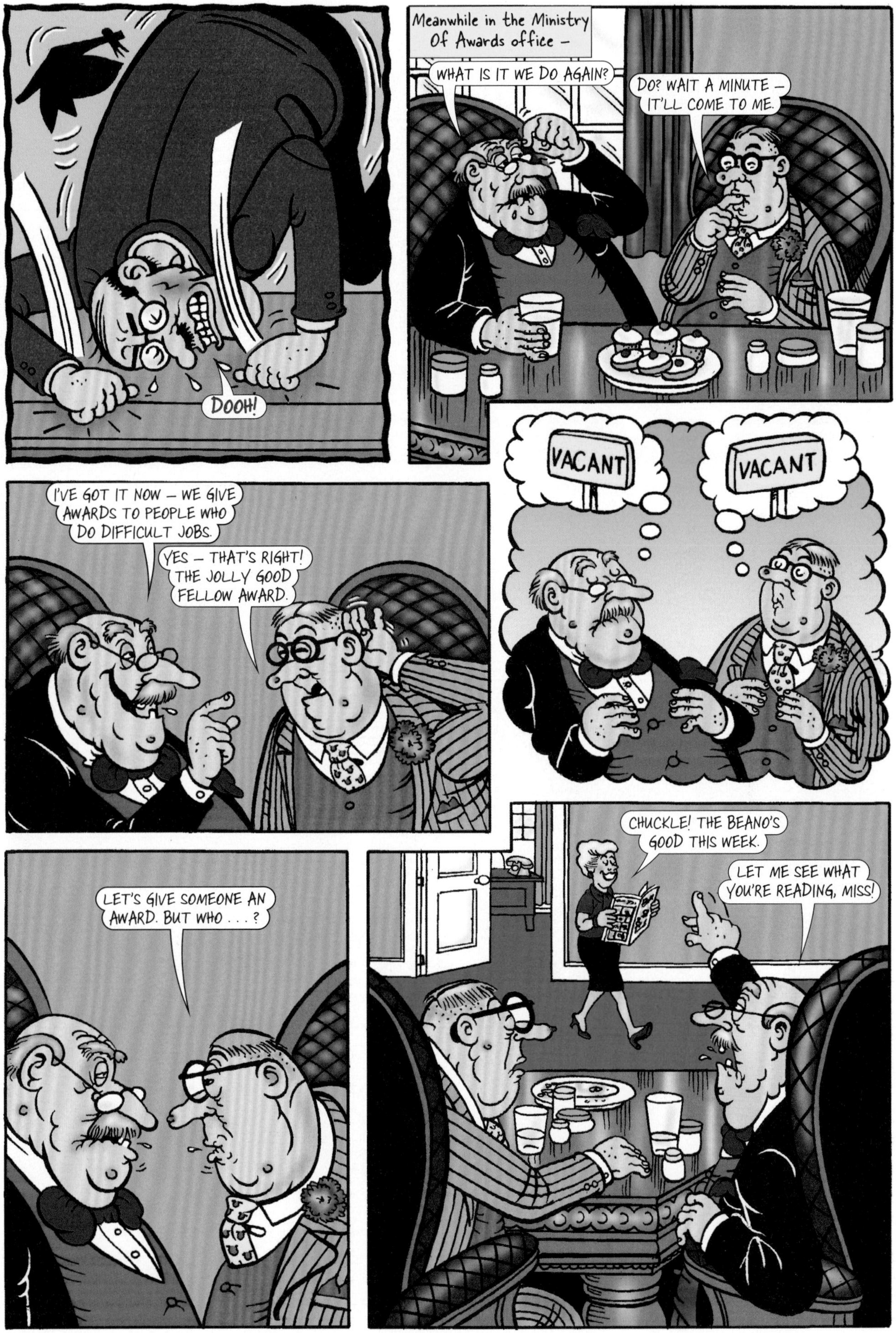
DOOH!
Meanwhile in the Ministry Of Awards office –
WHAT IS IT WE DO AGAIN?
DO? WAIT A MINUTE – IT'LL COME TO ME.
I'VE GOT IT NOW – WE GIVE AWARDS TO PEOPLE WHO DO DIFFICULT JOBS.
YES – THAT'S RIGHT! THE JOLLY GOOD FELLOW AWARD.
VACANT
VACANT
LET'S GIVE SOMEONE AN AWARD. BUT WHO . . . ?
CHUCKLE! THE BEANO'S GOOD THIS WEEK.
LET ME SEE WHAT YOU'RE READING, MISS!

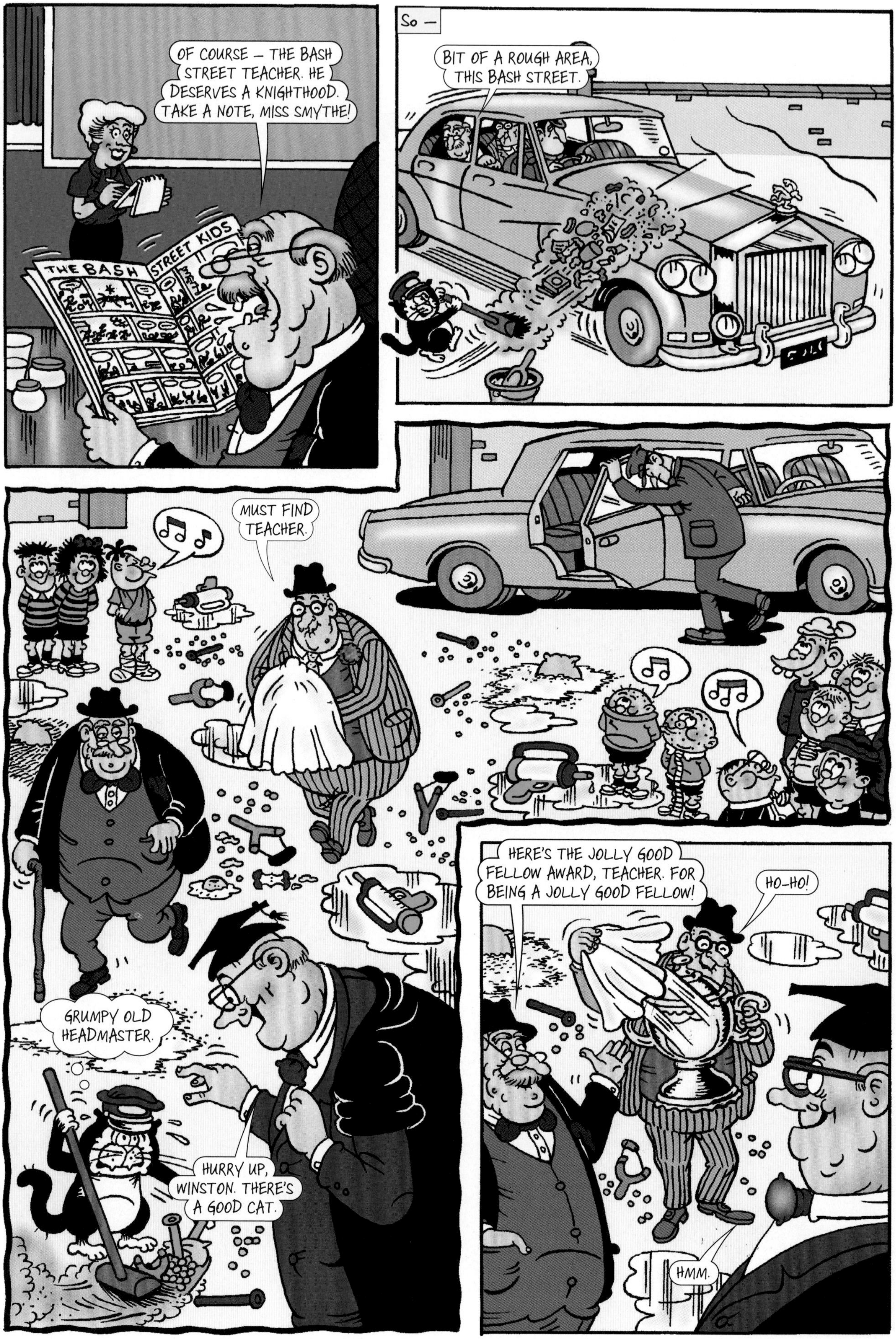
OF COURSE — THE BASH STREET TEACHER. HE DESERVES A KNIGHTHOOD. TAKE A NOTE, MISS SMYTHE!
THE BASH STREET KIDS
So —
BIT OF A ROUGH AREA, THIS BASH STREET.
MUST FIND TEACHER.
GRUMPY OLD HEADMASTER.
HURRY UP, WINSTON. THERE'S A GOOD CAT.
HERE'S THE JOLLY GOOD FELLOW AWARD, TEACHER. FOR BEING A JOLLY GOOD FELLOW!
HO-HO!
HMM.

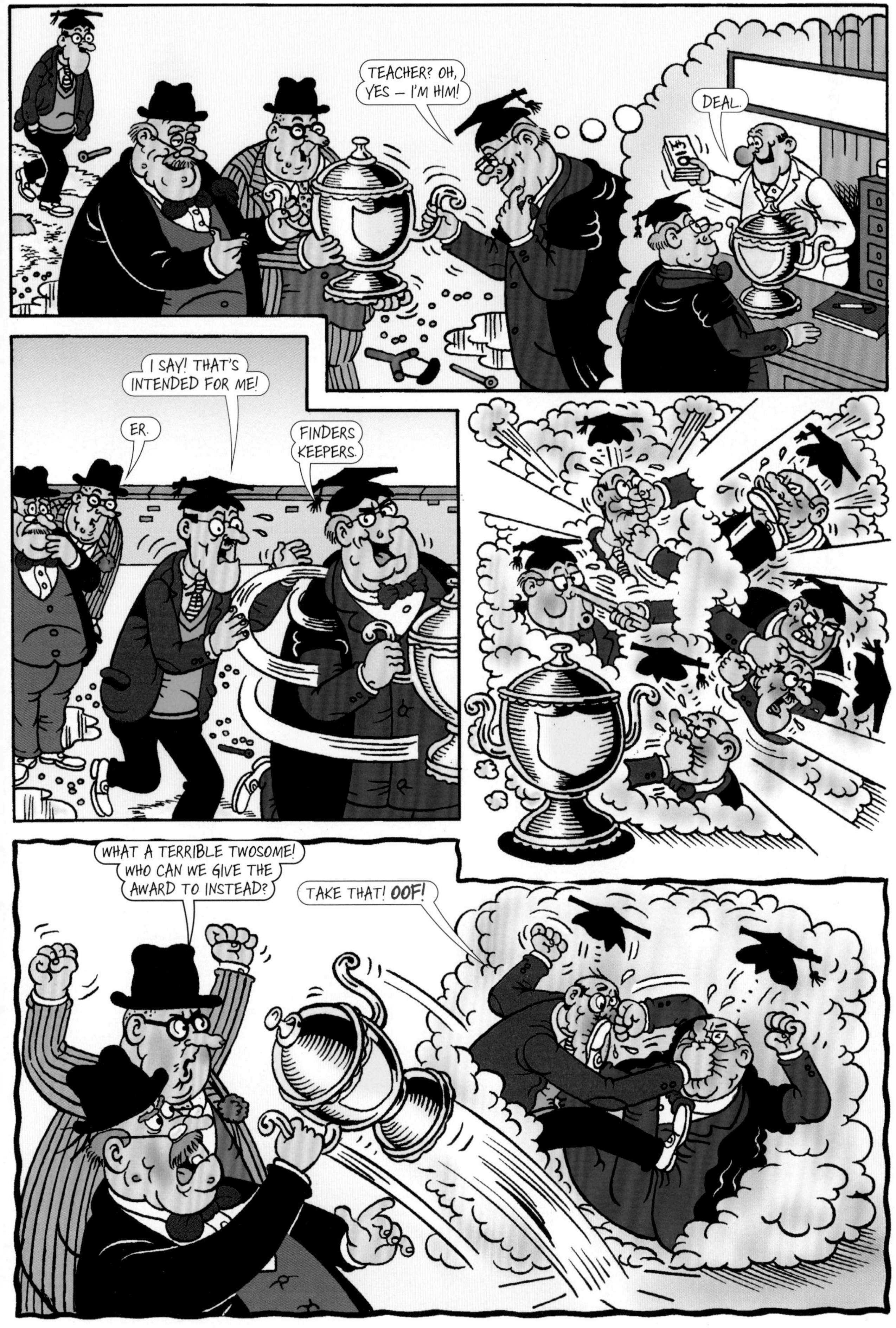
TEACHER? OH, YES – I'M HIM!
DEAL.
I SAY! THAT'S INTENDED FOR ME!
ER.
FINDERS KEEPERS.
WHAT A TERRIBLE TWOSOME! WHO CAN WE GIVE THE AWARD TO INSTEAD?
TAKE THAT! OOF!

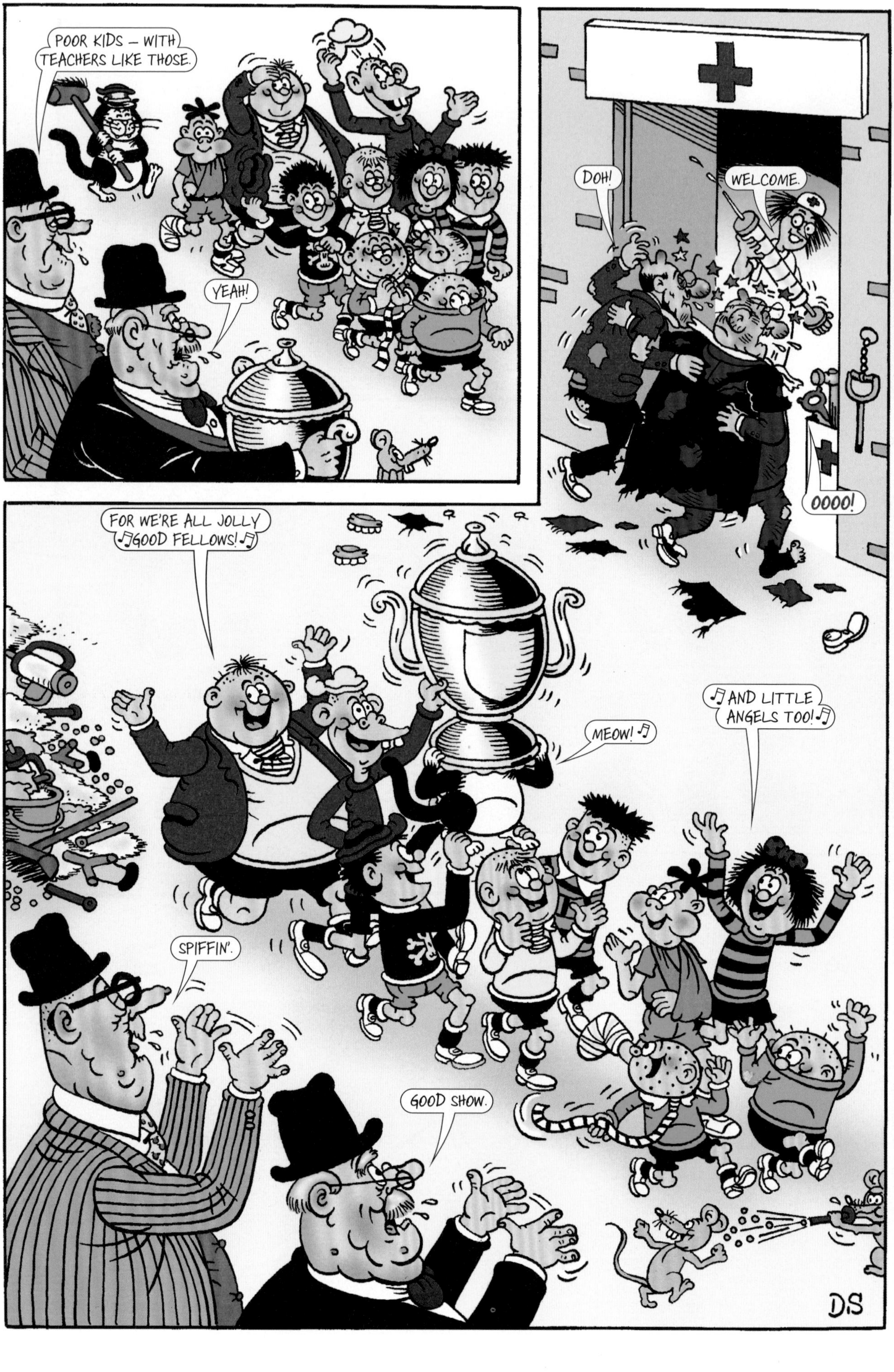
POOR KIDS — WITH TEACHERS LIKE THOSE.
YEAH!
DOH!
WELCOME.
OOOO!
FOR WE'RE ALL JOLLY ♫GOOD FELLOWS!♫
MEOW! ♫
♫AND LITTLE ANGELS TOO!♫
SPIFFIN'.
GOOD SHOW.
DS

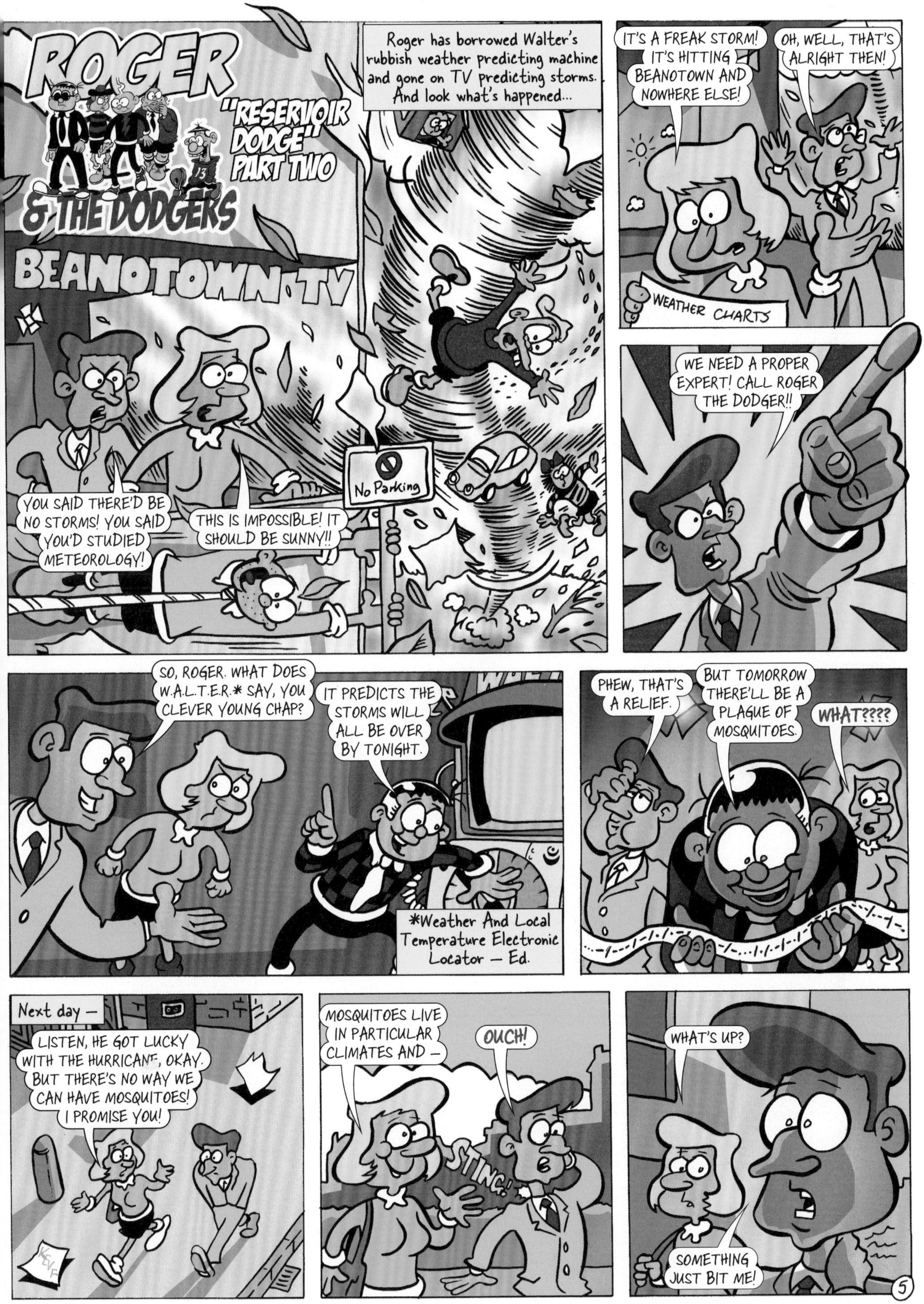
ROGER & THE DODGERS
"RESERVOIR DODGE" PART TWO
BEANOTOWN TV
Roger has borrowed Walter's rubbish weather predicting machine and gone on TV predicting storms. And look what's happened...
YOU SAID THERE'D BE NO STORMS! YOU SAID YOU'D STUDIED METEOROLOGY!
THIS IS IMPOSSIBLE! IT SHOULD BE SUNNY!!
No Parking
IT'S A FREAK STORM! IT'S HITTING BEANOTOWN AND NOWHERE ELSE!
OH, WELL, THAT'S ALRIGHT THEN!
WEATHER CHARTS
WE NEED A PROPER EXPERT! CALL ROGER THE DODGER!!
SO, ROGER. WHAT DOES W.A.L.T.E.R.* SAY, YOU CLEVER YOUNG CHAP?
IT PREDICTS THE STORMS WILL ALL BE OVER BY TONIGHT.
*Weather And Local Temperature Electronic Locator — Ed.
PHEW, THAT'S A RELIEF.
BUT TOMORROW THERE'LL BE A PLAGUE OF MOSQUITOES.
WHAT????
Next day —
LISTEN, HE GOT LUCKY WITH THE HURRICANE, OKAY. BUT THERE'S NO WAY WE CAN HAVE MOSQUITOES! I PROMISE YOU!
MOSQUITOES LIVE IN PARTICULAR CLIMATES AND —
OUCH!
STING!
WHAT'S UP?
SOMETHING JUST BIT ME!

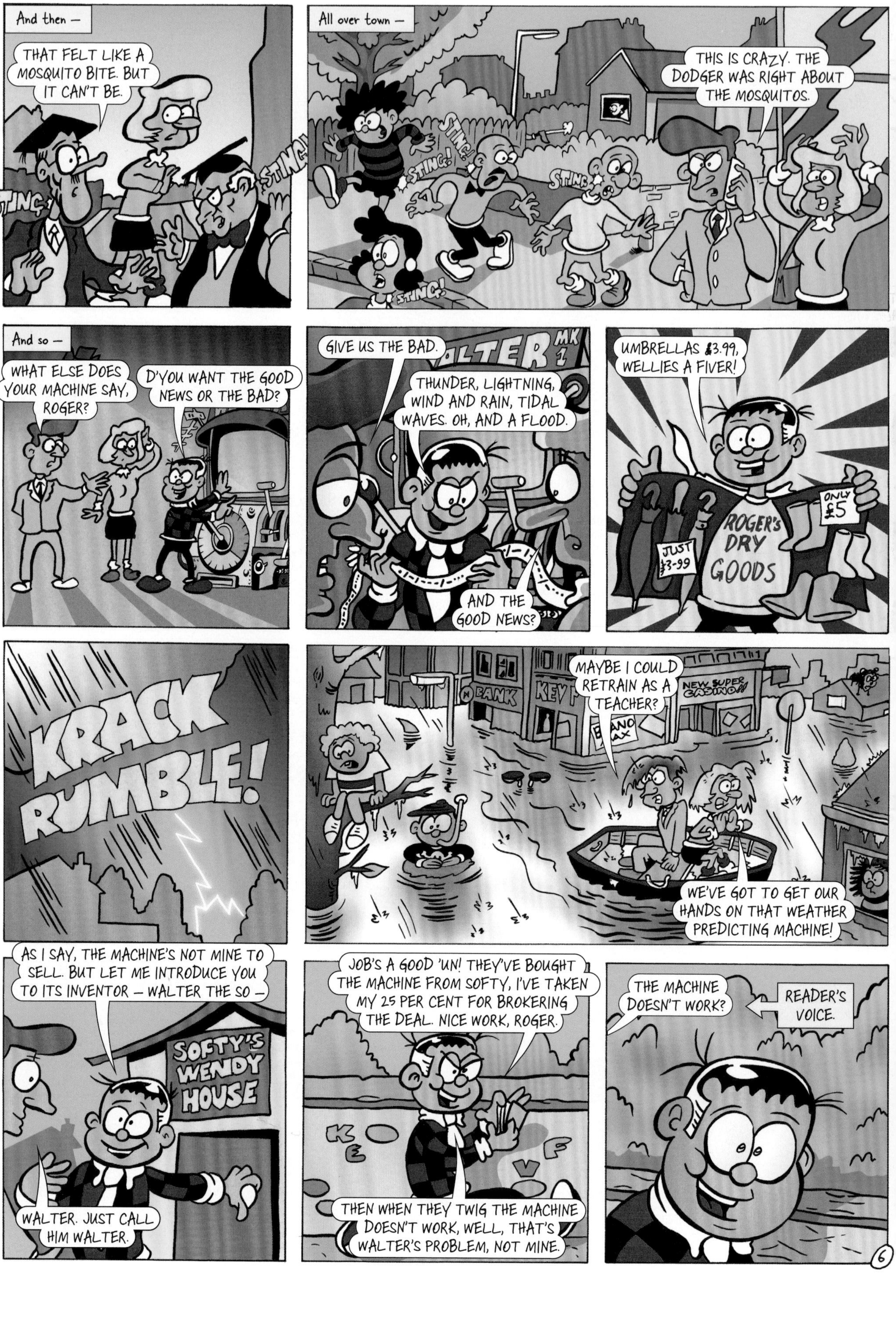
And then —
THAT FELT LIKE A MOSQUITO BITE. BUT IT CAN'T BE.
STING!
STING!
All over town —
THIS IS CRAZY. THE DODGER WAS RIGHT ABOUT THE MOSQUITOS.
STING!
STING!
STING!
STING!
And so —
WHAT ELSE DOES YOUR MACHINE SAY, ROGER?
D'YOU WANT THE GOOD NEWS OR THE BAD?
GIVE US THE BAD.
THUNDER, LIGHTNING, WIND AND RAIN, TIDAL WAVES. OH, AND A FLOOD.
AND THE GOOD NEWS?
UMBRELLAS £3.99, WELLIES A FIVER!
ROGER'S DRY GOODS
JUST £3-99
ONLY £5
KRACK RUMBLE!
MAYBE I COULD RETRAIN AS A TEACHER?
BANK
NEW SUPER CASINO!!
WE'VE GOT TO GET OUR HANDS ON THAT WEATHER PREDICTING MACHINE!
AS I SAY, THE MACHINE'S NOT MINE TO SELL. BUT LET ME INTRODUCE YOU TO ITS INVENTOR — WALTER THE SO —
SOFTY'S WENDY HOUSE
WALTER. JUST CALL HIM WALTER.
JOB'S A GOOD 'UN! THEY'VE BOUGHT THE MACHINE FROM SOFTY, I'VE TAKEN MY 25 PER CENT FOR BROKERING THE DEAL. NICE WORK, ROGER.
THEN WHEN THEY TWIG THE MACHINE DOESN'T WORK, WELL, THAT'S WALTER'S PROBLEM, NOT MINE.
THE MACHINE DOESN'T WORK?
READER'S VOICE.

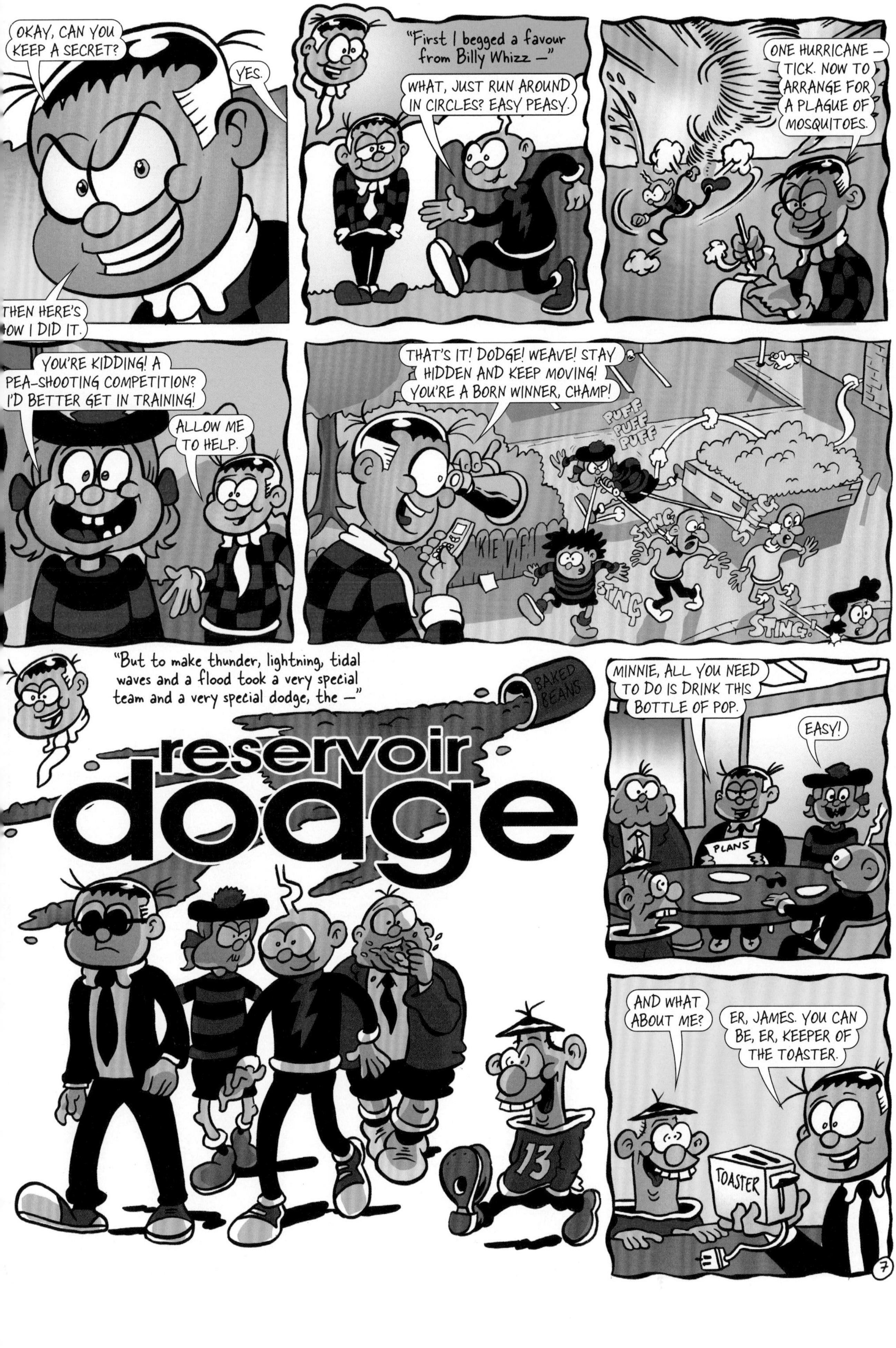
OKAY, CAN YOU KEEP A SECRET?
YES.
THEN HERE'S HOW I DID IT.
"First I begged a favour from Billy Whizz —"
WHAT, JUST RUN AROUND IN CIRCLES? EASY PEASY.
ONE HURRICANE — TICK. NOW TO ARRANGE FOR A PLAGUE OF MOSQUITOES.
YOU'RE KIDDING! A PEA-SHOOTING COMPETITION? I'D BETTER GET IN TRAINING!
ALLOW ME TO HELP.
THAT'S IT! DODGE! WEAVE! STAY HIDDEN AND KEEP MOVING! YOU'RE A BORN WINNER, CHAMP!
PUFF PUFF PUFF
STING
STING
STING
STING!
"But to make thunder, lightning, tidal waves and a flood took a very special team and a very special dodge, the —"
BAKED BEANS
reservoir dodge
13
MINNIE, ALL YOU NEED TO DO IS DRINK THIS BOTTLE OF POP.
EASY!
PLANS
AND WHAT ABOUT ME?
ER, JAMES. YOU CAN BE, ER, KEEPER OF THE TOASTER.
TOASTER

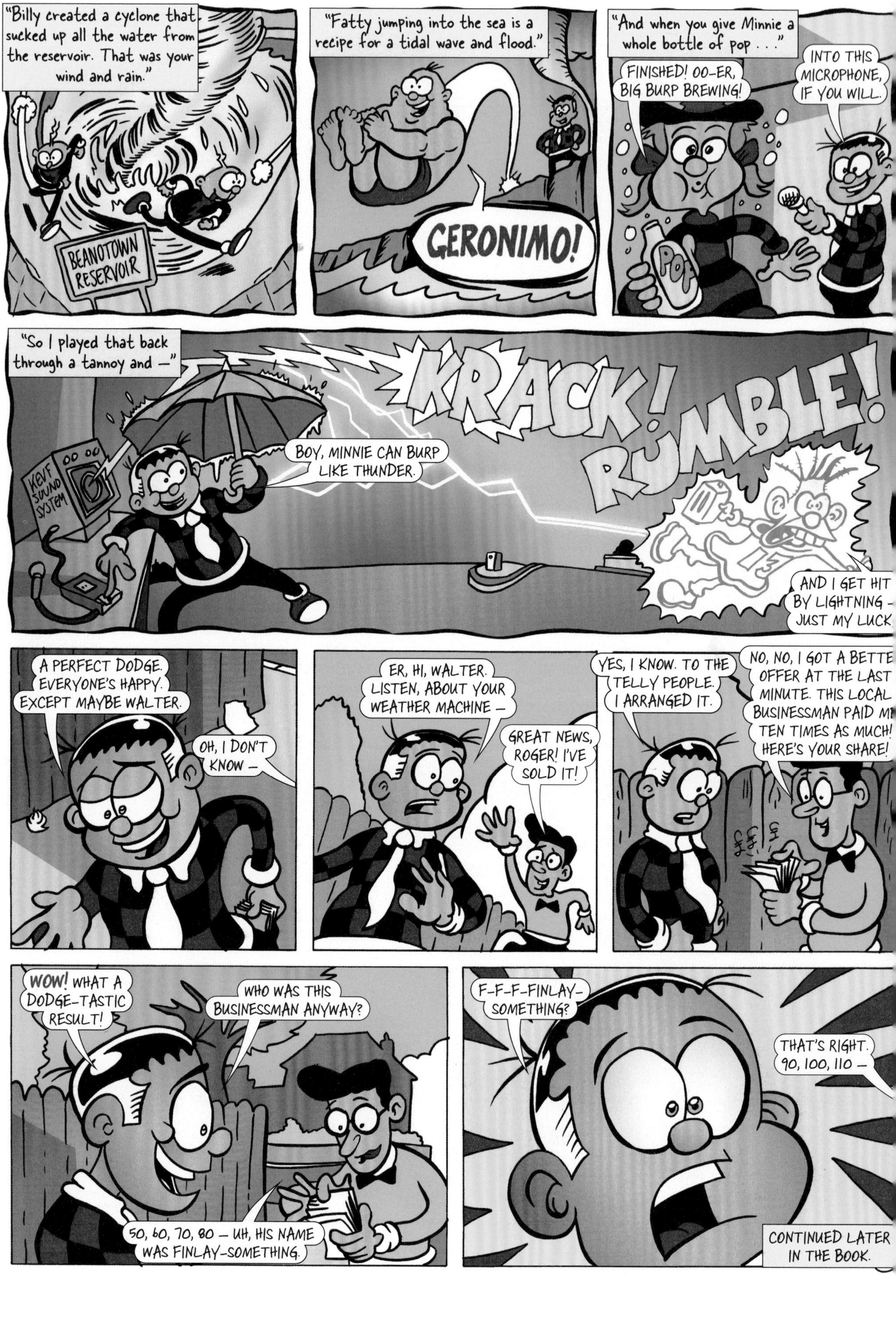
"Billy created a cyclone that sucked up all the water from the reservoir. That was your wind and rain."
BEANOTOWN RESERVOIR
"Fatty jumping into the sea is a recipe for a tidal wave and flood."
GERONIMO!
"And when you give Minnie a whole bottle of pop . . ."
FINISHED! OO-ER, BIG BURP BREWING!
INTO THIS MICROPHONE, IF YOU WILL.
POP
"So I played that back through a tannoy and –"
KRACK!
RUMBLE!
KEVF SOUND SYSTEM
BOY, MINNIE CAN BURP LIKE THUNDER.
AND I GET HIT
BY LIGHTNING –
JUST MY LUCK
A PERFECT DODGE. EVERYONE'S HAPPY. EXCEPT MAYBE WALTER.
OH, I DON'T KNOW –
ER, HI, WALTER. LISTEN, ABOUT YOUR WEATHER MACHINE –
GREAT NEWS, ROGER! I'VE SOLD IT!
YES, I KNOW. TO THE TELLY PEOPLE. I ARRANGED IT.
NO, NO, I GOT A BETTE OFFER AT THE LAST MINUTE. THIS LOCAL BUSINESSMAN PAID M TEN TIMES AS MUCH! HERE'S YOUR SHARE!
WOW! WHAT A DODGE-TASTIC RESULT!
WHO WAS THIS BUSINESSMAN ANYWAY?
50, 60, 70, 80 – UH, HIS NAME WAS FINLAY-SOMETHING.
F-F-F-FINLAY-SOMETHING?
THAT'S RIGHT. 90, 100, 110 –
CONTINUED LATER IN THE BOOK.

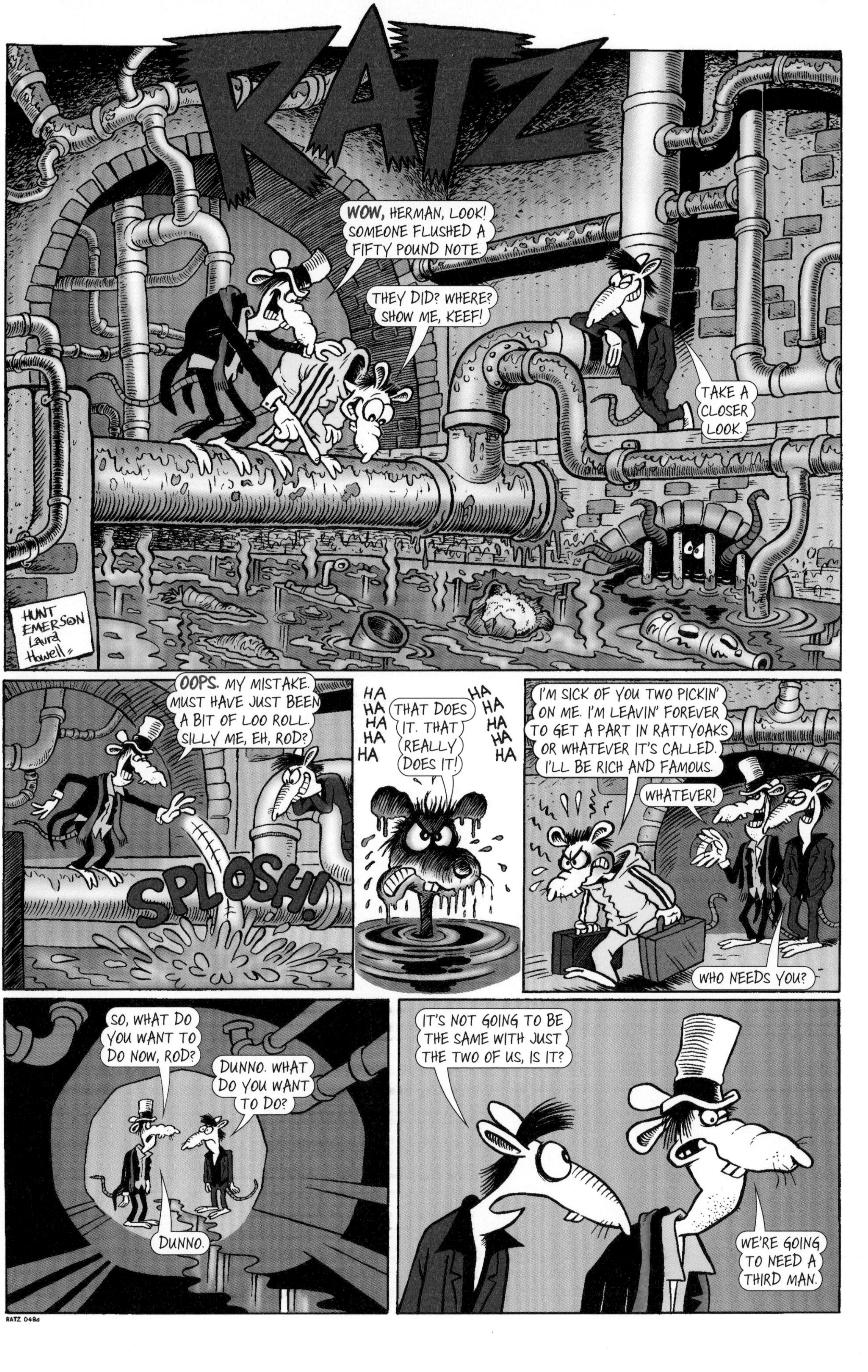
RATZ
WOW, HERMAN, LOOK! SOMEONE FLUSHED A FIFTY POUND NOTE.
THEY DID? WHERE? SHOW ME, KEEF!
TAKE A CLOSER LOOK.
HUNT EMERSON Laura Howell
OOPS. MY MISTAKE. MUST HAVE JUST BEEN A BIT OF LOO ROLL. SILLY ME, EH, ROD?
SPLOSH!
HA HA HA HA HA
THAT DOES IT. THAT REALLY DOES IT!
HA HA HA HA HA
I'M SICK OF YOU TWO PICKIN' ON ME. I'M LEAVIN' FOREVER TO GET A PART IN RATTYOAKS OR WHATEVER IT'S CALLED. I'LL BE RICH AND FAMOUS.
WHATEVER!
WHO NEEDS YOU?
SO, WHAT DO YOU WANT TO DO NOW, ROD?
DUNNO. WHAT DO YOU WANT TO DO?
DUNNO.
IT'S NOT GOING TO BE THE SAME WITH JUST THE TWO OF US, IS IT?
WE'RE GOING TO NEED A THIRD MAN.

RATZ 048a

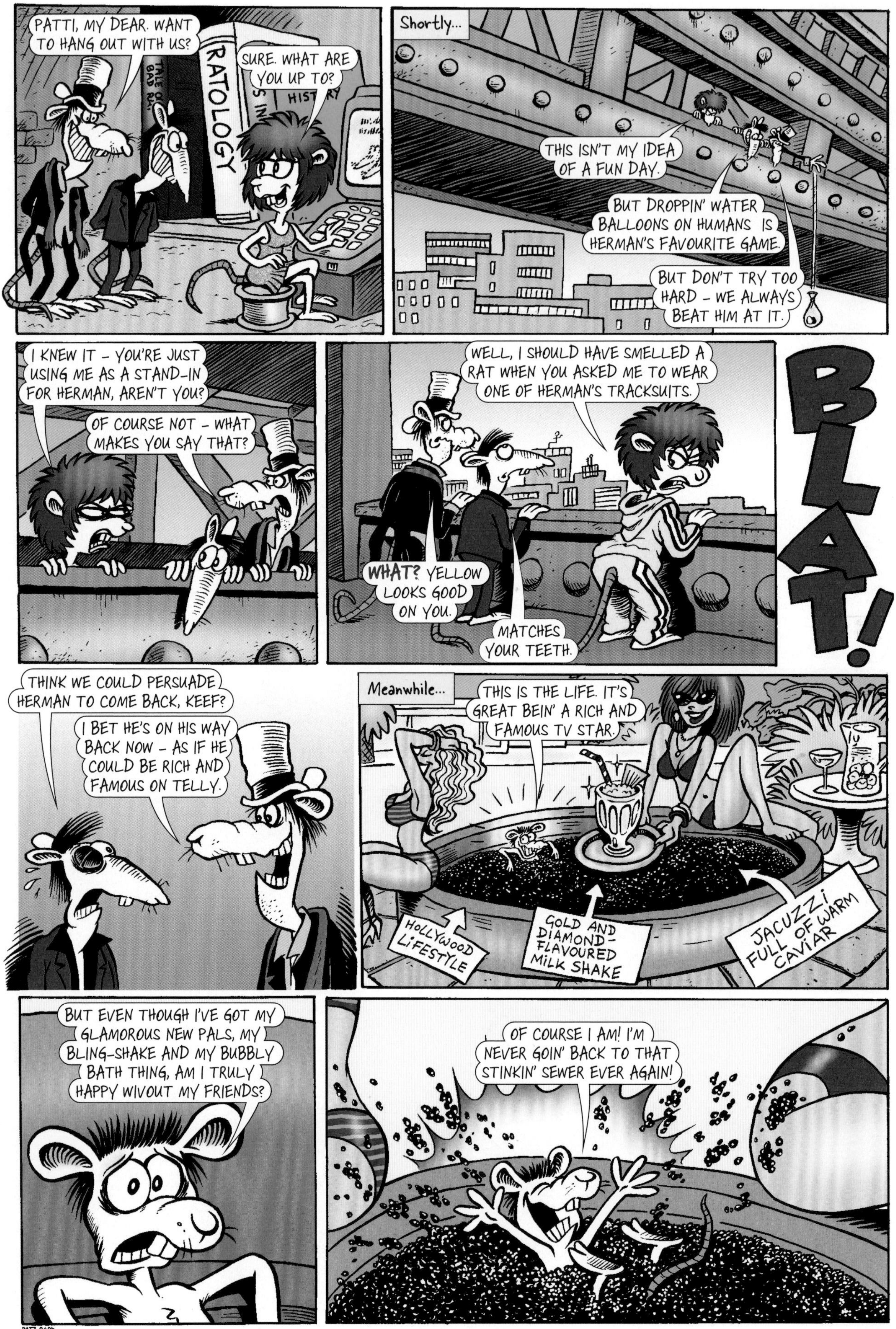
PATTI, MY DEAR. WANT TO HANG OUT WITH US?
TALE OF BAD RAT
RATOLOGY
HISTORY
SURE. WHAT ARE YOU UP TO?
Shortly...
THIS ISN'T MY IDEA OF A FUN DAY.
BUT DROPPIN' WATER BALLOONS ON HUMANS IS HERMAN'S FAVOURITE GAME.
BUT DON'T TRY TOO HARD - WE ALWAYS BEAT HIM AT IT.
I KNEW IT - YOU'RE JUST USING ME AS A STAND-IN FOR HERMAN, AREN'T YOU?
OF COURSE NOT - WHAT MAKES YOU SAY THAT?
WELL, I SHOULD HAVE SMELLED A RAT WHEN YOU ASKED ME TO WEAR ONE OF HERMAN'S TRACKSUITS.
WHAT? YELLOW LOOKS GOOD ON YOU.
MATCHES YOUR TEETH.
BLAT!
THINK WE COULD PERSUADE HERMAN TO COME BACK, KEEF?
I BET HE'S ON HIS WAY BACK NOW - AS IF HE COULD BE RICH AND FAMOUS ON TELLY.
Meanwhile...
THIS IS THE LIFE. IT'S GREAT BEIN' A RICH AND FAMOUS TV STAR.
HOLLYWOOD LIFESTYLE
GOLD AND DIAMOND-FLAVOURED MILK SHAKE
JACUZZI FULL OF WARM CAVIAR
BUT EVEN THOUGH I'VE GOT MY GLAMOROUS NEW PALS, MY BLING-SHAKE AND MY BUBBLY BATH THING, AM I TRULY HAPPY WIVOUT MY FRIENDS?
OF COURSE I AM! I'M NEVER GOIN' BACK TO THAT STINKIN' SEWER EVER AGAIN!
RATZ 048b

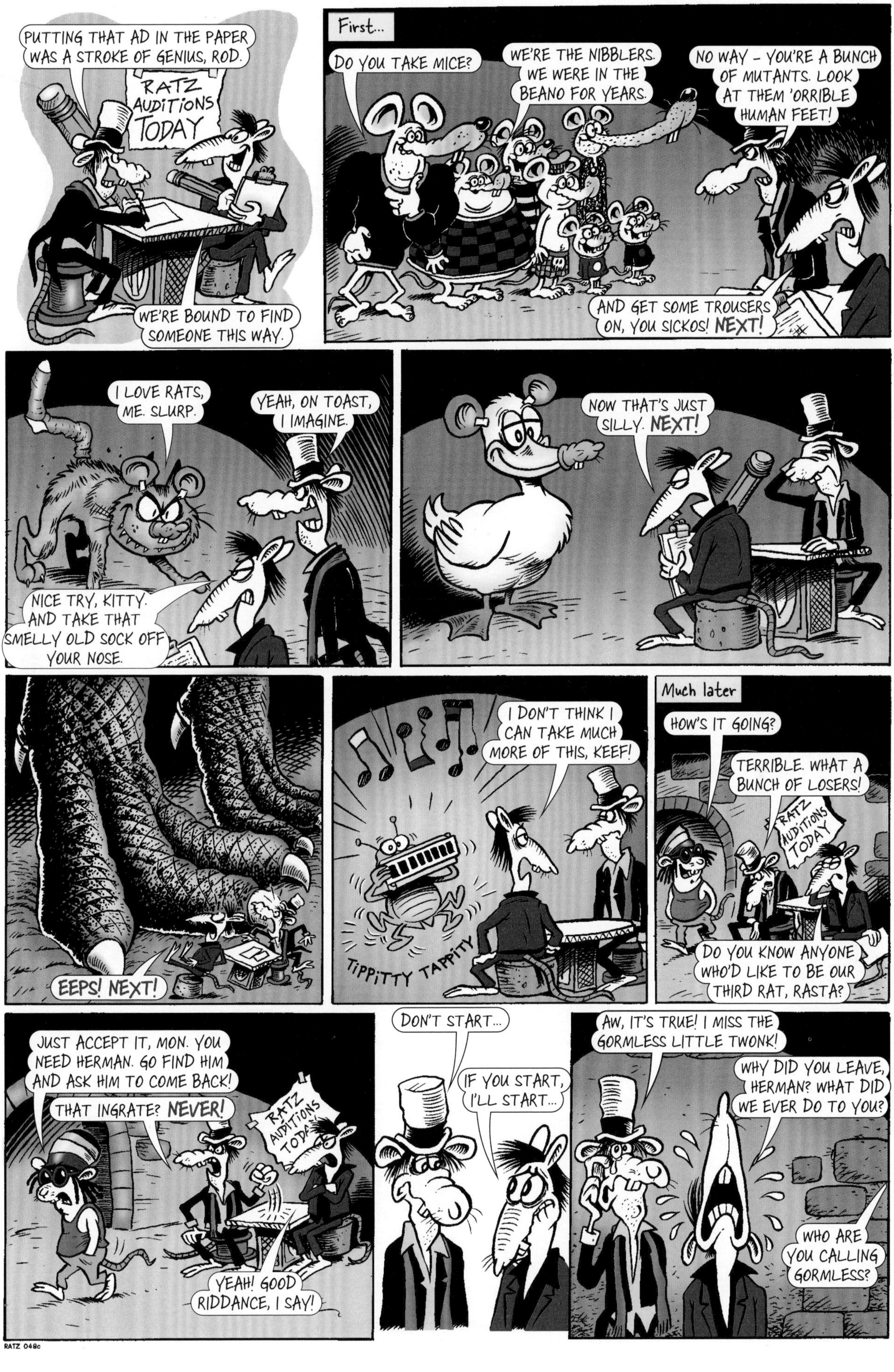
PUTTING THAT AD IN THE PAPER WAS A STROKE OF GENIUS, ROD.
RATZ AUDITIONS TODAY
WE'RE BOUND TO FIND SOMEONE THIS WAY.
First...
DO YOU TAKE MICE?
WE'RE THE NIBBLERS. WE WERE IN THE BEANO FOR YEARS.
NO WAY – YOU'RE A BUNCH OF MUTANTS. LOOK AT THEM 'ORRIBLE HUMAN FEET!
AND GET SOME TROUSERS ON, YOU SICKOS! NEXT!
I LOVE RATS, ME. SLURP.
YEAH, ON TOAST, I IMAGINE.
NICE TRY, KITTY. AND TAKE THAT SMELLY OLD SOCK OFF YOUR NOSE.
NOW THAT'S JUST SILLY. NEXT!
EEPS! NEXT!
I DON'T THINK I CAN TAKE MUCH MORE OF THIS, KEEF!
TIPPITTY TAPPITY
Much later
HOW'S IT GOING?
TERRIBLE. WHAT A BUNCH OF LOSERS!
RATZ AUDITIONS TODAY
DO YOU KNOW ANYONE WHO'D LIKE TO BE OUR THIRD RAT, RASTA?
JUST ACCEPT IT, MON. YOU NEED HERMAN. GO FIND HIM AND ASK HIM TO COME BACK!
THAT INGRATE? NEVER!
RATZ AUDITIONS TODAY
YEAH! GOOD RIDDANCE, I SAY!
DON'T START...
IF YOU START, I'LL START...
AW, IT'S TRUE! I MISS THE GORMLESS LITTLE TWONK!
WHY DID YOU LEAVE, HERMAN? WHAT DID WE EVER DO TO YOU?
WHO ARE YOU CALLING GORMLESS?

RATZ 048c

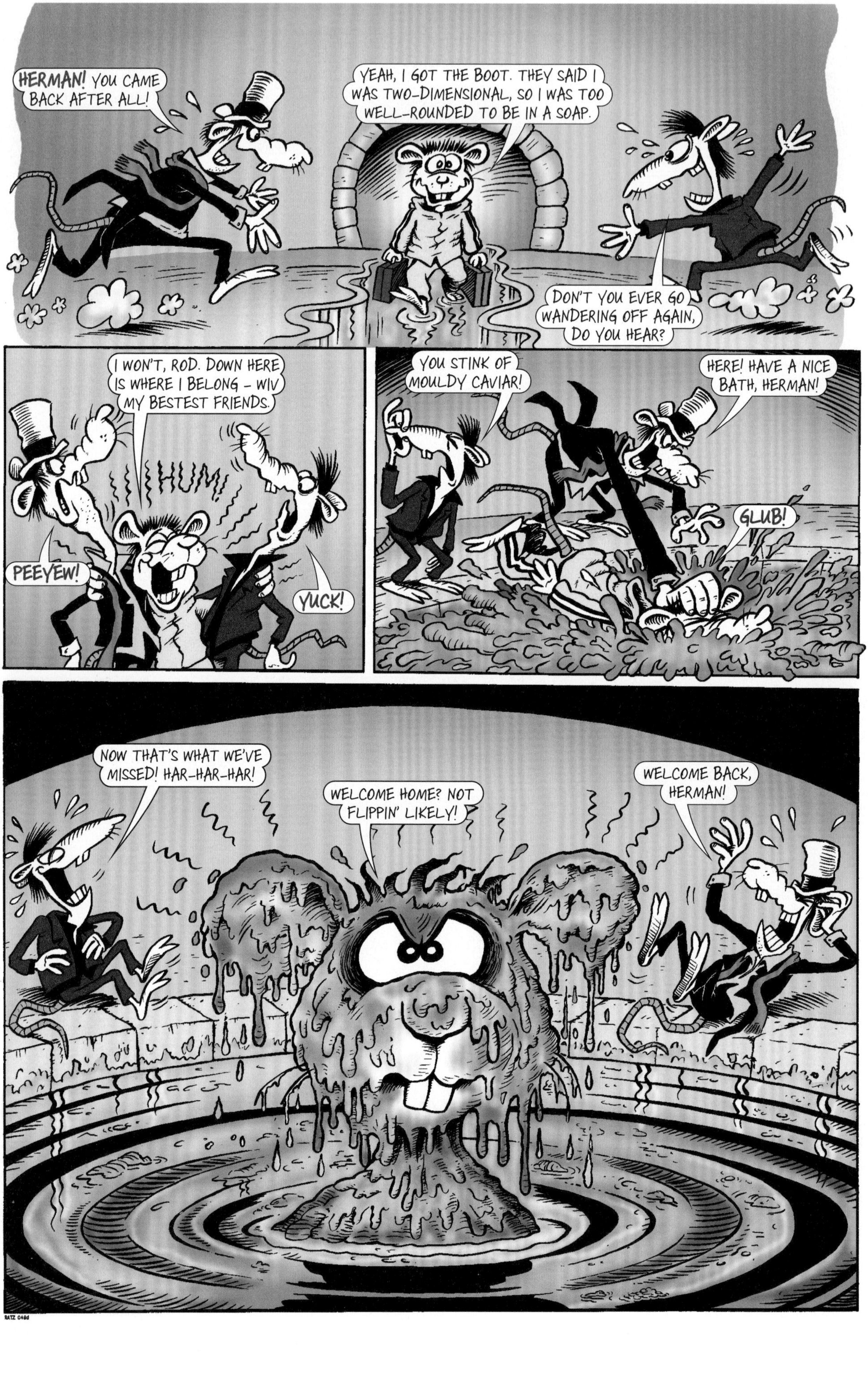
HERMAN! YOU CAME BACK AFTER ALL!
YEAH, I GOT THE BOOT. THEY SAID I WAS TWO-DIMENSIONAL, SO I WAS TOO WELL-ROUNDED TO BE IN A SOAP.
DON'T YOU EVER GO WANDERING OFF AGAIN, DO YOU HEAR?
I WON'T, ROD. DOWN HERE IS WHERE I BELONG - WIV MY BESTEST FRIENDS.
HUM!
PEEYEW!
YUCK!
YOU STINK OF MOULDY CAVIAR!
HERE! HAVE A NICE BATH, HERMAN!
GLUB!
NOW THAT'S WHAT WE'VE MISSED! HAR-HAR-HAR!
WELCOME HOME? NOT FLIPPIN' LIKELY!
WELCOME BACK, HERMAN!

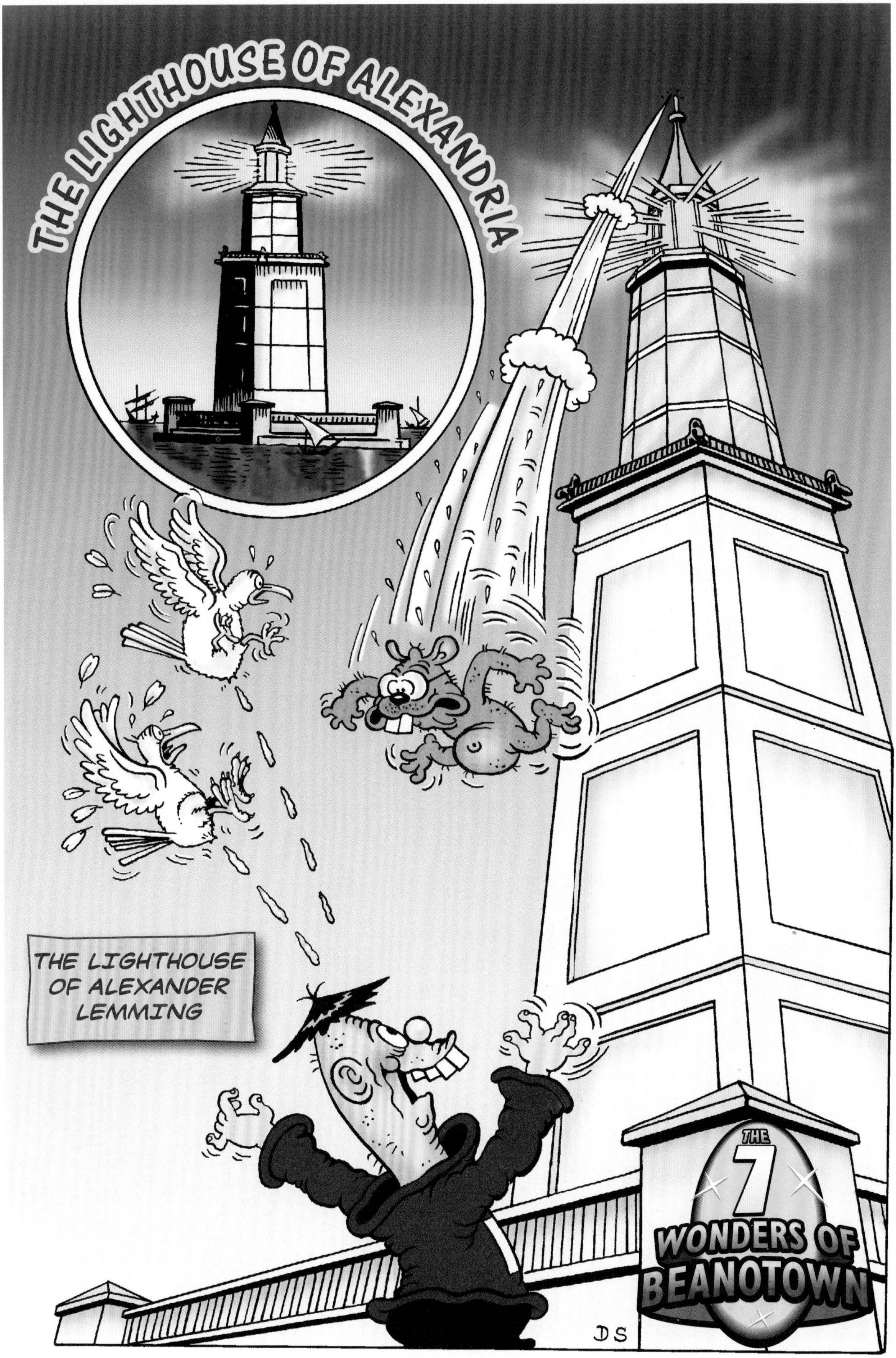
THE LIGHTHOUSE OF ALEXANDRIA
THE LIGHTHOUSE OF ALEXANDER LEMMING
THE 7 WONDERS OF BEANOTOWN
DS

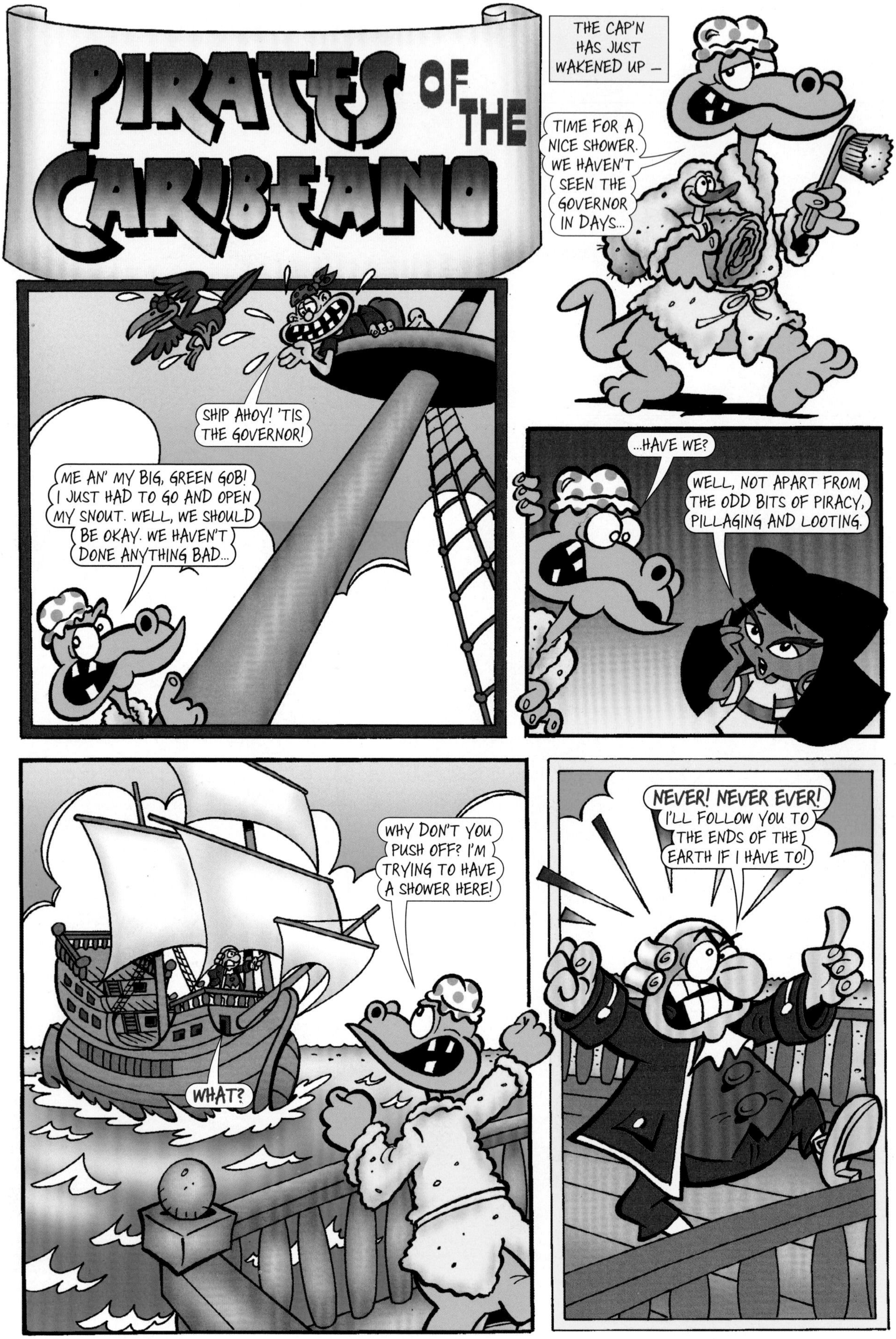
PIRATES OF THE CARIBEANO
THE CAP'N HAS JUST WAKENED UP –
TIME FOR A NICE SHOWER. WE HAVEN'T SEEN THE GOVERNOR IN DAYS...
SHIP AHOY! 'TIS THE GOVERNOR!
ME AN' MY BIG, GREEN GOB! I JUST HAD TO GO AND OPEN MY SNOUT. WELL, WE SHOULD BE OKAY. WE HAVEN'T DONE ANYTHING BAD...
...HAVE WE?
WELL, NOT APART FROM THE ODD BITS OF PIRACY, PILLAGING AND LOOTING.
WHY DON'T YOU PUSH OFF? I'M TRYING TO HAVE A SHOWER HERE!
WHAT?
NEVER! NEVER EVER! I'LL FOLLOW YOU TO THE ENDS OF THE EARTH IF I HAVE TO!

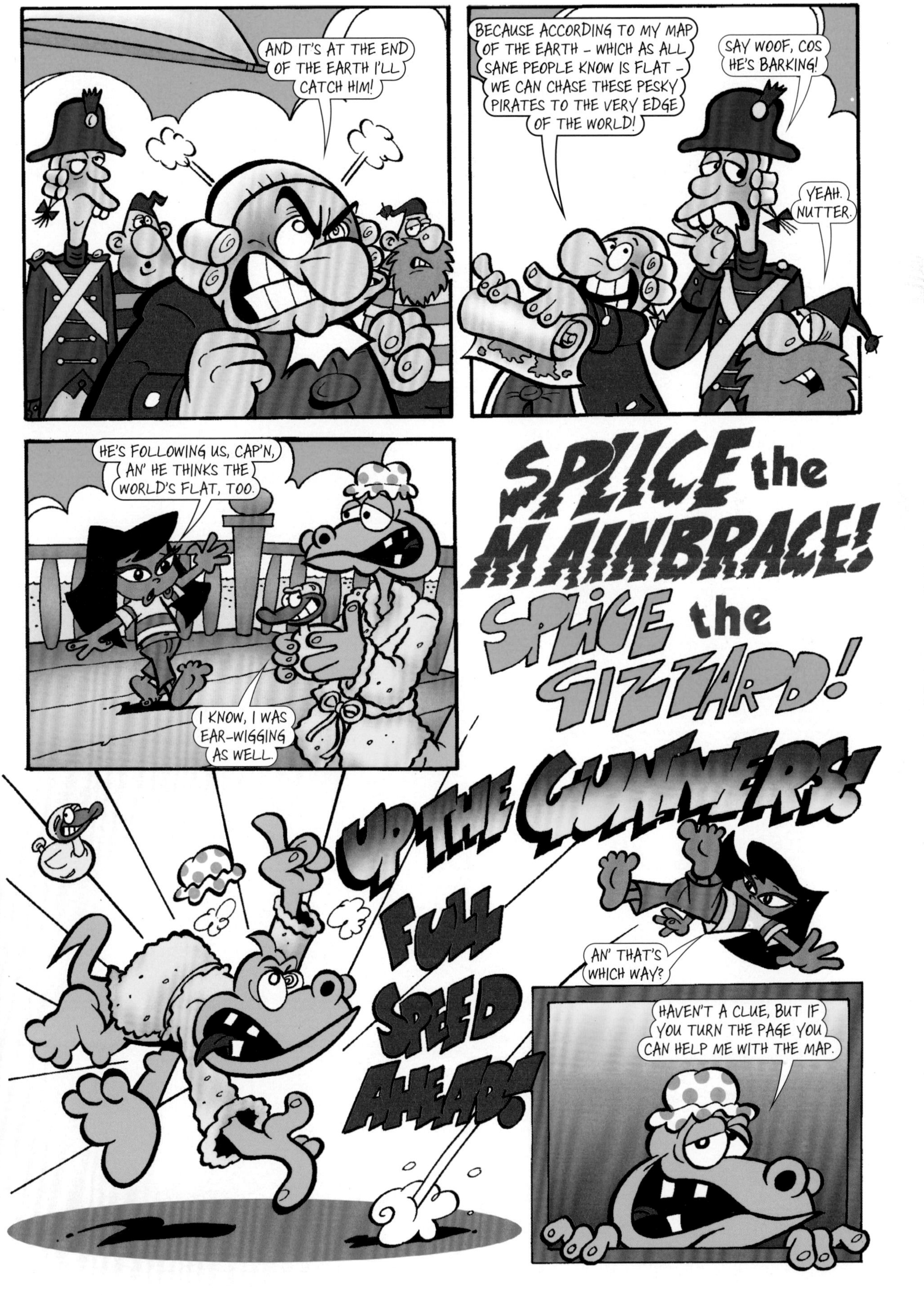
AND IT'S AT THE END OF THE EARTH I'LL CATCH HIM!
BECAUSE ACCORDING TO MY MAP OF THE EARTH – WHICH AS ALL SANE PEOPLE KNOW IS FLAT – WE CAN CHASE THESE PESKY PIRATES TO THE VERY EDGE OF THE WORLD!
SAY WOOF, COS HE'S BARKING!
YEAH. NUTTER.
HE'S FOLLOWING US, CAP'N, AN' HE THINKS THE WORLD'S FLAT, TOO.
I KNOW, I WAS EAR-WIGGING AS WELL.
SPLICE the MAINBRACE!
SPLICE the GIZZARD!
UP THE GUNNERS!
FULL SPEED AHEAD!
AN' THAT'S WHICH WAY?
HAVEN'T A CLUE, BUT IF YOU TURN THE PAGE YOU CAN HELP ME WITH THE MAP.

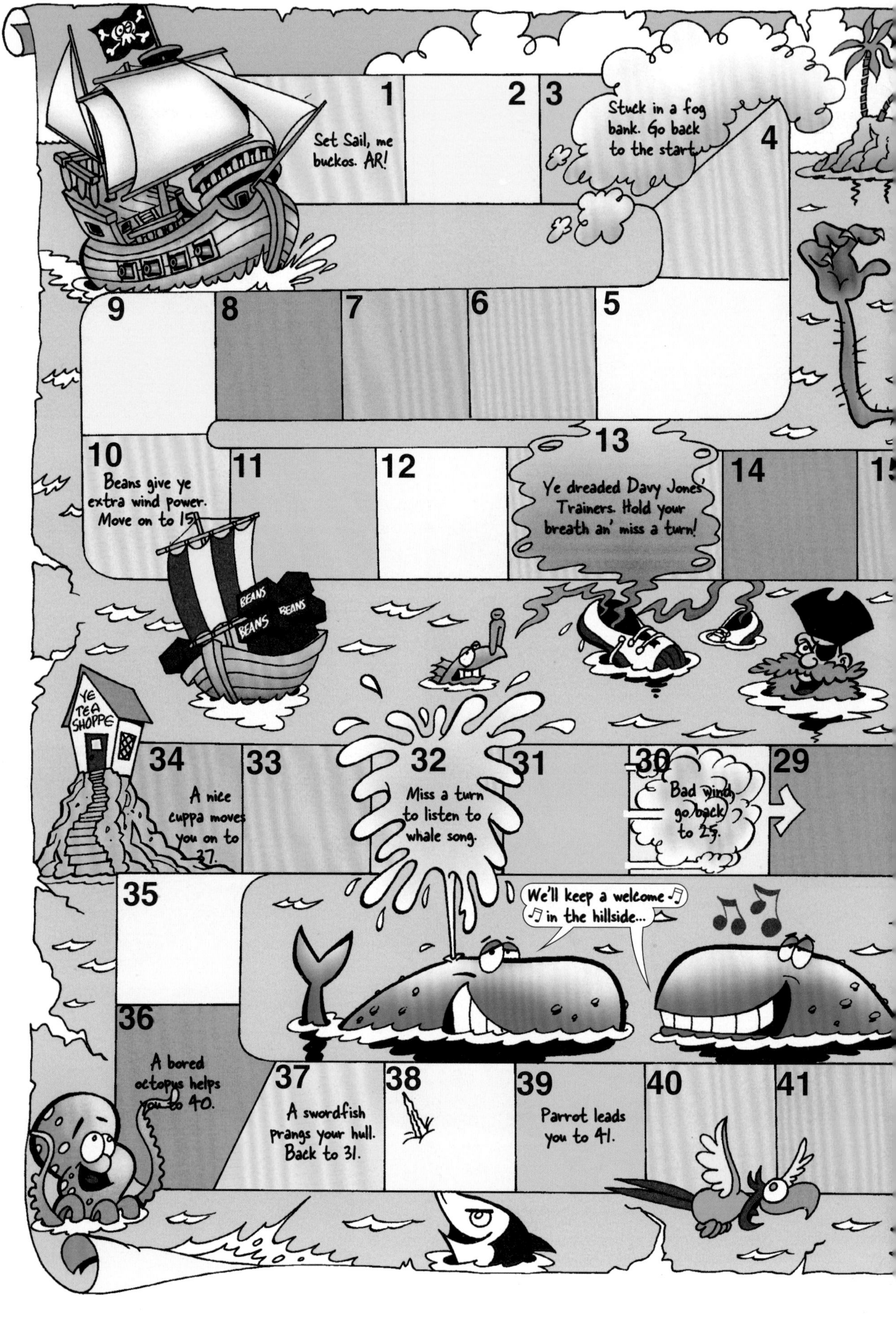

1
Set Sail, me buckos. AR!
2
3
Stuck in a fog bank. Go back to the start.
4
5
6
7
8
9
10
Beans give ye extra wind power. Move on to 15.
11
12
13
Ye dreaded Davy Jones' Trainers. Hold your breath an' miss a turn!
14
BEANS
BEANS
BEANS
YE TEA SHOPPE
34
A nice cuppa moves you on to 37.
33
32
Miss a turn to listen to whale song.
31
30
Bad wind, go back to 25.
29
35
We'll keep a welcome ♫ ♫ in the hillside...
36
A bored octopus helps you to 40.
37
A swordfish prangs your hull. Back to 31.
38
39
Parrot leads you to 41.
40
41

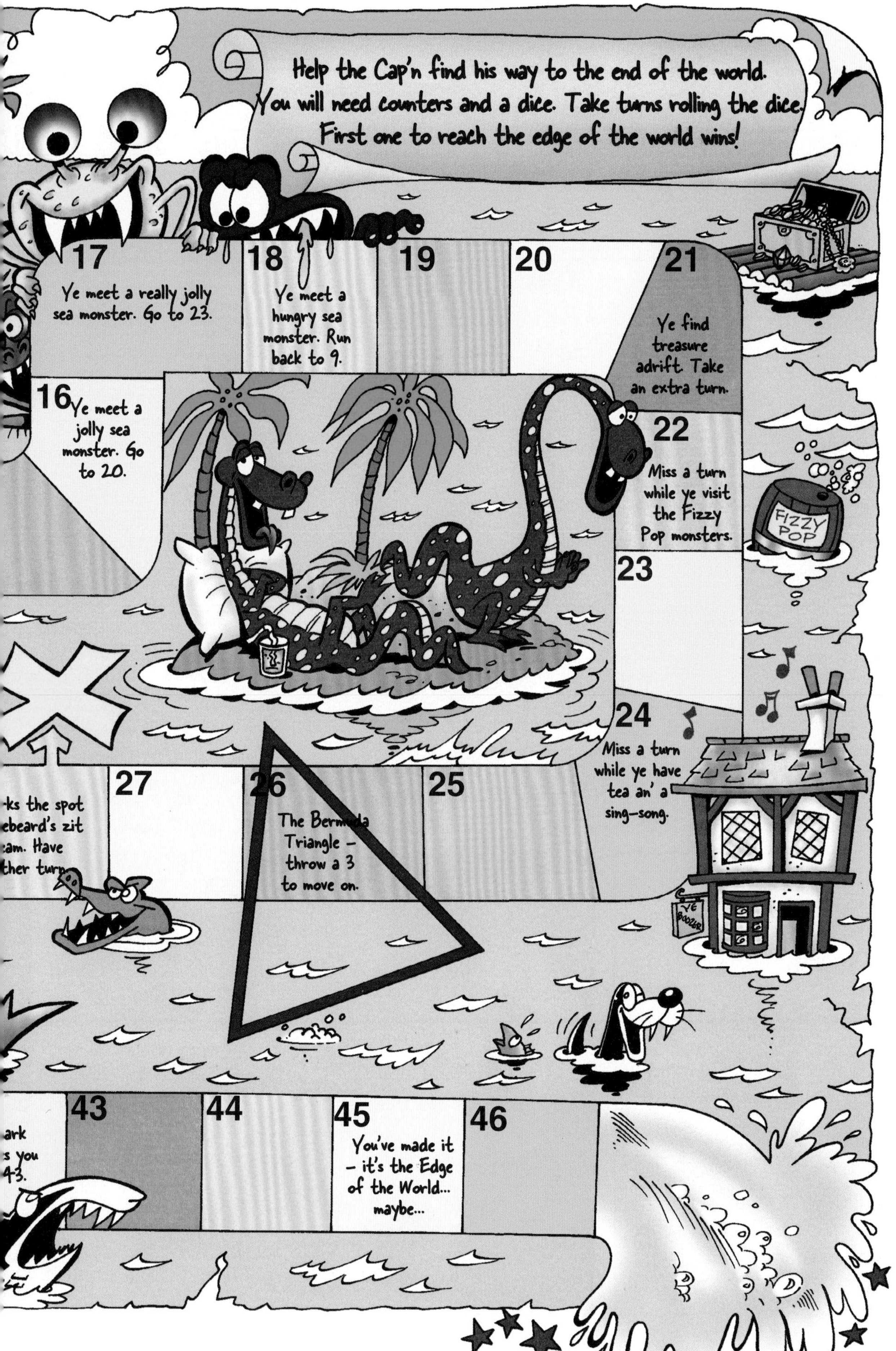
Help the Cap'n find his way to the end of the world. You will need counters and a dice. Take turns rolling the dice. First one to reach the edge of the world wins!
17 Ye meet a really jolly sea monster. Go to 23.
18 Ye meet a hungry sea monster. Run back to 9.
19
20
21 Ye find treasure adrift. Take an extra turn.
16 Ye meet a jolly sea monster. Go to 20.
22 Miss a turn while ye visit the Fizzy Pop monsters.
FIZZY POP
23
24 Miss a turn while ye have tea an' a sing-song.
27
-ks the spot
-ebeard's zit
-am. Have
-ther turn
26 The Bermuda Triangle – throw a 3 to move on.
25
-ark
-s you
-43.
43
44
45 You've made it – it's the Edge of the World... maybe...
46

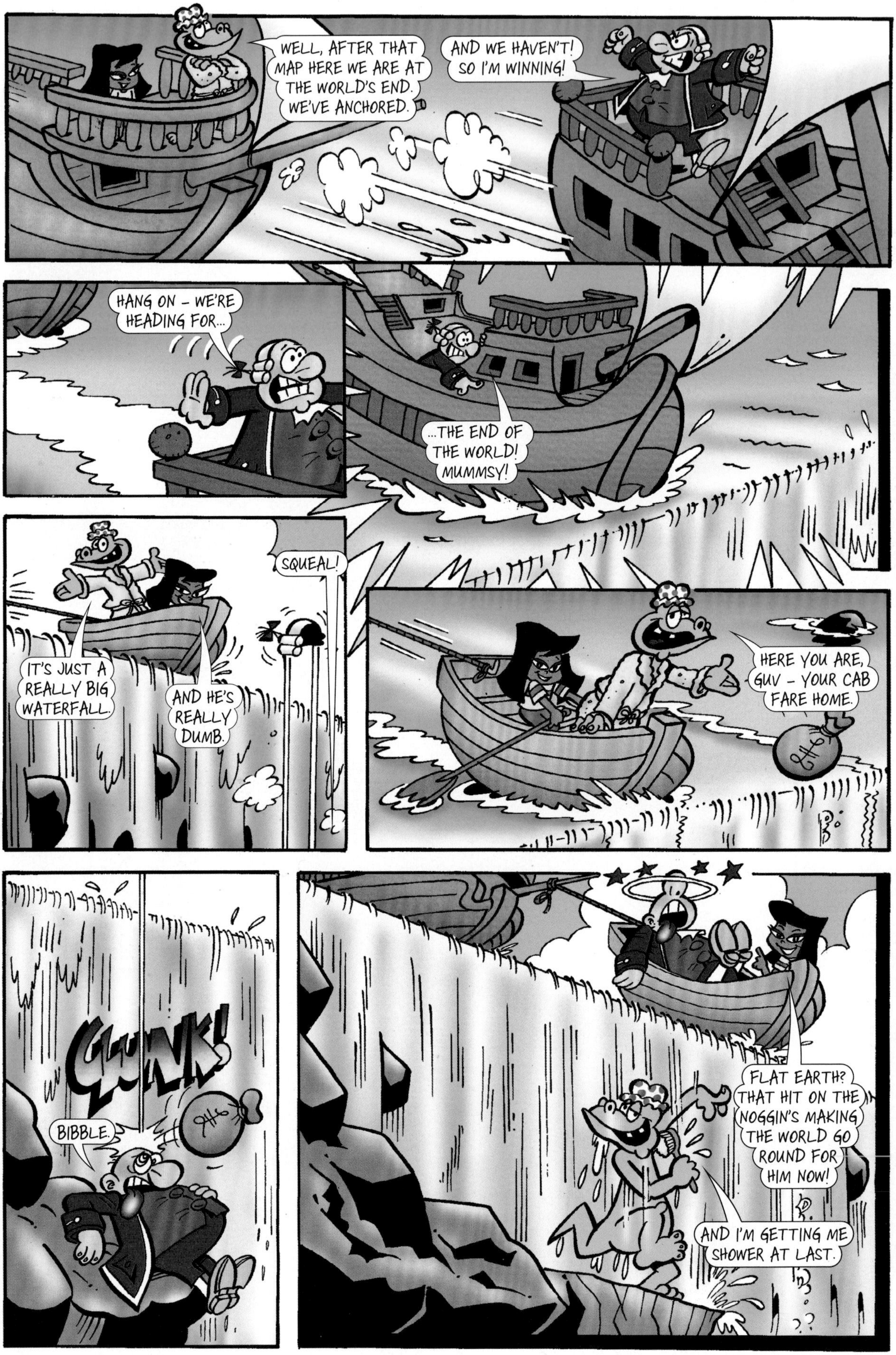
WELL, AFTER THAT MAP HERE WE ARE AT THE WORLD'S END. WE'VE ANCHORED.
AND WE HAVEN'T! SO I'M WINNING!
HANG ON – WE'RE HEADING FOR...
...THE END OF THE WORLD! MUMMSY!
SQUEAL!
IT'S JUST A REALLY BIG WATERFALL.
AND HE'S REALLY DUMB.
HERE YOU ARE, GUV – YOUR CAB FARE HOME.
GLUNK!
BIBBLE.
FLAT EARTH? THAT HIT ON THE NOGGIN'S MAKING THE WORLD GO ROUND FOR HIM NOW!
AND I'M GETTING ME SHOWER AT LAST.

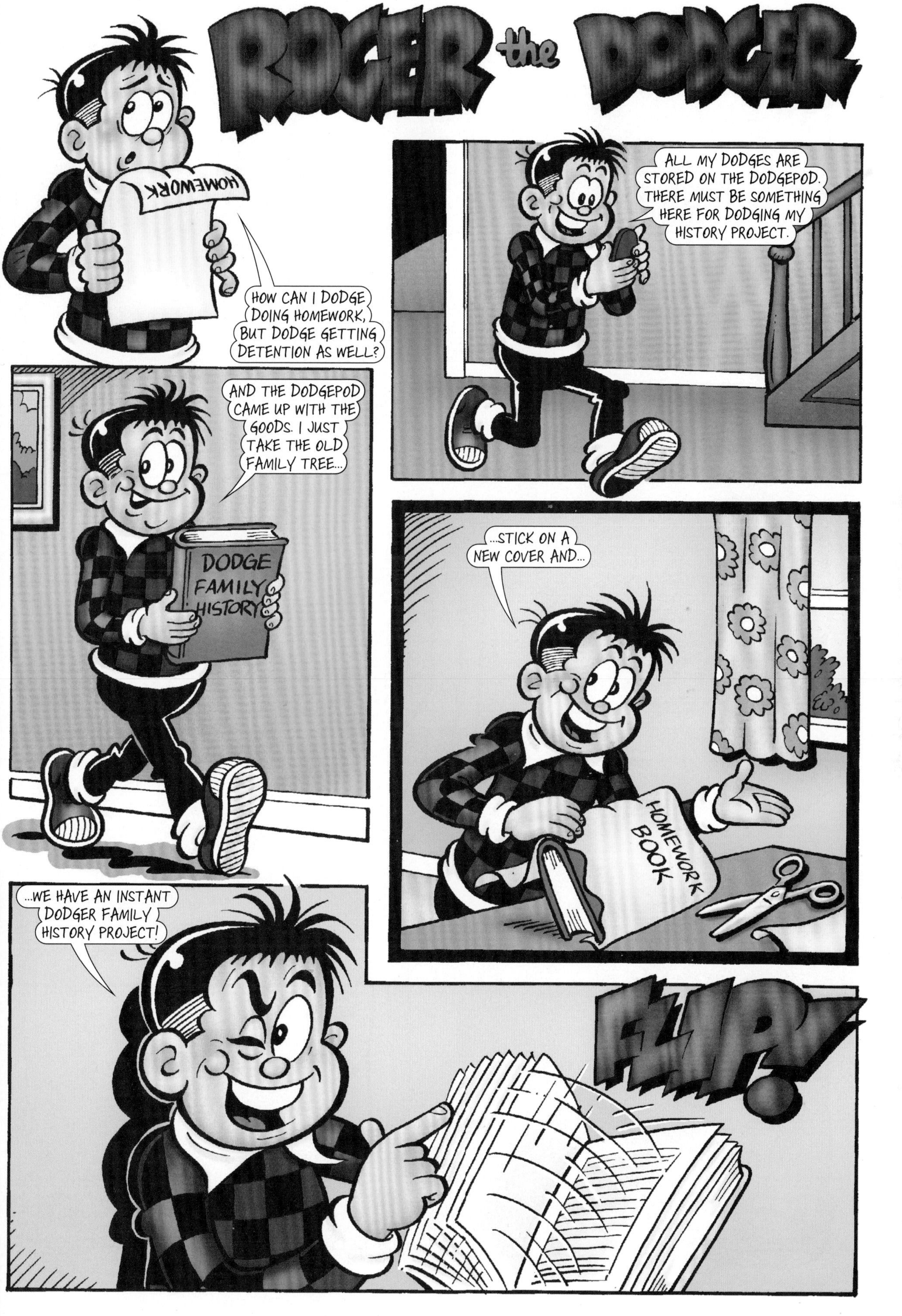
ROGER the DODGER
HOMEWORK
HOW CAN I DODGE DOING HOMEWORK, BUT DODGE GETTING DETENTION AS WELL?
ALL MY DODGES ARE STORED ON THE DODGEPOD. THERE MUST BE SOMETHING HERE FOR DODGING MY HISTORY PROJECT.
AND THE DODGEPOD CAME UP WITH THE GOODS. I JUST TAKE THE OLD FAMILY TREE...
DODGE FAMILY HISTORY
...STICK ON A NEW COVER AND...
HOMEWORK BOOK
...WE HAVE AN INSTANT DODGER FAMILY HISTORY PROJECT!
FLIP!

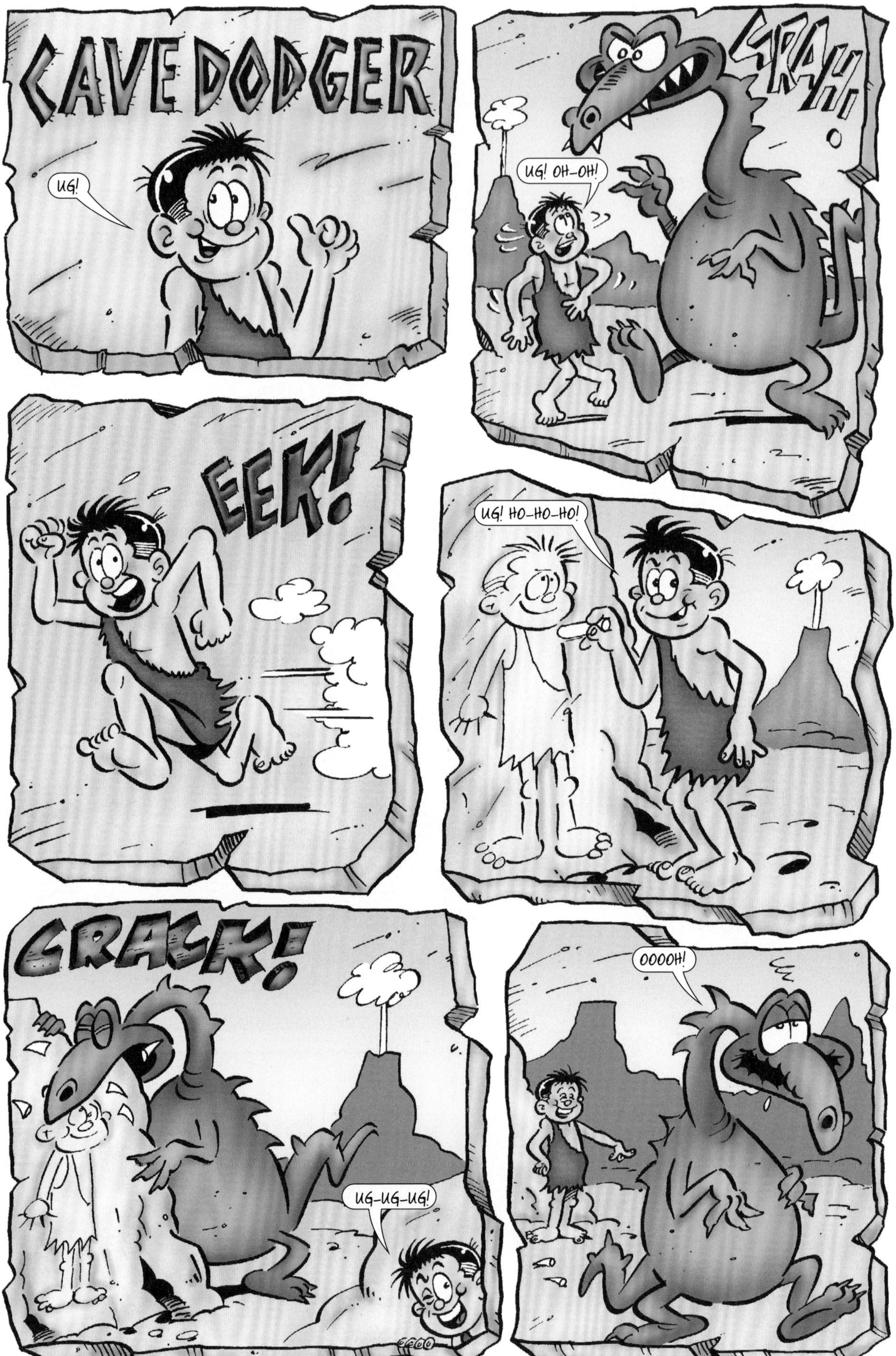
CAVE DODGER
UG!
SRAH!
UG! OH-OH!
EEK!
UG! HO-HO-HO!
CRACK!
UG-UG-UG!
OOOOH!

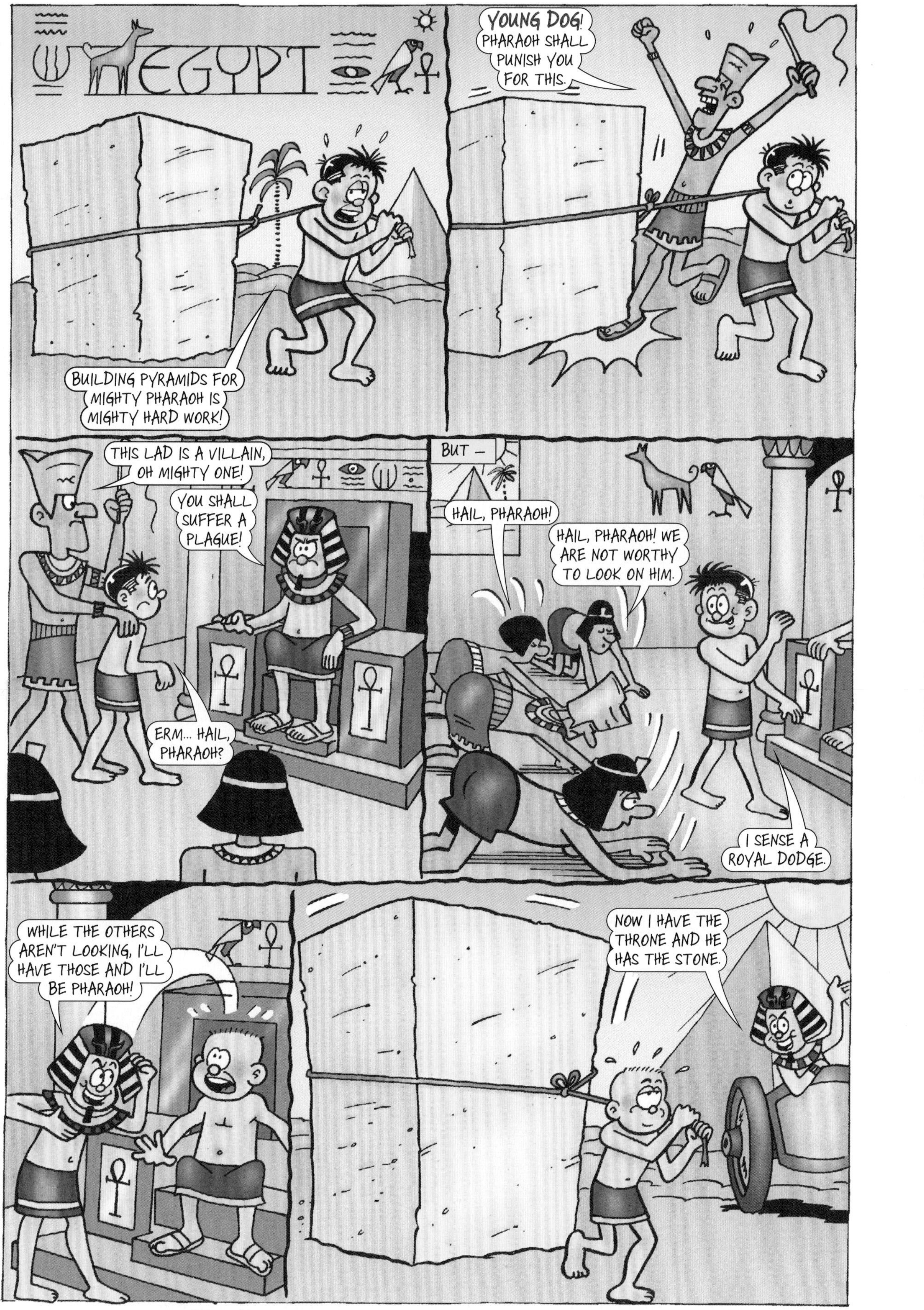
EGYPT
BUILDING PYRAMIDS FOR MIGHTY PHARAOH IS MIGHTY HARD WORK!
YOUNG DOG! PHARAOH SHALL PUNISH YOU FOR THIS.
THIS LAD IS A VILLAIN, OH MIGHTY ONE!
YOU SHALL SUFFER A PLAGUE!
ERM... HAIL, PHARAOH?
BUT —
HAIL, PHARAOH!
HAIL, PHARAOH! WE ARE NOT WORTHY TO LOOK ON HIM.
I SENSE A ROYAL DODGE.
WHILE THE OTHERS AREN'T LOOKING, I'LL HAVE THOSE AND I'LL BE PHARAOH!
NOW I HAVE THE THRONE AND HE HAS THE STONE.

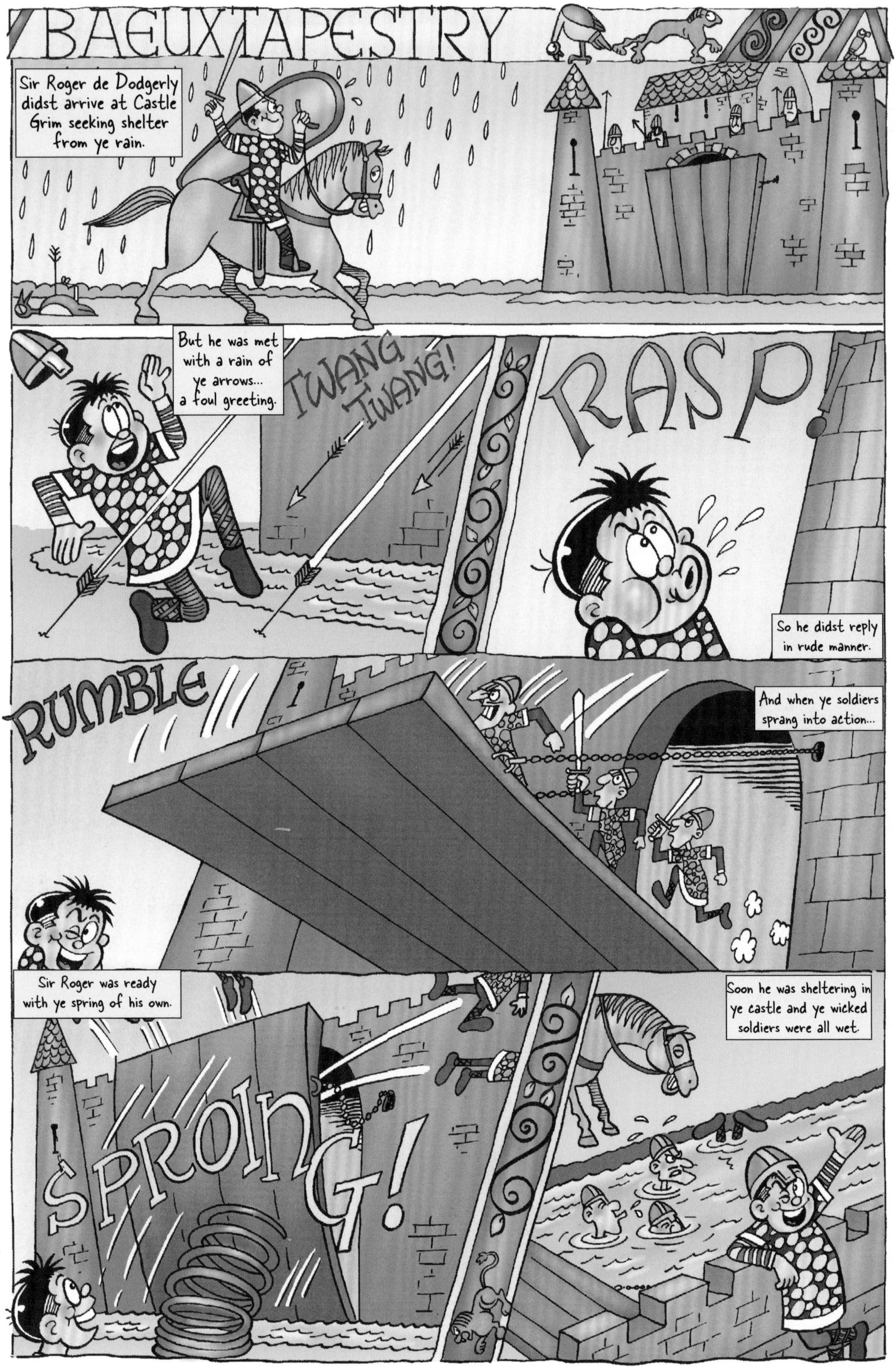

BAEUX TAPESTRY
Sir Roger de Dodgerly didst arrive at Castle Grim seeking shelter from ye rain.
But he was met with a rain of ye arrows... a foul greeting.
TWANG TWANG!
RASP!
So he didst reply in rude manner.
RUMBLE
And when ye soldiers sprang into action...
Sir Roger was ready with ye spring of his own.
SPROING!
Soon he was sheltering in ye castle and ye wicked soldiers were all wet.

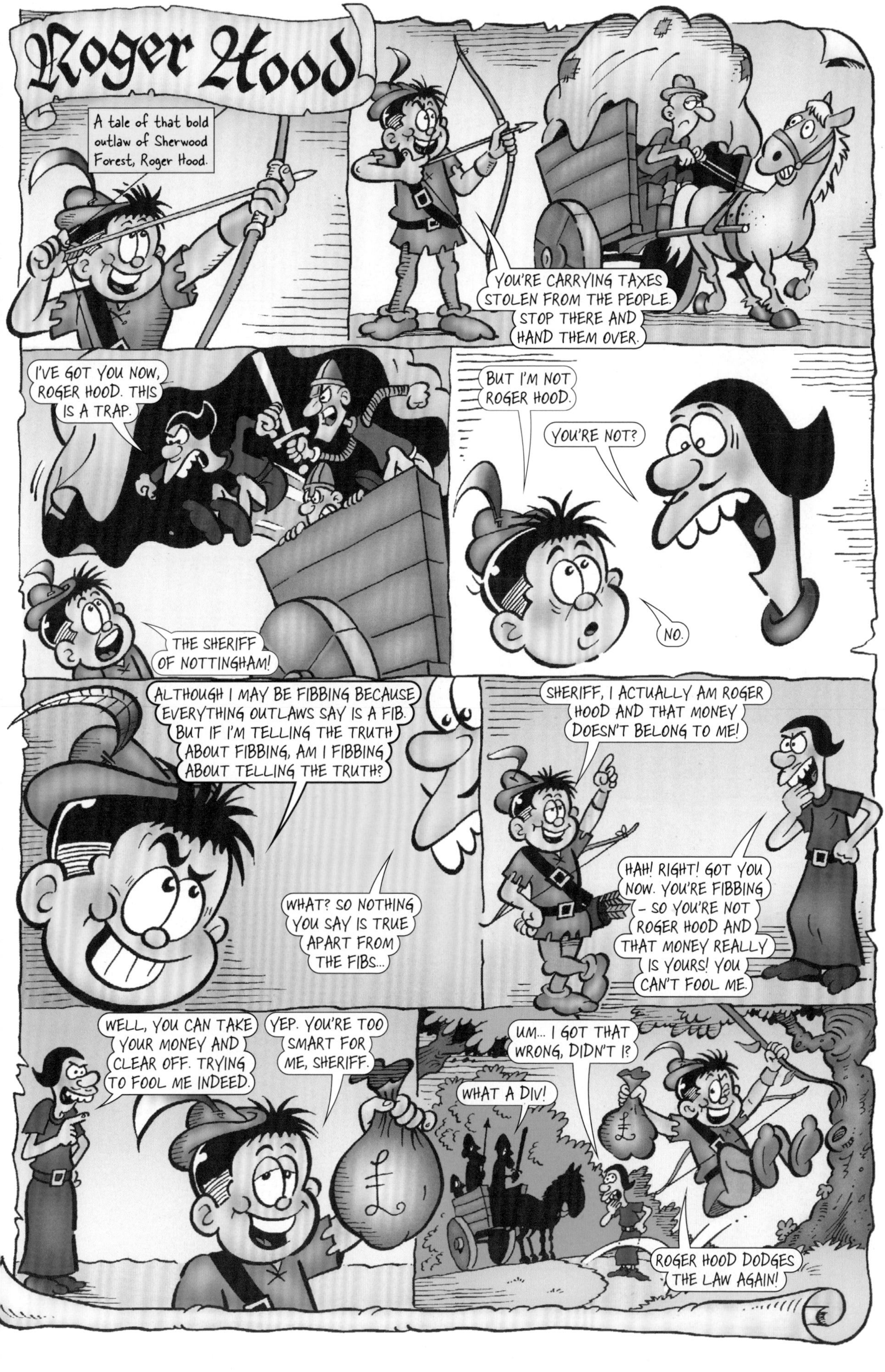
Roger Hood
A tale of that bold outlaw of Sherwood Forest, Roger Hood.
YOU'RE CARRYING TAXES STOLEN FROM THE PEOPLE. STOP THERE AND HAND THEM OVER.
I'VE GOT YOU NOW, ROGER HOOD. THIS IS A TRAP.
THE SHERIFF OF NOTTINGHAM!
BUT I'M NOT ROGER HOOD.
YOU'RE NOT?
NO.
ALTHOUGH I MAY BE FIBBING BECAUSE EVERYTHING OUTLAWS SAY IS A FIB. BUT IF I'M TELLING THE TRUTH ABOUT FIBBING, AM I FIBBING ABOUT TELLING THE TRUTH?
WHAT? SO NOTHING YOU SAY IS TRUE APART FROM THE FIBS...
SHERIFF, I ACTUALLY AM ROGER HOOD AND THAT MONEY DOESN'T BELONG TO ME!
HAH! RIGHT! GOT YOU NOW. YOU'RE FIBBING – SO YOU'RE NOT ROGER HOOD AND THAT MONEY REALLY IS YOURS! YOU CAN'T FOOL ME.
WELL, YOU CAN TAKE YOUR MONEY AND CLEAR OFF. TRYING TO FOOL ME INDEED.
YEP. YOU'RE TOO SMART FOR ME, SHERIFF.
UM... I GOT THAT WRONG, DIDN'T I?
WHAT A DIV!
ROGER HOOD DODGES THE LAW AGAIN!

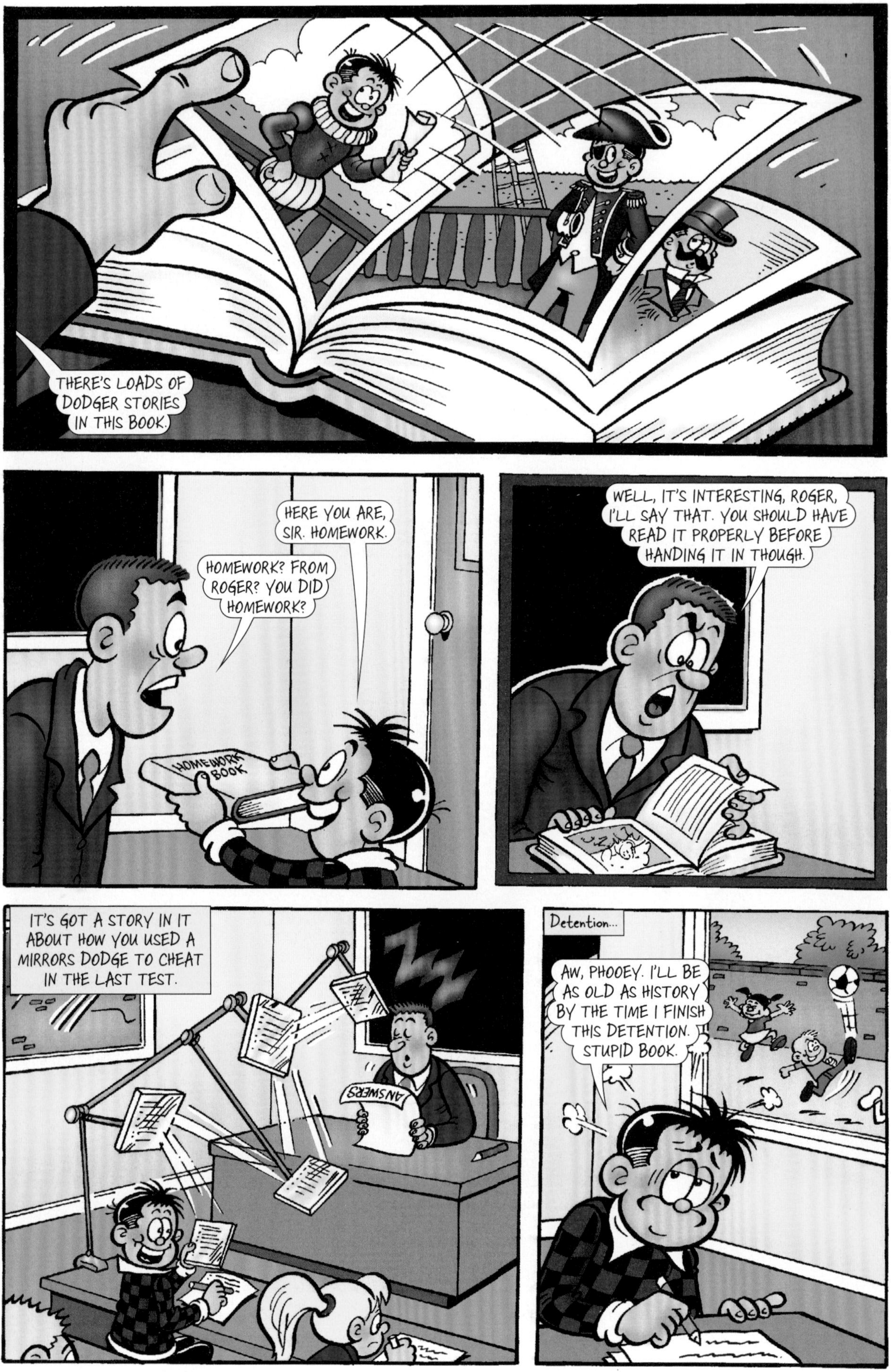
THERE'S LOADS OF DODGER STORIES IN THIS BOOK.
HERE YOU ARE, SIR. HOMEWORK.
HOMEWORK? FROM ROGER? YOU DID HOMEWORK?
HOMEWORK BOOK
WELL, IT'S INTERESTING, ROGER, I'LL SAY THAT. YOU SHOULD HAVE READ IT PROPERLY BEFORE HANDING IT IN THOUGH.
IT'S GOT A STORY IN IT ABOUT HOW YOU USED A MIRRORS DODGE TO CHEAT IN THE LAST TEST.
ANSWERS
Detention...
AW, PHOOEY. I'LL BE AS OLD AS HISTORY BY THE TIME I FINISH THIS DETENTION. STUPID BOOK.

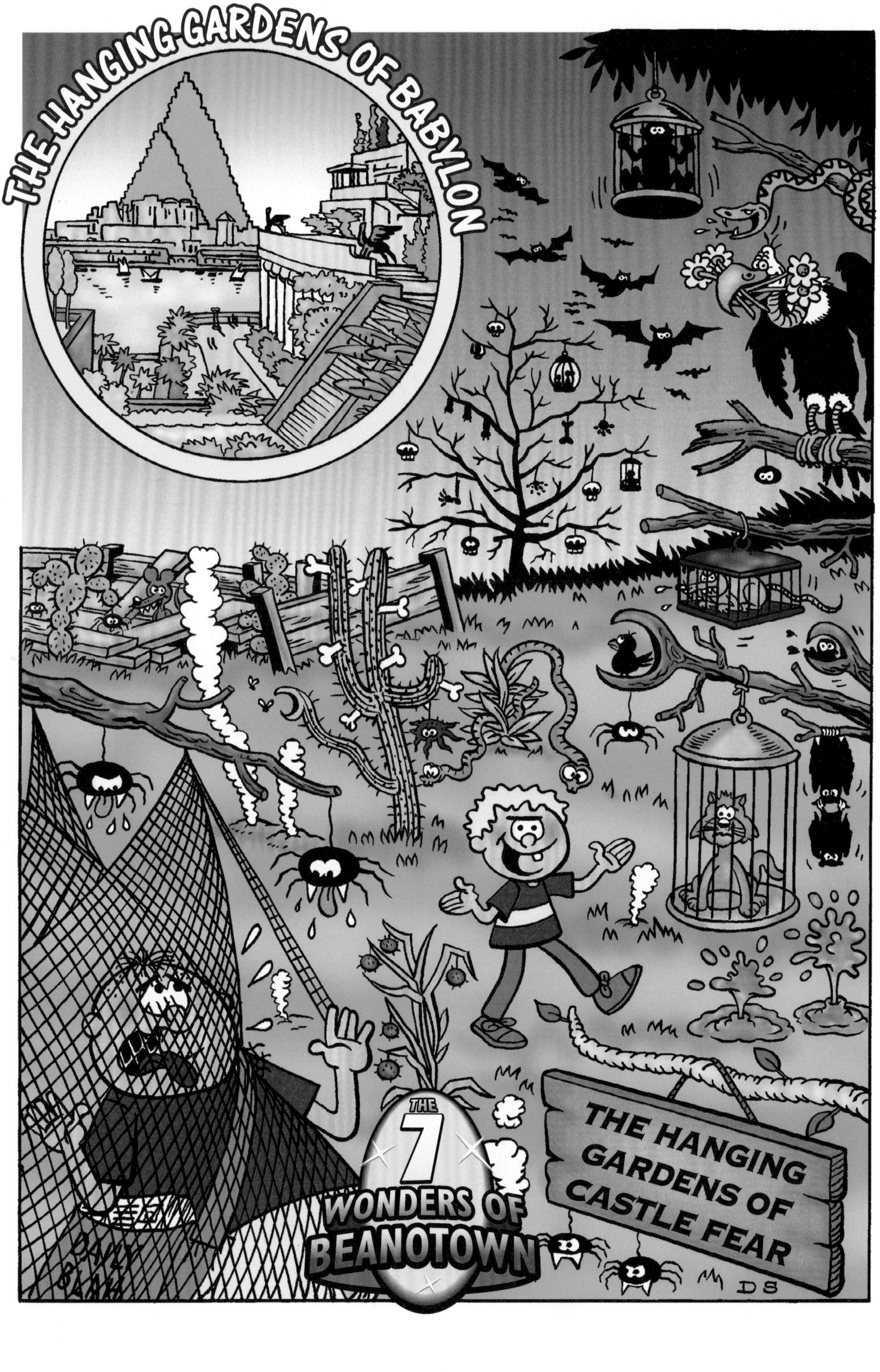
THE HANGING GARDENS OF BABYLON
THE 7 WONDERS OF BEANOTOWN
THE HANGING GARDENS OF CASTLE FEAR
DS

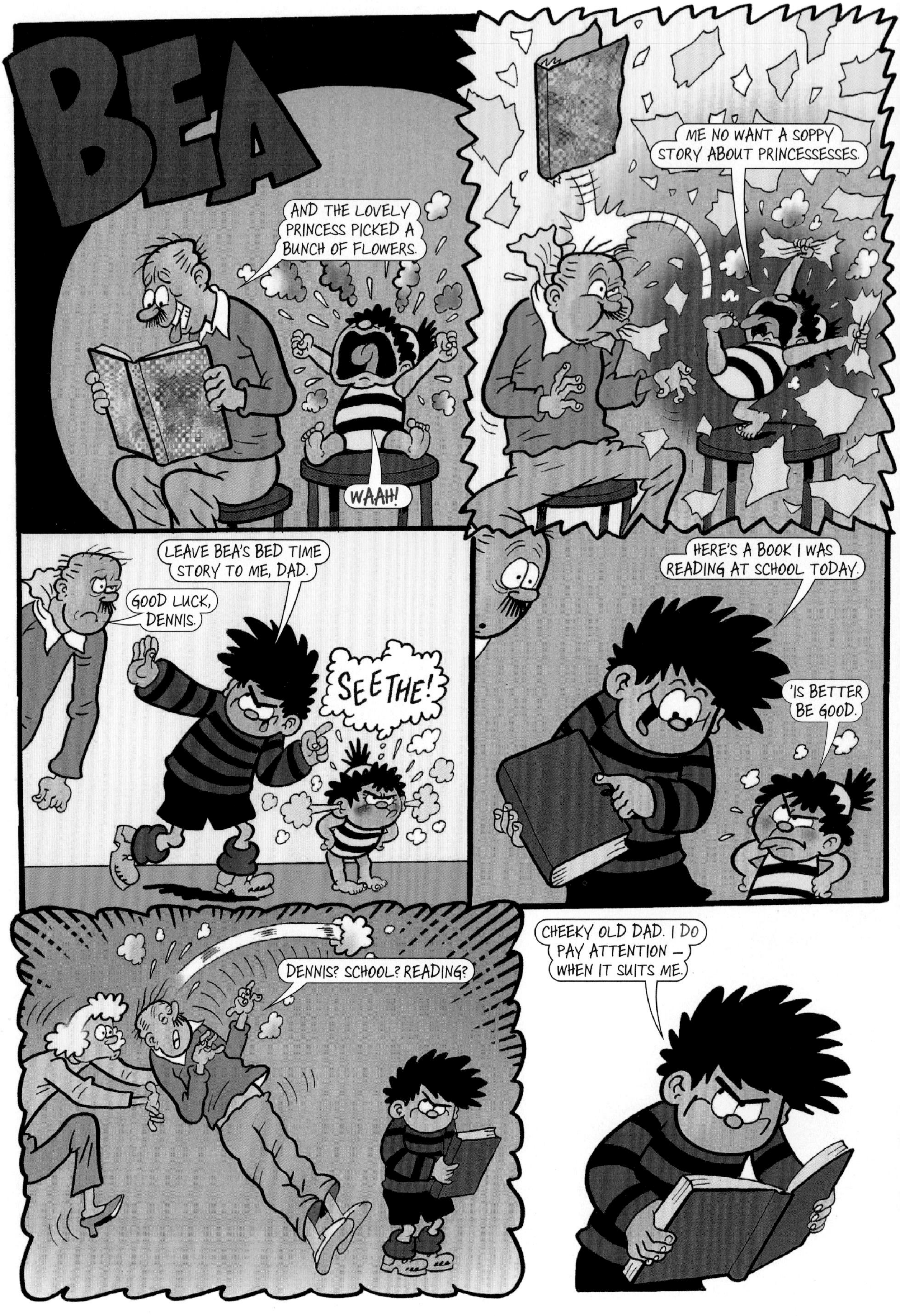
BEA
AND THE LOVELY PRINCESS PICKED A BUNCH OF FLOWERS.
WAAH!
ME NO WANT A SOPPY STORY ABOUT PRINCESSESSES.
LEAVE BEA'S BED TIME STORY TO ME, DAD.
GOOD LUCK, DENNIS.
SEETHE!
HERE'S A BOOK I WAS READING AT SCHOOL TODAY.
'IS BETTER BE GOOD.
DENNIS? SCHOOL? READING?
CHEEKY OLD DAD. I DO PAY ATTENTION — WHEN IT SUITS ME.

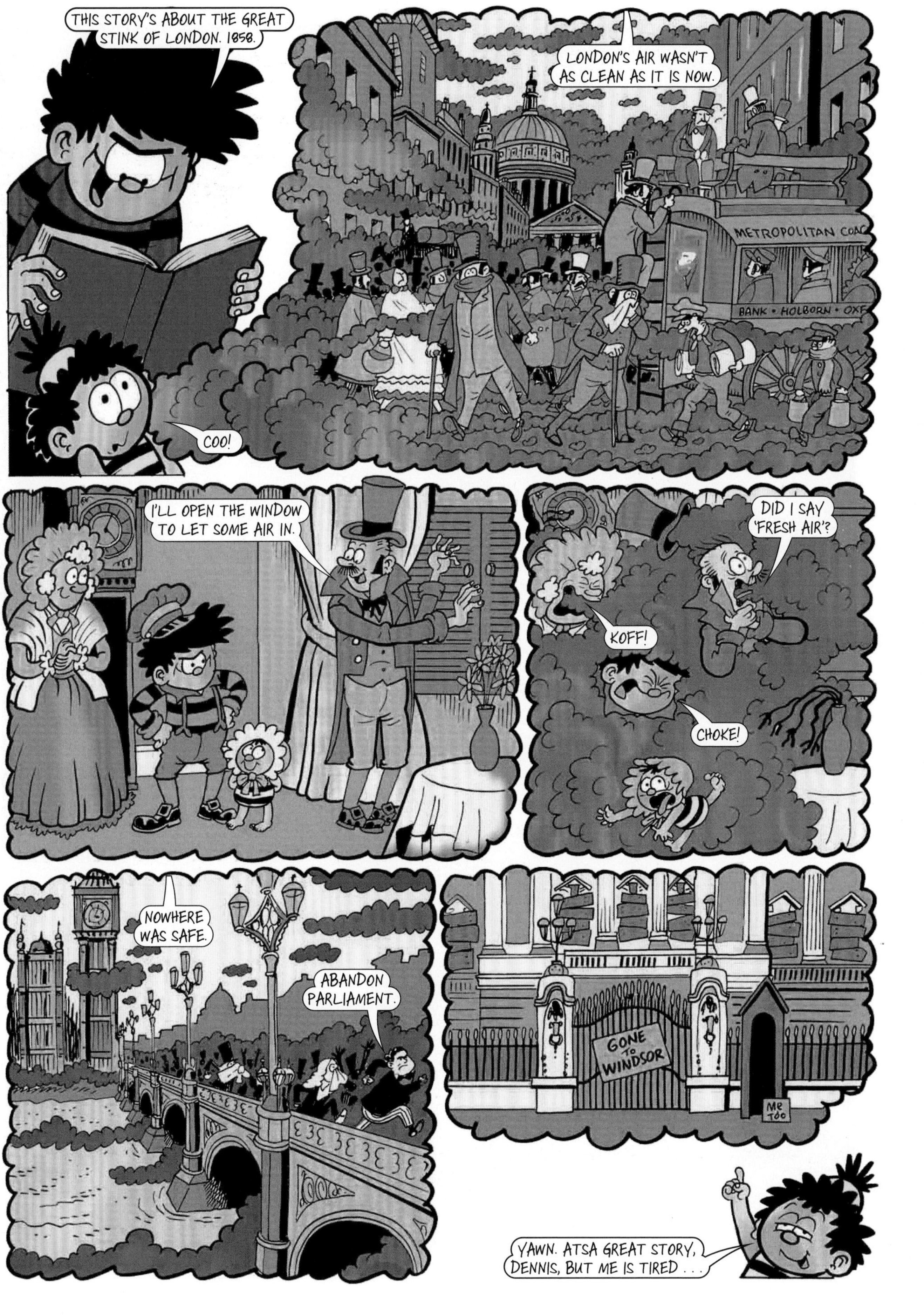
THIS STORY'S ABOUT THE GREAT STINK OF LONDON. 1858.
LONDON'S AIR WASN'T AS CLEAN AS IT IS NOW.
METROPOLITAN COAC
BANK • HOLBORN • OXF
COO!
I'LL OPEN THE WINDOW TO LET SOME AIR IN.
DID I SAY 'FRESH AIR'?
KOFF!
CHOKE!
NOWHERE WAS SAFE.
ABANDON PARLIAMENT.
GONE TO WINDSOR
ME TOO
YAWN. ATSA GREAT STORY, DENNIS, BUT ME IS TIRED . . .

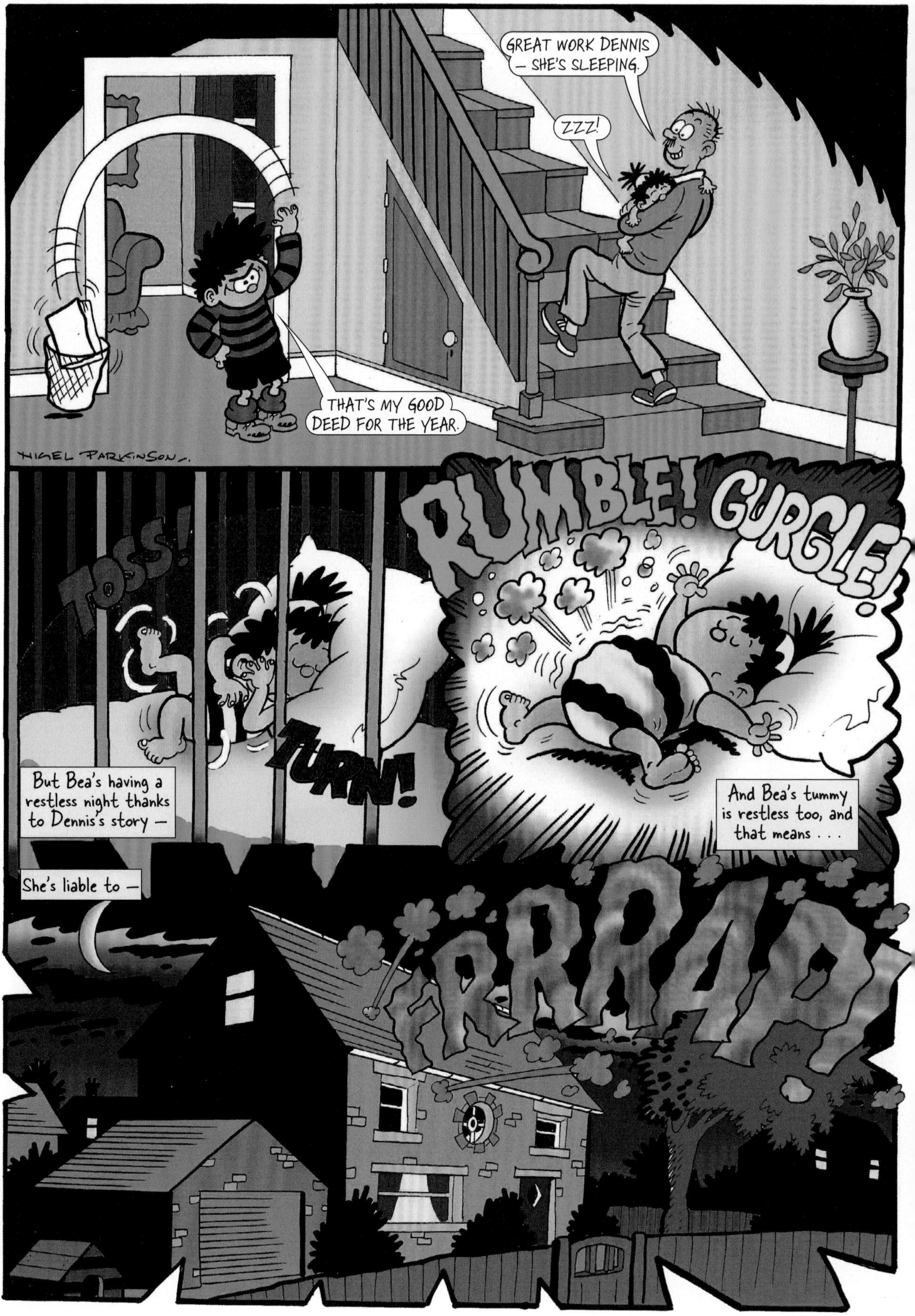
GREAT WORK DENNIS — SHE'S SLEEPING.
ZZZ!
THAT'S MY GOOD DEED FOR THE YEAR.
NIGEL PARKINSON
TOSS!
TURN!
But Bea's having a restless night thanks to Dennis's story —
RUMBLE! GURGLE!
And Bea's tummy is restless too, and that means . . .
She's liable to —
PRRRAP!

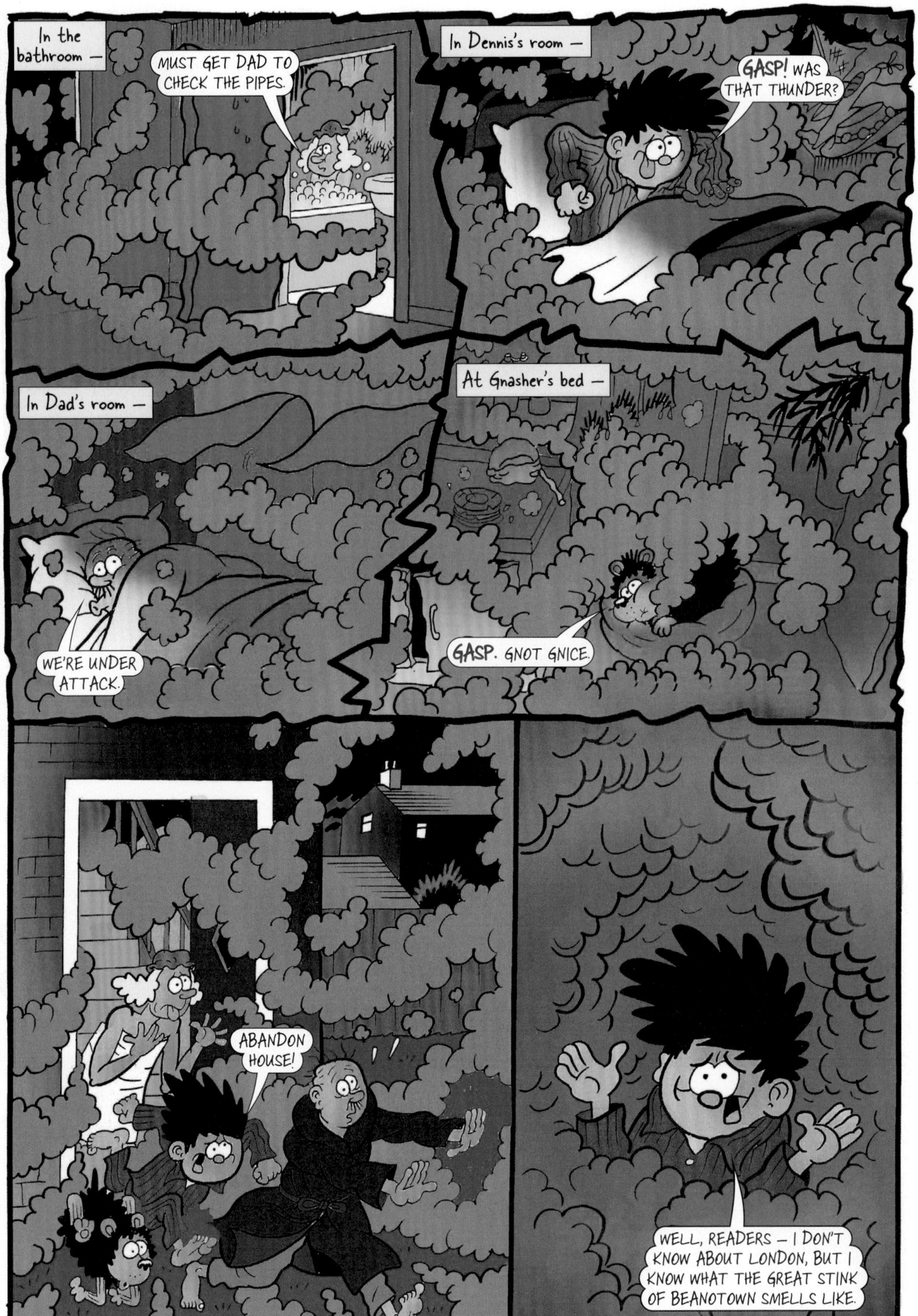
In the bathroom —
MUST GET DAD TO CHECK THE PIPES.
In Dennis's room —
GASP! WAS THAT THUNDER?
In Dad's room —
WE'RE UNDER ATTACK.
At Gnasher's bed —
GASP. GNOT GNICE.
ABANDON HOUSE!
WELL, READERS — I DON'T KNOW ABOUT LONDON, BUT I KNOW WHAT THE GREAT STINK OF BEANOTOWN SMELLS LIKE.

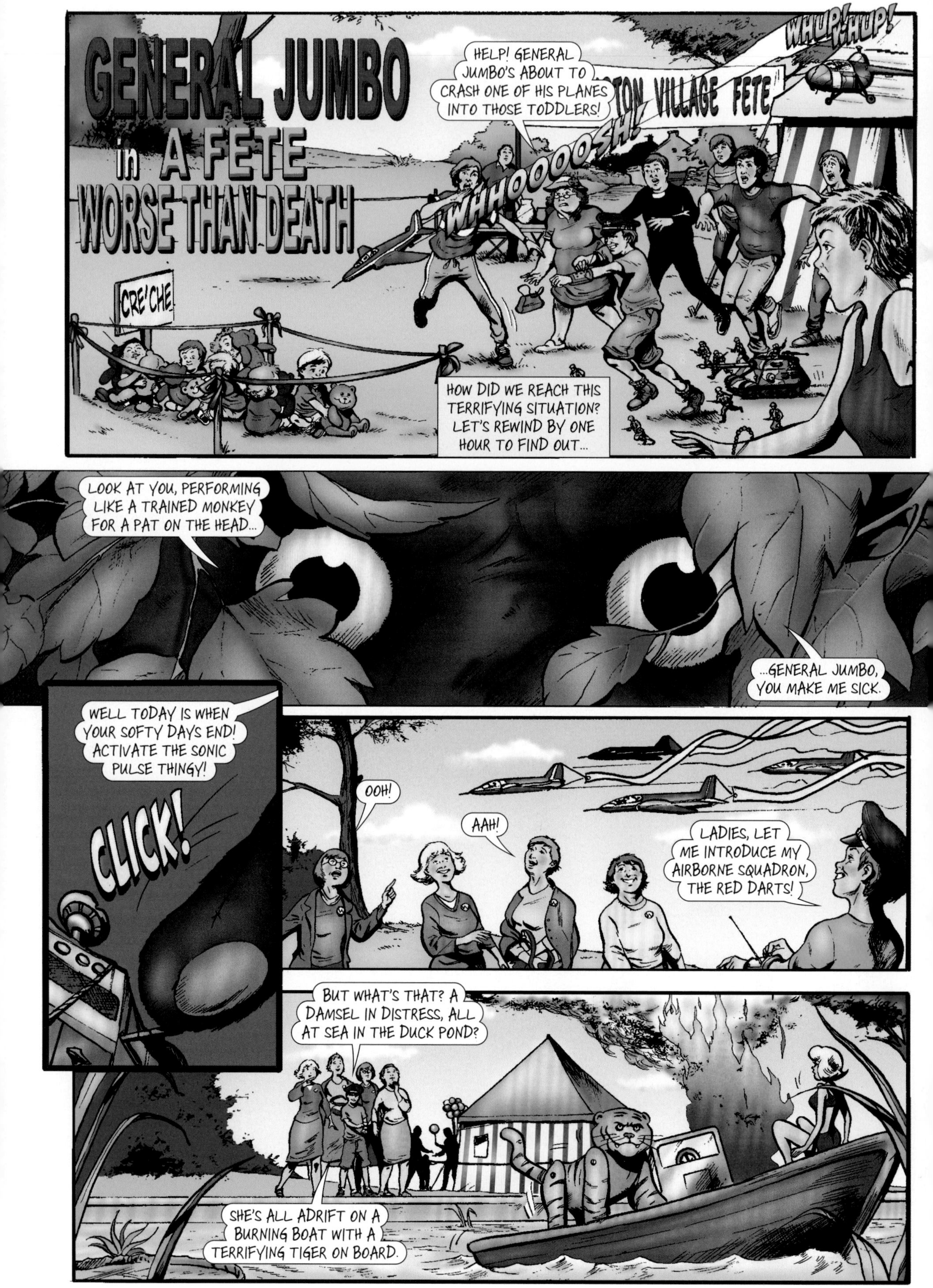
GENERAL JUMBO
in A FETE WORSE THAN DEATH
HELP! GENERAL JUMBO'S ABOUT TO CRASH ONE OF HIS PLANES INTO THOSE TODDLERS!
WHUP! WHUP!
TON VILLAGE FETE
WHHOOOOOSH!
CRE'CHE
HOW DID WE REACH THIS TERRIFYING SITUATION? LET'S REWIND BY ONE HOUR TO FIND OUT...
LOOK AT YOU, PERFORMING LIKE A TRAINED MONKEY FOR A PAT ON THE HEAD...
...GENERAL JUMBO, YOU MAKE ME SICK.
WELL TODAY IS WHEN YOUR SOFTY DAYS END! ACTIVATE THE SONIC PULSE THINGY!
CLICK!
OOH!
AAH!
LADIES, LET ME INTRODUCE MY AIRBORNE SQUADRON, THE RED DARTS!
BUT WHAT'S THAT? A DAMSEL IN DISTRESS, ALL AT SEA IN THE DUCK POND?
SHE'S ALL ADRIFT ON A BURNING BOAT WITH A TERRIFYING TIGER ON BOARD.

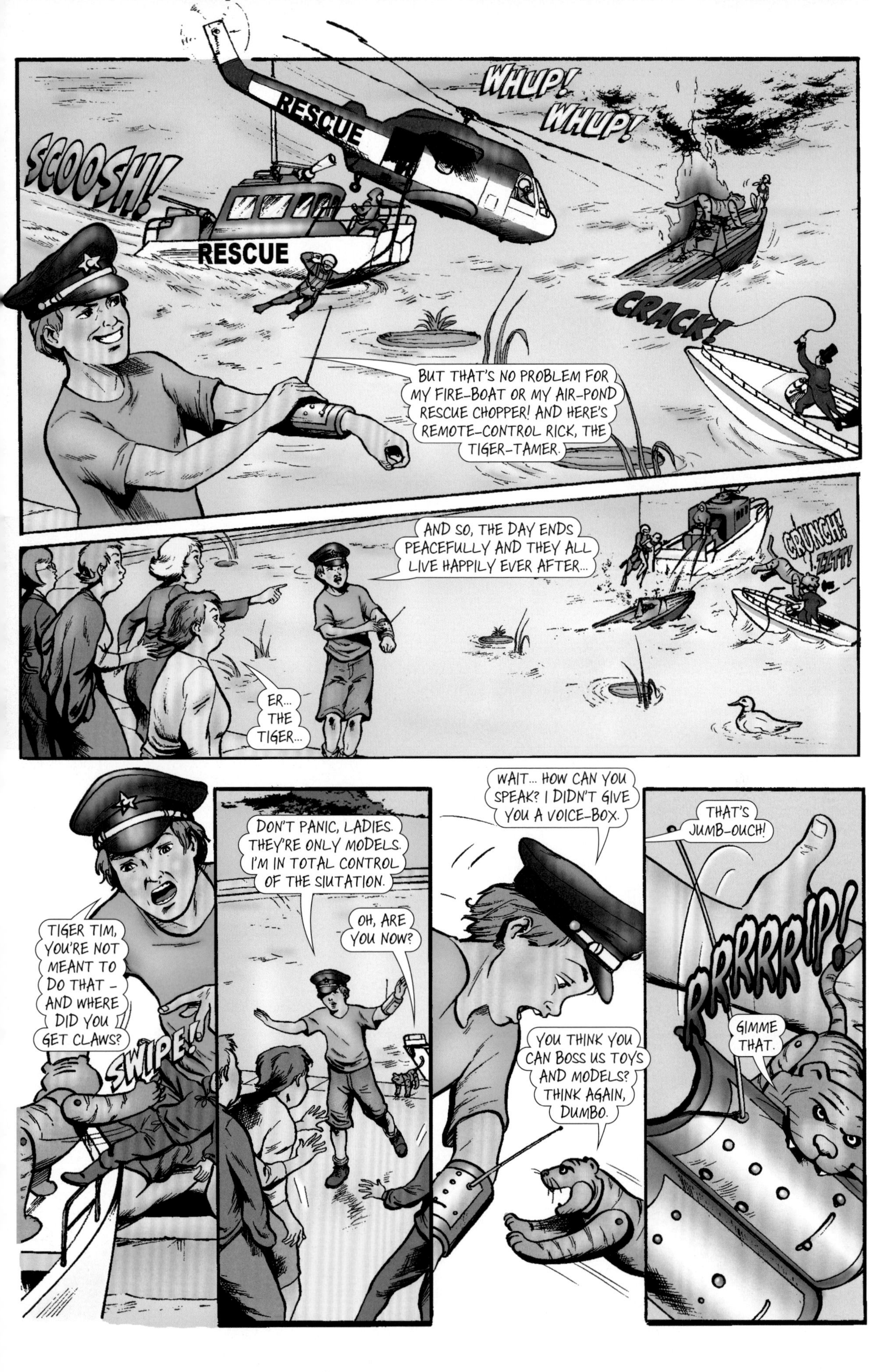

SCOOSH!
WHUP! WHUP!
RESCUE
RESCUE
CRACK!
BUT THAT'S NO PROBLEM FOR MY FIRE-BOAT OR MY AIR-POND RESCUE CHOPPER! AND HERE'S REMOTE-CONTROL RICK, THE TIGER-TAMER.
AND SO, THE DAY ENDS PEACEFULLY AND THEY ALL LIVE HAPPILY EVER AFTER...
CRUNCH!
ZZTT!
ER... THE TIGER...
TIGER TIM, YOU'RE NOT MEANT TO DO THAT - AND WHERE DID YOU GET CLAWS?
SWIPE!
DON'T PANIC, LADIES. THEY'RE ONLY MODELS. I'M IN TOTAL CONTROL OF THE SIUTATION.
OH, ARE YOU NOW?
WAIT... HOW CAN YOU SPEAK? I DIDN'T GIVE YOU A VOICE-BOX.
YOU THINK YOU CAN BOSS US TOYS AND MODELS? THINK AGAIN, DUMBO.
THAT'S JUMB-OUCH!
RRRRRIP!
GIMME THAT.

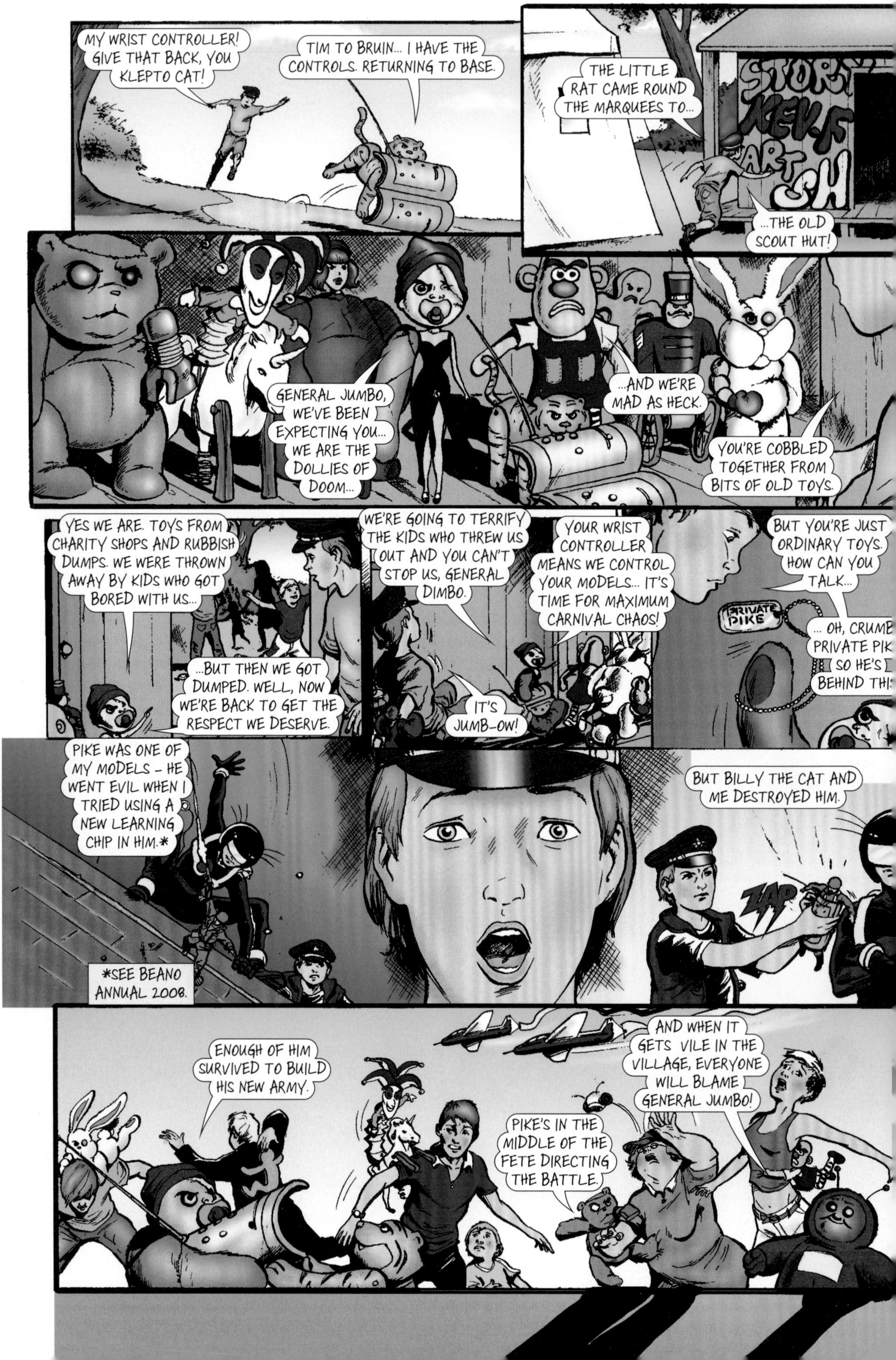
MY WRIST CONTROLLER! GIVE THAT BACK, YOU KLEPTO CAT!
TIM TO BRUIN... I HAVE THE CONTROLS. RETURNING TO BASE.
THE LITTLE RAT CAME ROUND THE MARQUEES TO...
...THE OLD SCOUT HUT!
GENERAL JUMBO, WE'VE BEEN EXPECTING YOU... WE ARE THE DOLLIES OF DOOM...
...AND WE'RE MAD AS HECK.
YOU'RE COBBLED TOGETHER FROM BITS OF OLD TOYS.
YES WE ARE. TOYS FROM CHARITY SHOPS AND RUBBISH DUMPS. WE WERE THROWN AWAY BY KIDS WHO GOT BORED WITH US...
...BUT THEN WE GOT DUMPED. WELL, NOW WE'RE BACK TO GET THE RESPECT WE DESERVE.
WE'RE GOING TO TERRIFY THE KIDS WHO THREW US OUT AND YOU CAN'T STOP US, GENERAL DIMBO.
YOUR WRIST CONTROLLER MEANS WE CONTROL YOUR MODELS... IT'S TIME FOR MAXIMUM CARNIVAL CHAOS!
IT'S JUMB-OW!
BUT YOU'RE JUST ORDINARY TOYS. HOW CAN YOU TALK...
PRIVATE PIKE
... OH, CRUMB
PRIVATE PIK
SO HE'S
BEHIND THI
PIKE WAS ONE OF MY MODELS – HE WENT EVIL WHEN I TRIED USING A NEW LEARNING CHIP IN HIM.*
*SEE BEANO ANNUAL 2008.
BUT BILLY THE CAT AND ME DESTROYED HIM.
ZAP
ENOUGH OF HIM SURVIVED TO BUILD HIS NEW ARMY.
PIKE'S IN THE MIDDLE OF THE FETE DIRECTING THE BATTLE.
AND WHEN IT GETS VILE IN THE VILLAGE, EVERYONE WILL BLAME GENERAL JUMBO!

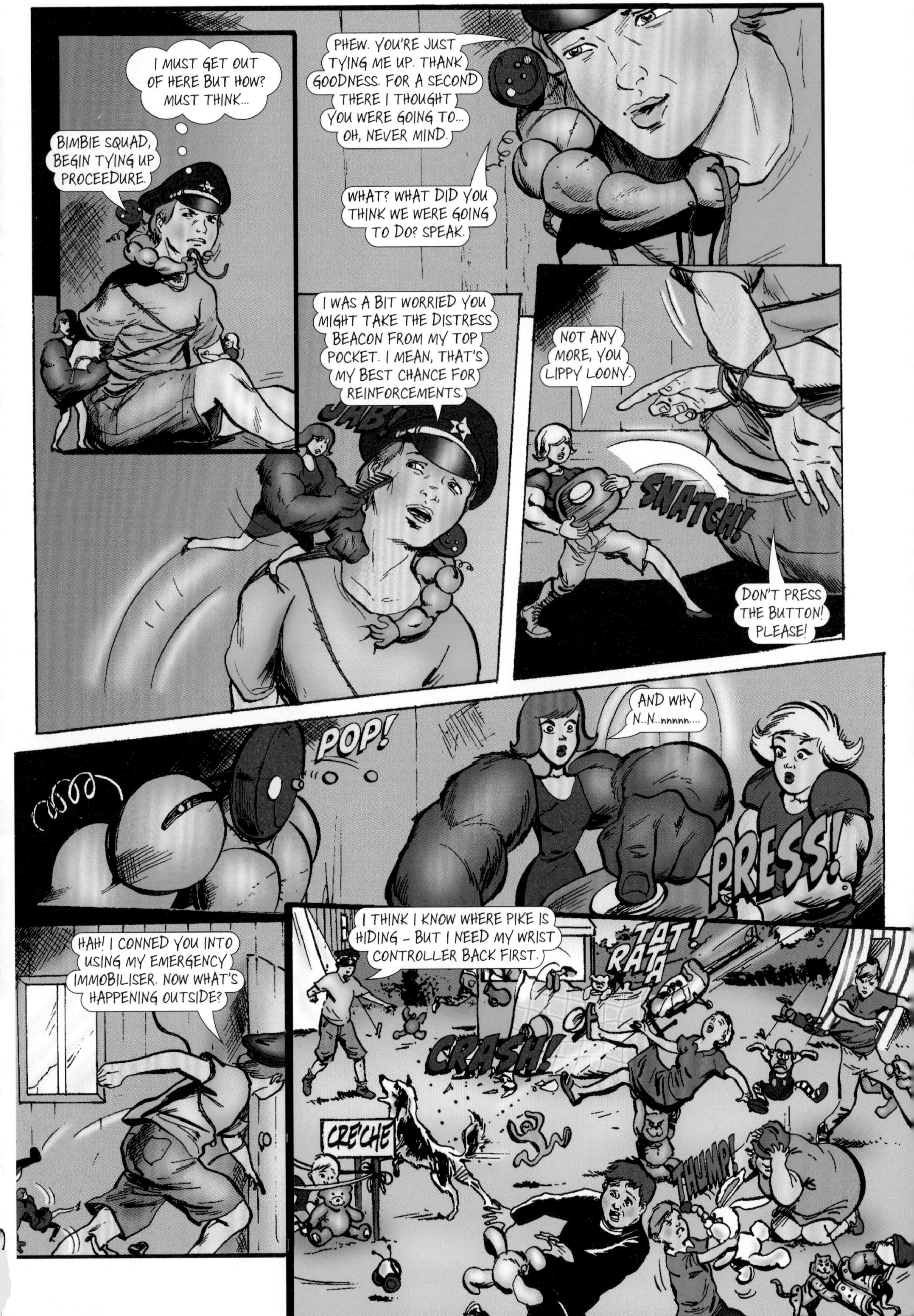
I MUST GET OUT OF HERE BUT HOW? MUST THINK...
BIMBIE SQUAD, BEGIN TYING UP PROCEEDURE.
PHEW. YOU'RE JUST TYING ME UP. THANK GOODNESS. FOR A SECOND THERE I THOUGHT YOU WERE GOING TO... OH, NEVER MIND.
WHAT? WHAT DID YOU THINK WE WERE GOING TO DO? SPEAK.
I WAS A BIT WORRIED YOU MIGHT TAKE THE DISTRESS BEACON FROM MY TOP POCKET. I MEAN, THAT'S MY BEST CHANCE FOR REINFORCEMENTS.
NOT ANY MORE, YOU LIPPY LOONY.
SNATCH!
DON'T PRESS THE BUTTON! PLEASE!
POP!
AND WHY N..N..nnnnn....
PRESS!
HAH! I CONNED YOU INTO USING MY EMERGENCY IMMOBILISER. NOW WHAT'S HAPPENING OUTSIDE?
I THINK I KNOW WHERE PIKE IS HIDING - BUT I NEED MY WRIST CONTROLLER BACK FIRST.
RATATAT!
CRASH!
CRE'CHE
THUMP!

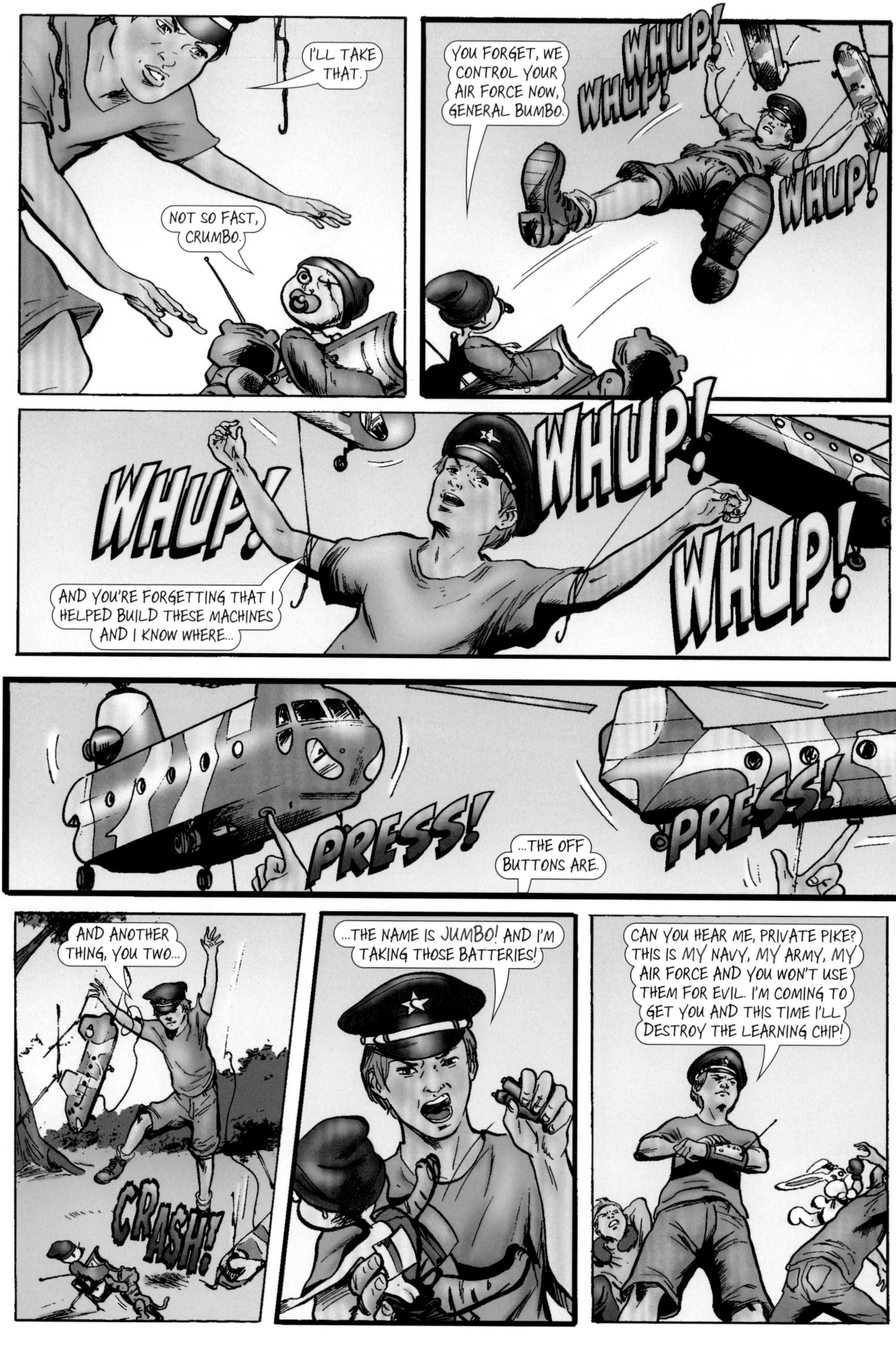
I'LL TAKE THAT.
NOT SO FAST, CRUMBO.
YOU FORGET, WE CONTROL YOUR AIR FORCE NOW, GENERAL BUMBO.
WHUP! WHUP!
WHUP!
WHUP!
WHUP!
WHUP!
WHUP!
AND YOU'RE FORGETTING THAT I HELPED BUILD THESE MACHINES AND I KNOW WHERE...
PRESS!
...THE OFF BUTTONS ARE.
PRESS!
AND ANOTHER THING, YOU TWO...
CRASH!
...THE NAME IS JUMBO! AND I'M TAKING THOSE BATTERIES!
CAN YOU HEAR ME, PRIVATE PIKE? THIS IS MY NAVY, MY ARMY, MY AIR FORCE AND YOU WON'T USE THEM FOR EVIL. I'M COMING TO GET YOU AND THIS TIME I'LL DESTROY THE LEARNING CHIP!

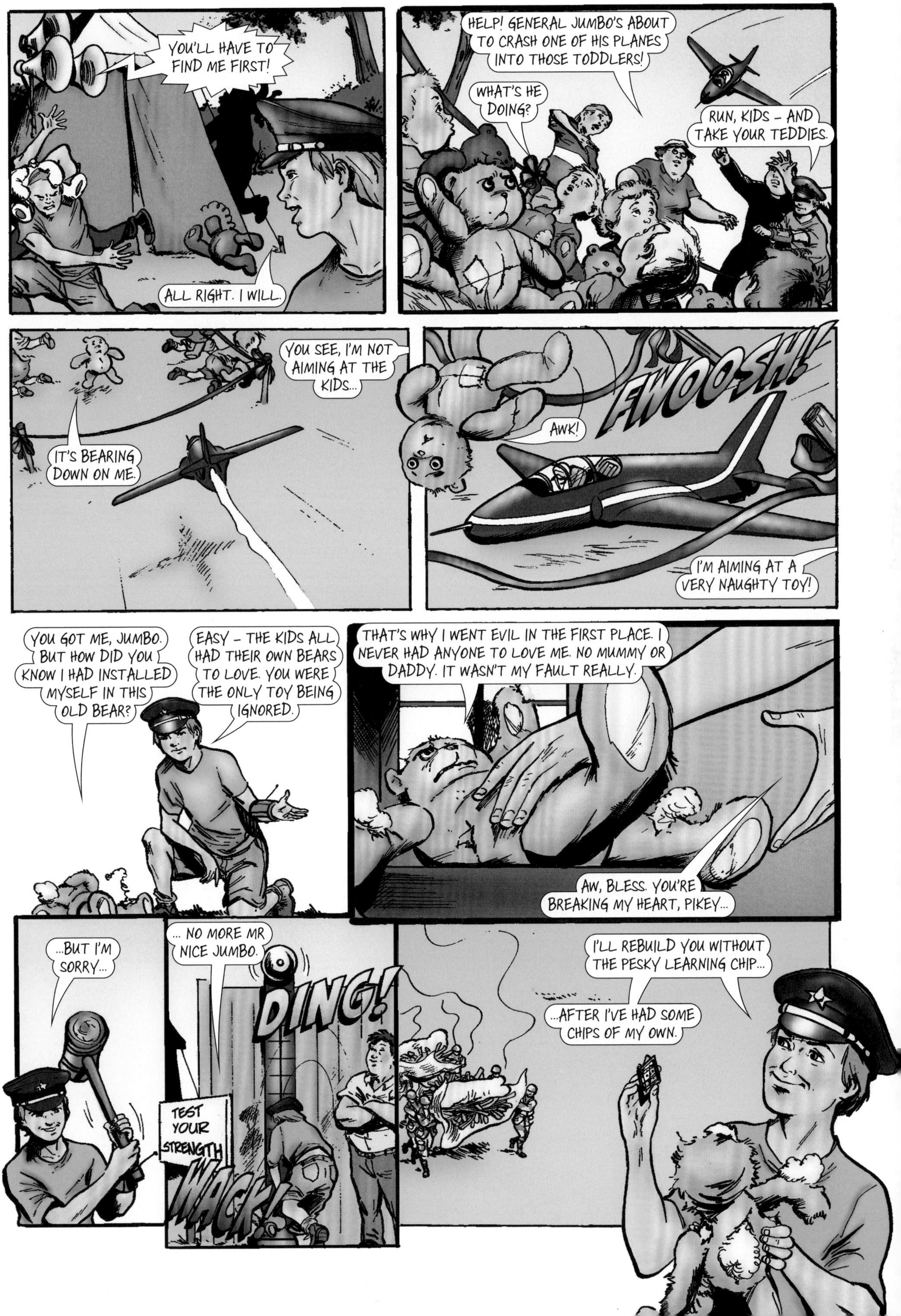
YOU'LL HAVE TO FIND ME FIRST!
ALL RIGHT. I WILL.
HELP! GENERAL JUMBO'S ABOUT TO CRASH ONE OF HIS PLANES INTO THOSE TODDLERS!
WHAT'S HE DOING?
RUN, KIDS – AND TAKE YOUR TEDDIES.
YOU SEE, I'M NOT AIMING AT THE KIDS...
IT'S BEARING DOWN ON ME.
FWOOSH!
AWK!
I'M AIMING AT A VERY NAUGHTY TOY!
YOU GOT ME, JUMBO. BUT HOW DID YOU KNOW I HAD INSTALLED MYSELF IN THIS OLD BEAR?
EASY – THE KIDS ALL HAD THEIR OWN BEARS TO LOVE. YOU WERE THE ONLY TOY BEING IGNORED.
THAT'S WHY I WENT EVIL IN THE FIRST PLACE. I NEVER HAD ANYONE TO LOVE ME. NO MUMMY OR DADDY. IT WASN'T MY FAULT REALLY.
AW, BLESS. YOU'RE BREAKING MY HEART, PIKEY...
...BUT I'M SORRY...
... NO MORE MR NICE JUMBO.
DING!
TEST YOUR STRENGTH
WACK!
I'LL REBUILD YOU WITHOUT THE PESKY LEARNING CHIP...
...AFTER I'VE HAD SOME CHIPS OF MY OWN.

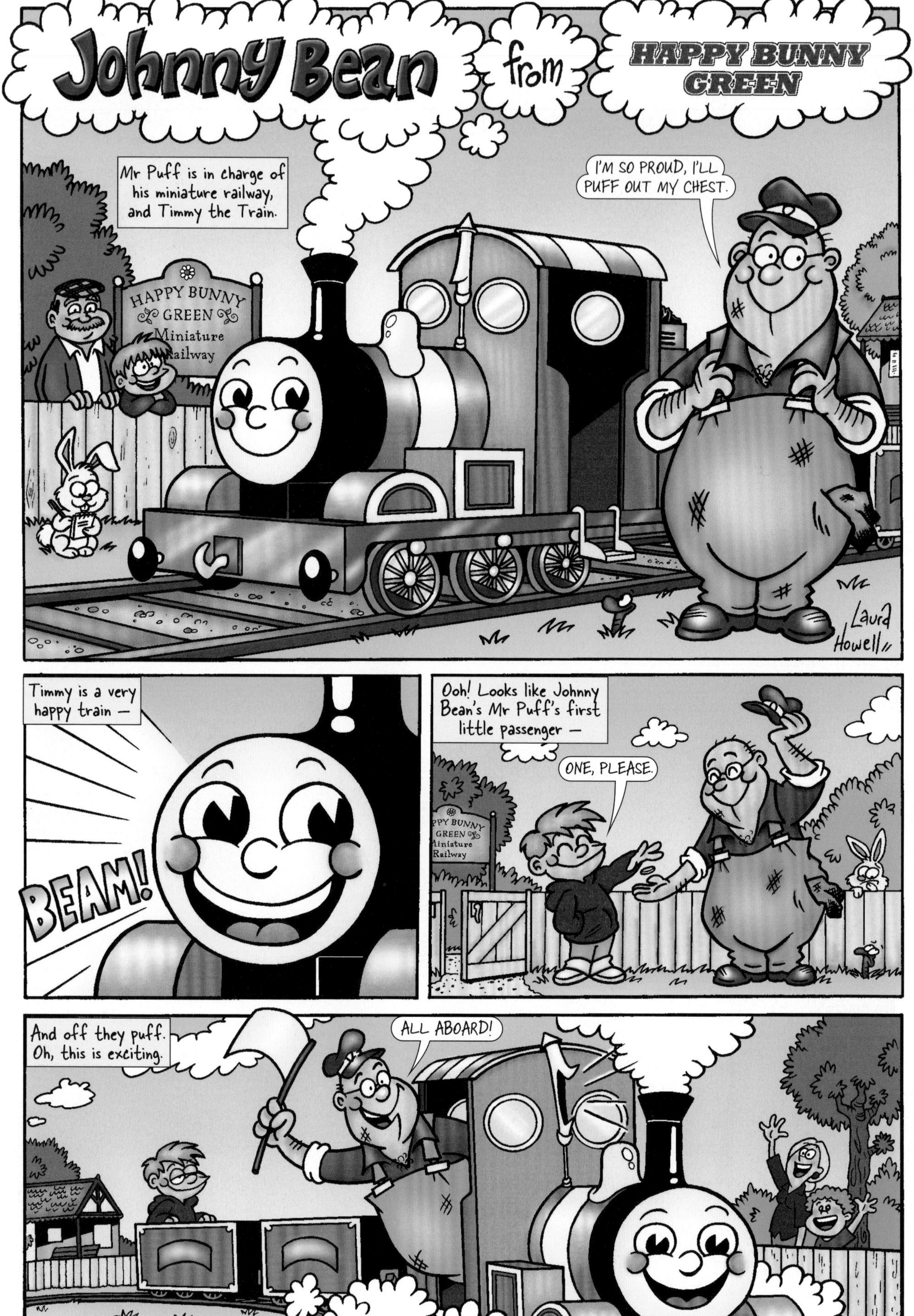
Johnny Bean from HAPPY BUNNY GREEN
Mr Puff is in charge of his miniature railway, and Timmy the Train.
HAPPY BUNNY GREEN Miniature Railway
I'M SO PROUD, I'LL PUFF OUT MY CHEST.
Laura Howell
Timmy is a very happy train —
BEAM!
Ooh! Looks like Johnny Bean's Mr Puff's first little passenger —
ONE, PLEASE.
And off they puff. Oh, this is exciting.
ALL ABOARD!

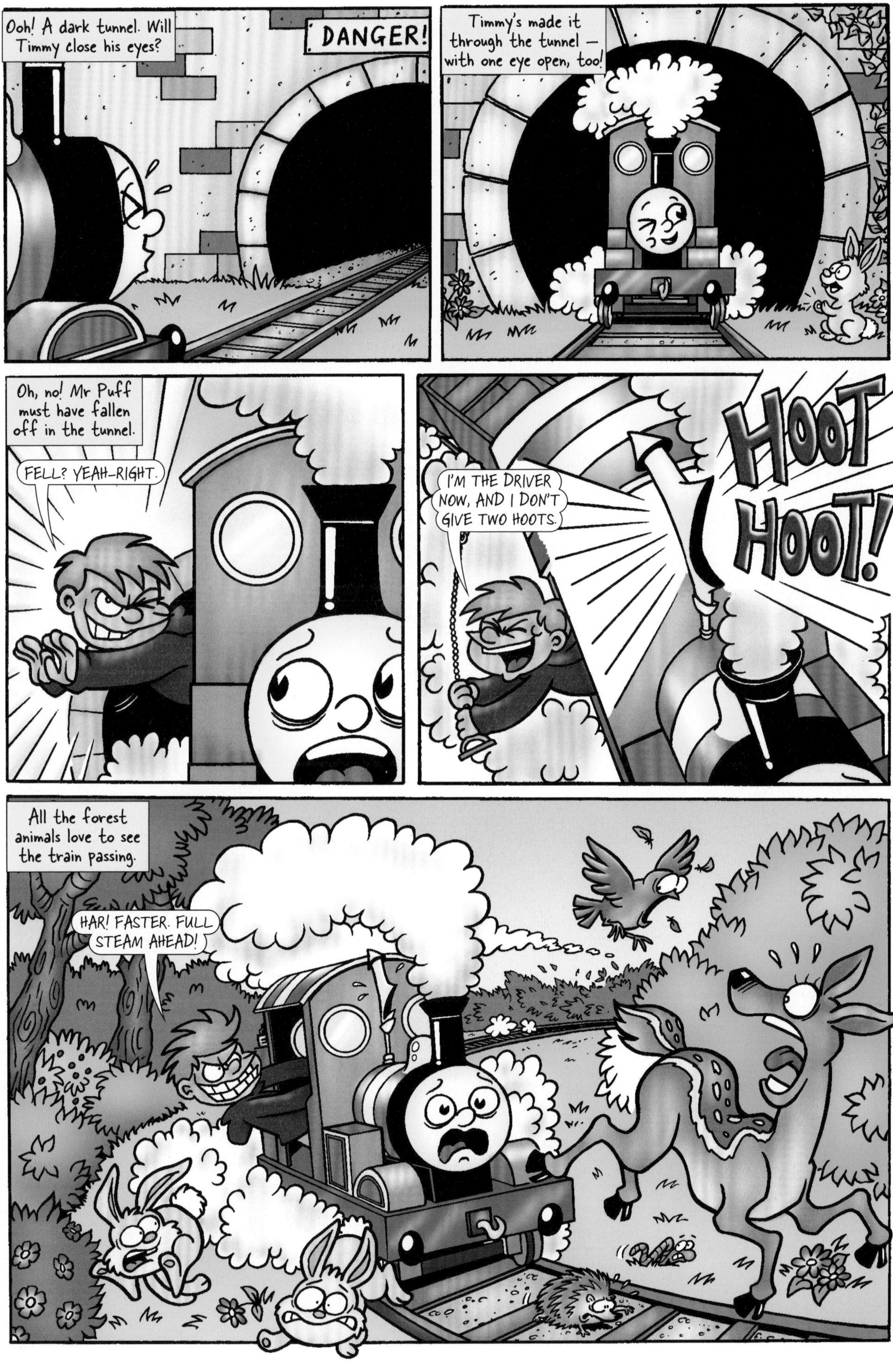
Ooh! A dark tunnel. Will Timmy close his eyes?
DANGER!
Timmy's made it through the tunnel — with one eye open, too!
Oh, no! Mr Puff must have fallen off in the tunnel.
FELL? YEAH–RIGHT.
I'M THE DRIVER NOW, AND I DON'T GIVE TWO HOOTS.
HOOT HOOT!
All the forest animals love to see the train passing.
HAR! FASTER. FULL STEAM AHEAD!

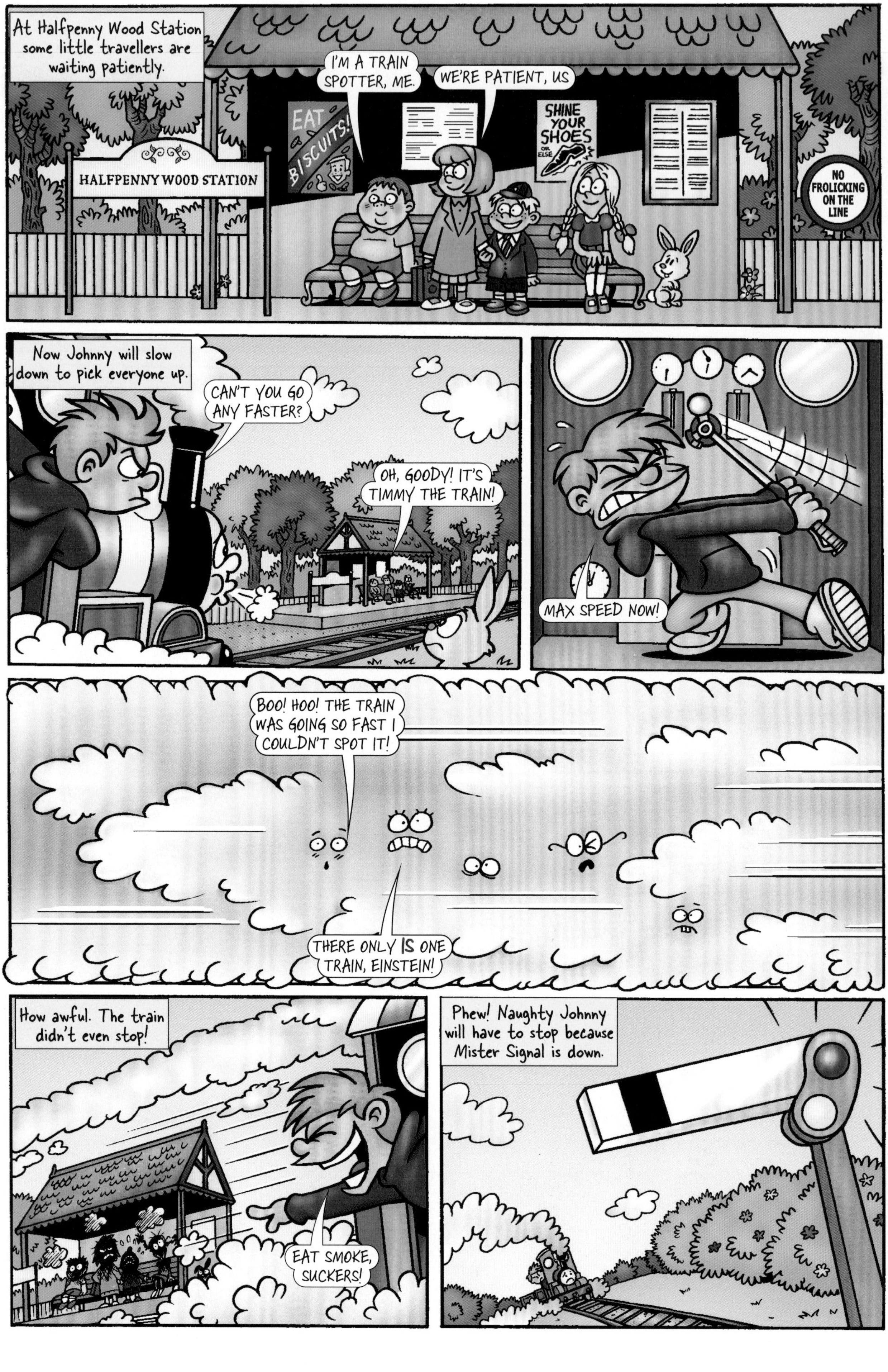
At Halfpenny Wood Station some little travellers are waiting patiently.
HALFPENNY WOOD STATION
EAT BISCUITS!
I'M A TRAIN SPOTTER, ME.
WE'RE PATIENT, US
SHINE YOUR SHOES OR ELSE
NO FROLICKING ON THE LINE
Now Johnny will slow down to pick everyone up.
CAN'T YOU GO ANY FASTER?
OH, GOODY! IT'S TIMMY THE TRAIN!
MAX SPEED NOW!
BOO! HOO! THE TRAIN WAS GOING SO FAST I COULDN'T SPOT IT!
THERE ONLY IS ONE TRAIN, EINSTEIN!
How awful. The train didn't even stop!
EAT SMOKE, SUCKERS!
Phew! Naughty Johnny will have to stop because Mister Signal is down.

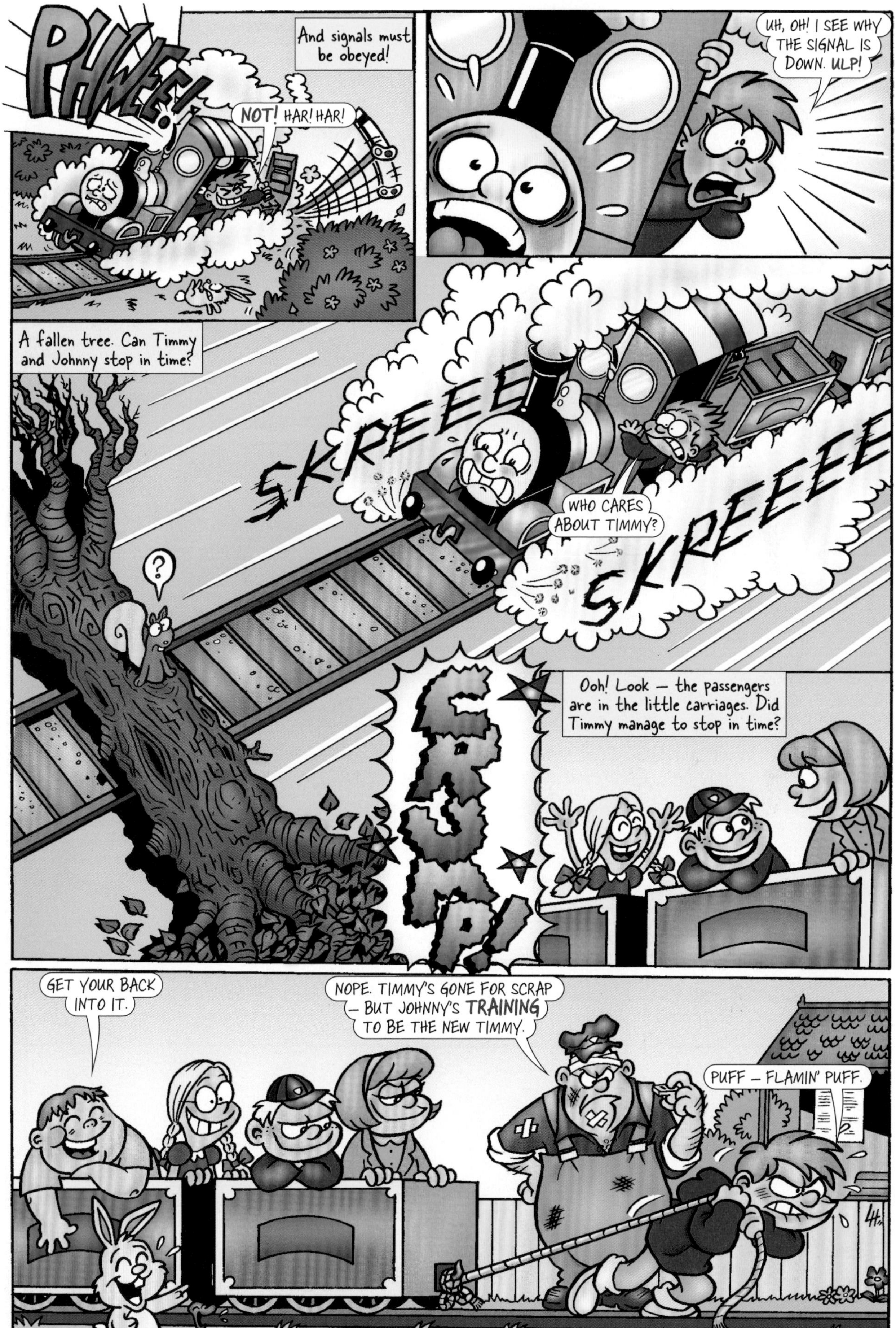

PHWEE!
And signals must be obeyed!
NOT! HAR! HAR!
UH, OH! I SEE WHY THE SIGNAL IS DOWN. ULP!
A fallen tree. Can Timmy and Johnny stop in time?
SKREEEE!
WHO CARES ABOUT TIMMY?
SKREEEEE
?
CRUMP!
Ooh! Look — the passengers are in the little carriages. Did Timmy manage to stop in time?
GET YOUR BACK INTO IT.
NOPE. TIMMY'S GONE FOR SCRAP — BUT JOHNNY'S TRAINING TO BE THE NEW TIMMY.
PUFF — FLAMIN' PUFF.

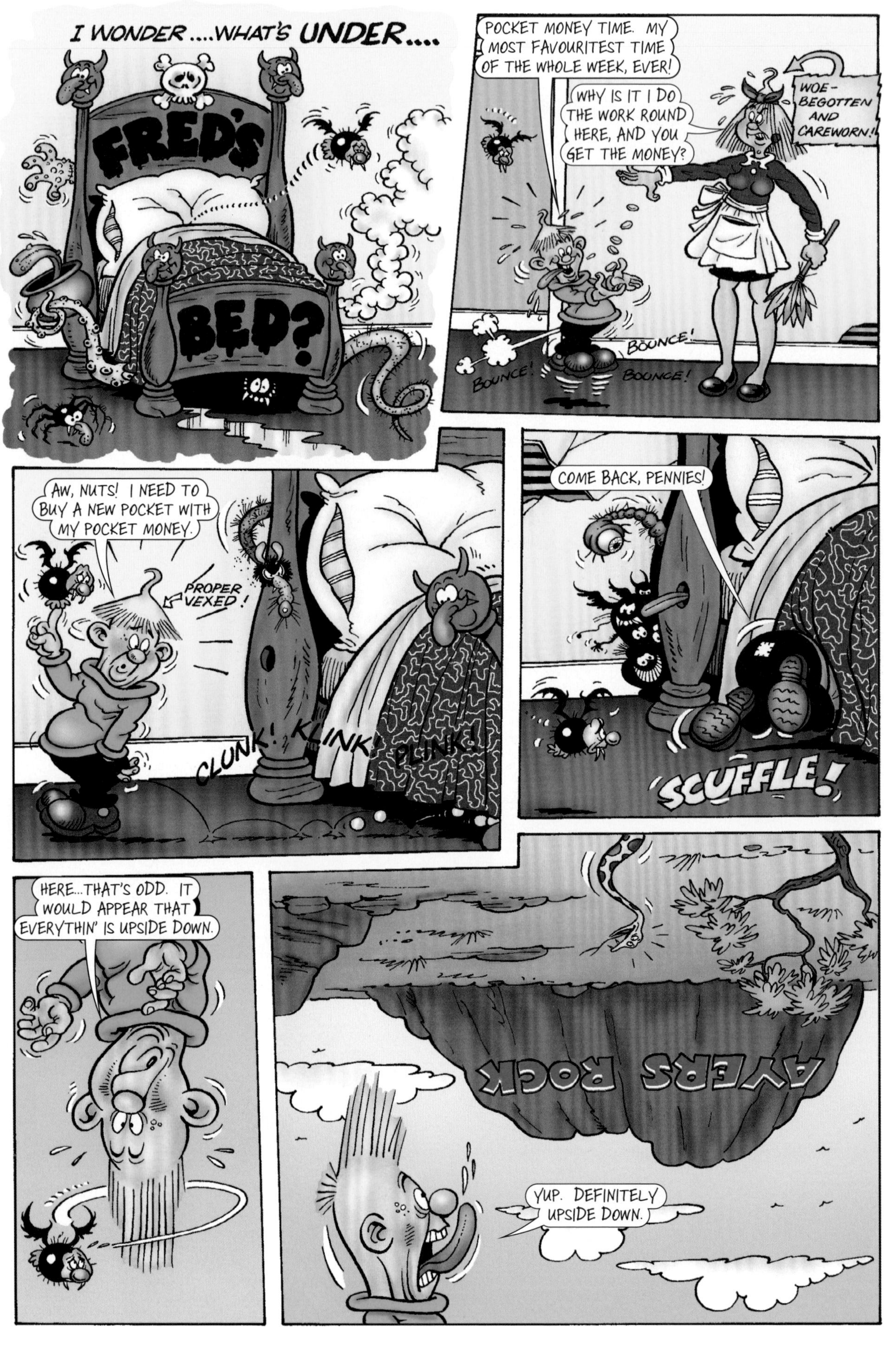
I WONDER....WHAT'S UNDER....
FRED'S BED?
POCKET MONEY TIME. MY MOST FAVOURITEST TIME OF THE WHOLE WEEK, EVER!
WHY IS IT I DO THE WORK ROUND HERE, AND YOU GET THE MONEY?
WOE-BEGOTTEN AND CAREWORN!
BOUNCE! BOUNCE! BOUNCE!
AW, NUTS! I NEED TO BUY A NEW POCKET WITH MY POCKET MONEY.
PROPER VEXED!
CLUNK! KLINK! PLINK!
COME BACK, PENNIES!
SCUFFLE!
HERE...THAT'S ODD. IT WOULD APPEAR THAT EVERYTHIN' IS UPSIDE DOWN.
AYERS ROCK
YUP. DEFINITELY UPSIDE DOWN.

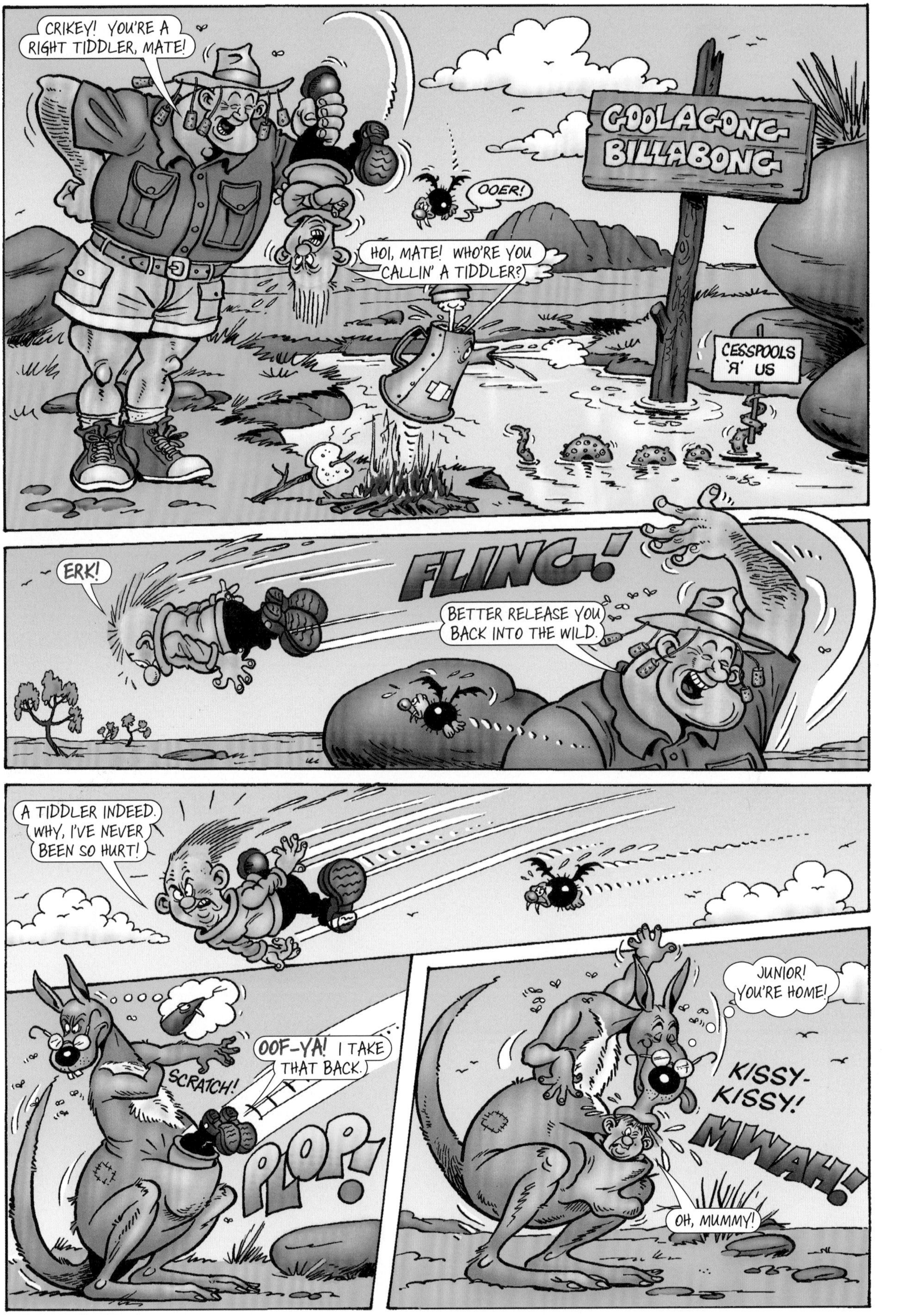
CRIKEY! YOU'RE A RIGHT TIDDLER, MATE!
GOOLAGONG BILLABONG
OOER!
HOI, MATE! WHO'RE YOU CALLIN' A TIDDLER?
CESSPOOLS 'R' US
ERK!
FLING!
BETTER RELEASE YOU BACK INTO THE WILD.
A TIDDLER INDEED. WHY, I'VE NEVER BEEN SO HURT!
SCRATCH!
OOF-YA! I TAKE THAT BACK.
PLOP!
JUNIOR! YOU'RE HOME!
KISSY-KISSY!
MWAH!
OH, MUMMY!

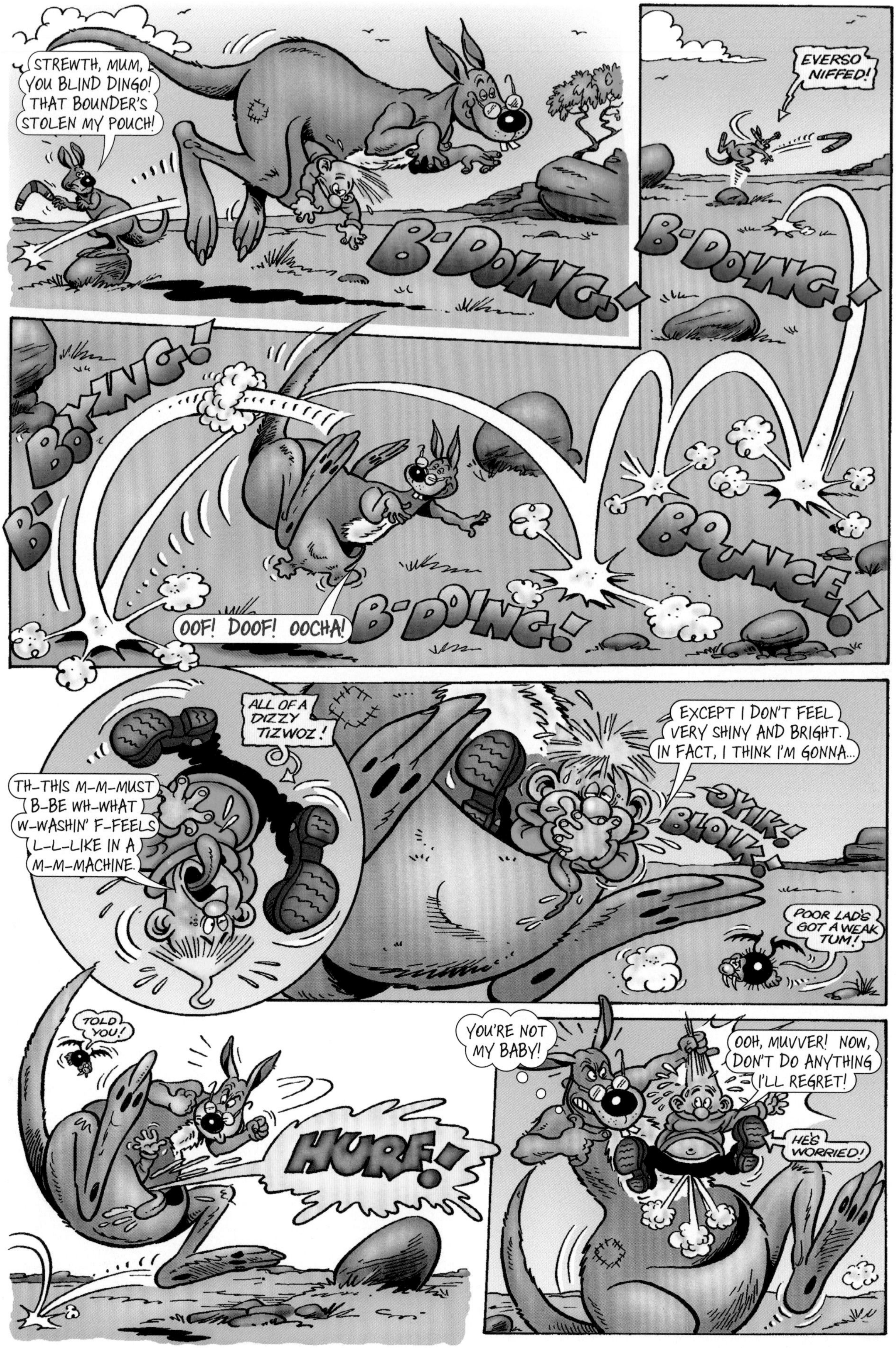
STREWTH, MUM, YOU BLIND DINGO! THAT BOUNDER'S STOLEN MY POUCH!
B-DOING!
EVERSO NIFFED!
B-DOING!
B-BOING!
BOUNCE!
OOF! DOOF! OOCHA!
B-DOING!
ALL OF A DIZZY TIZWOZ!
TH-THIS M-M-MUST B-BE WH-WHAT W-WASHIN' F-FEELS L-L-LIKE IN A M-M-MACHINE.
EXCEPT I DON'T FEEL VERY SHINY AND BRIGHT. IN FACT, I THINK I'M GONNA...
OYIK!
BLOIK!
POOR LAD'S GOT A WEAK TUM!
TOLD YOU!
HURF!
YOU'RE NOT MY BABY!
OOH, MUVVER! NOW, DON'T DO ANYTHING I'LL REGRET!
HE'S WORRIED!

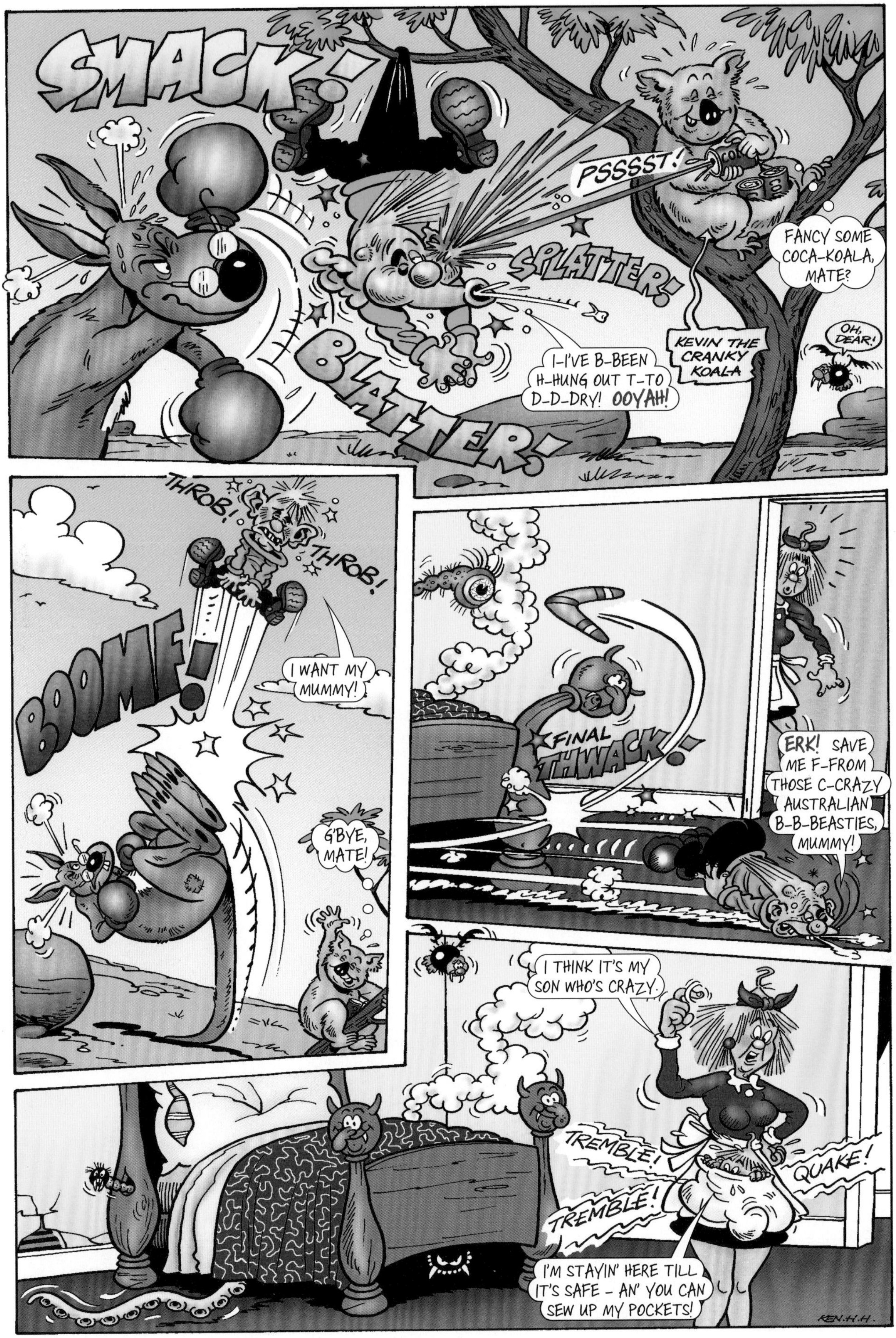
SMACK!
PSSSST!
SPLATTER!
BLATTER!
I-I'VE B-BEEN H-HUNG OUT T-TO D-D-DRY! OOYAH!
KEVIN THE CRANKY KOALA
FANCY SOME COCA-KOALA, MATE?
OH, DEAR!
THROB!
THROB!
BOOMF!
I WANT MY MUMMY!
G'BYE, MATE!
FINAL THWACK!
ERK! SAVE ME F-FROM THOSE C-CRAZY AUSTRALIAN B-B-BEASTIES, MUMMY!
I THINK IT'S MY SON WHO'S CRAZY.
TREMBLE!
TREMBLE!
QUAKE!
I'M STAYIN' HERE TILL IT'S SAFE - AN' YOU CAN SEW UP MY POCKETS!
KEN.H.H.

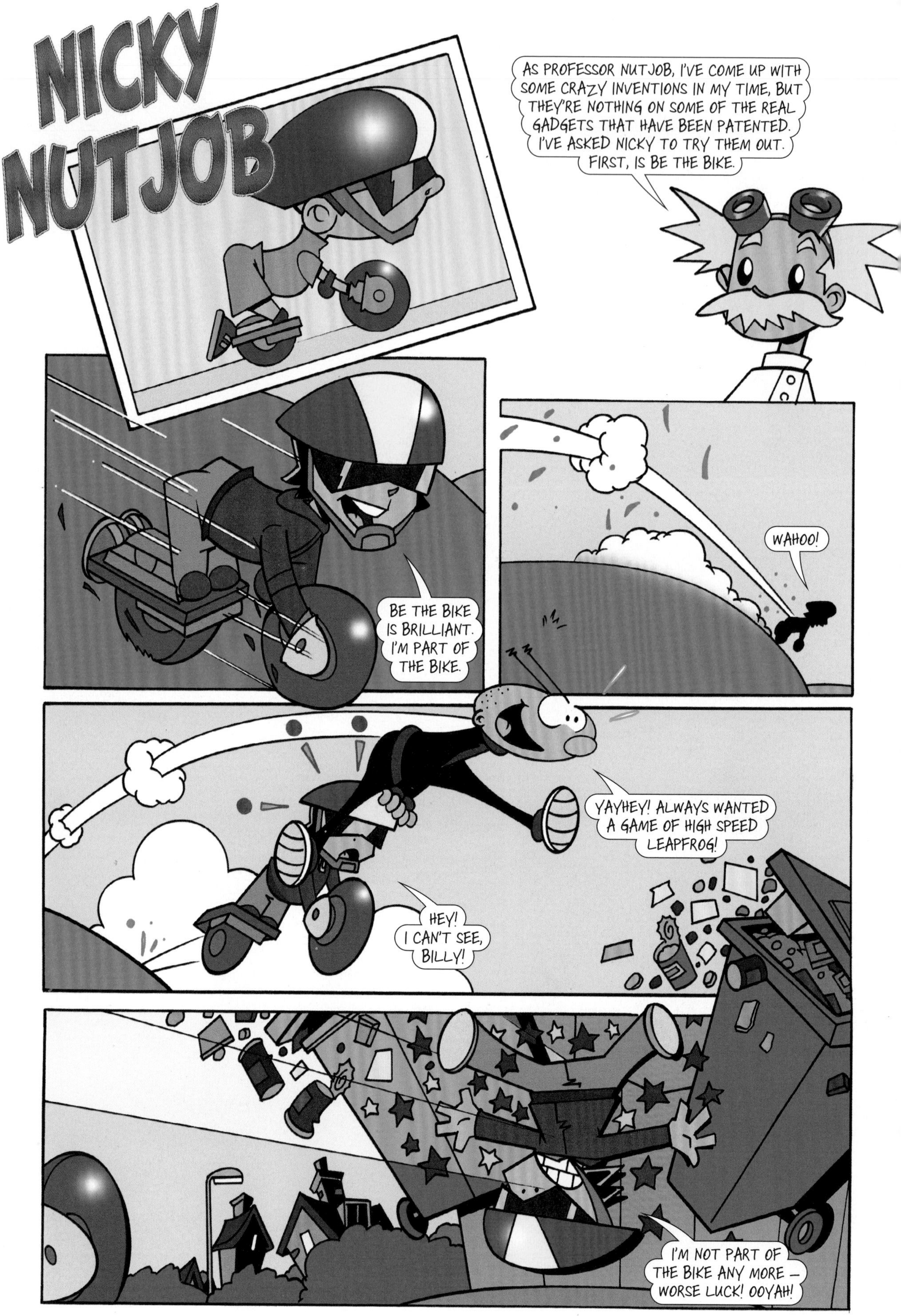
NICKY NUTJOB
AS PROFESSOR NUTJOB, I'VE COME UP WITH SOME CRAZY INVENTIONS IN MY TIME, BUT THEY'RE NOTHING ON SOME OF THE REAL GADGETS THAT HAVE BEEN PATENTED. I'VE ASKED NICKY TO TRY THEM OUT. FIRST, IS BE THE BIKE.
BE THE BIKE IS BRILLIANT. I'M PART OF THE BIKE.
WAHOO!
YAYHEY! ALWAYS WANTED A GAME OF HIGH SPEED LEAPFROG!
HEY! I CAN'T SEE, BILLY!
I'M NOT PART OF THE BIKE ANY MORE – WORSE LUCK! OOYAH!

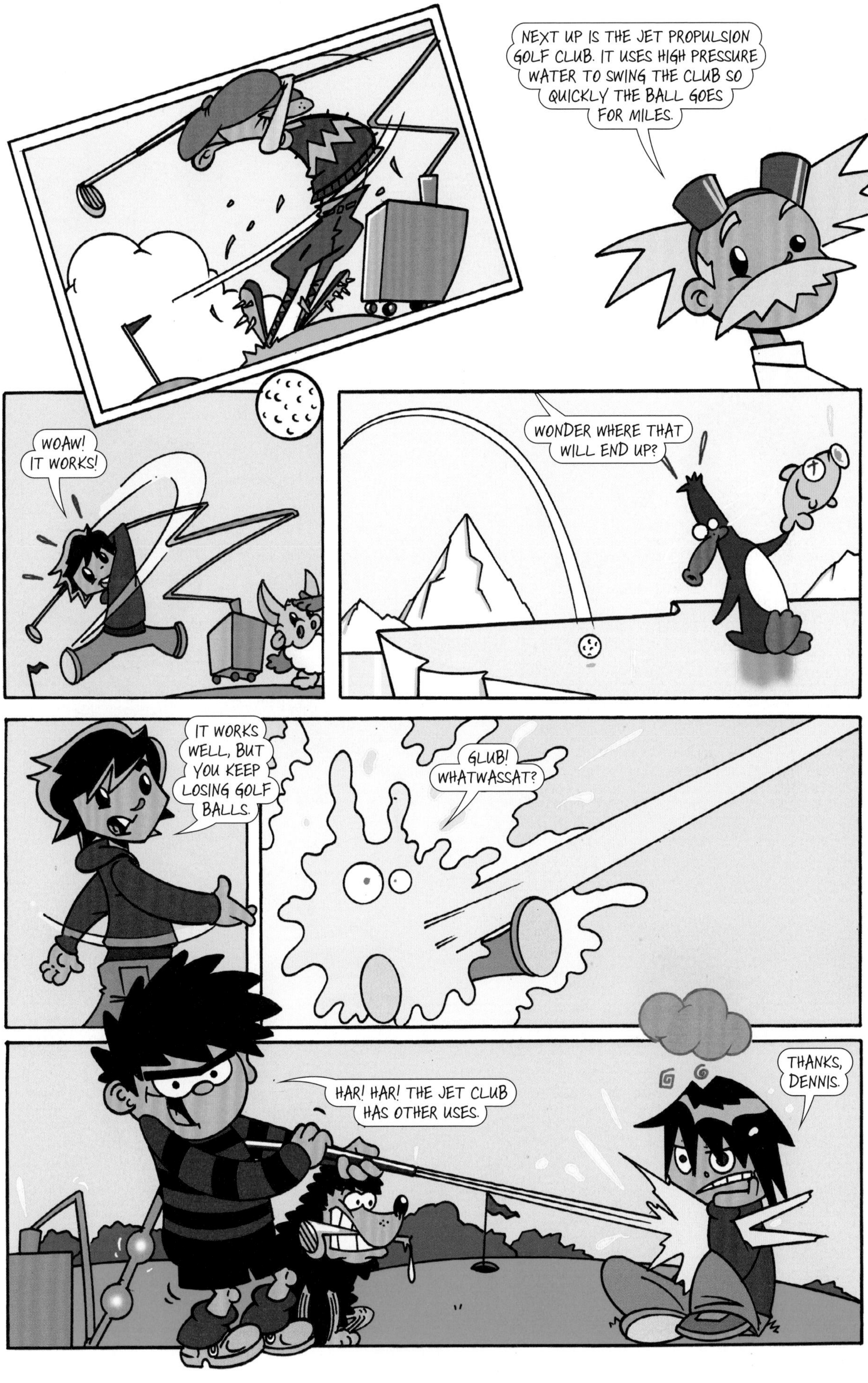
NEXT UP IS THE JET PROPULSION GOLF CLUB. IT USES HIGH PRESSURE WATER TO SWING THE CLUB SO QUICKLY THE BALL GOES FOR MILES.
WOAW! IT WORKS!
WONDER WHERE THAT WILL END UP?
IT WORKS WELL, BUT YOU KEEP LOSING GOLF BALLS.
GLUB! WHATWASSAT?
HAR! HAR! THE JET CLUB HAS OTHER USES.
THANKS, DENNIS.

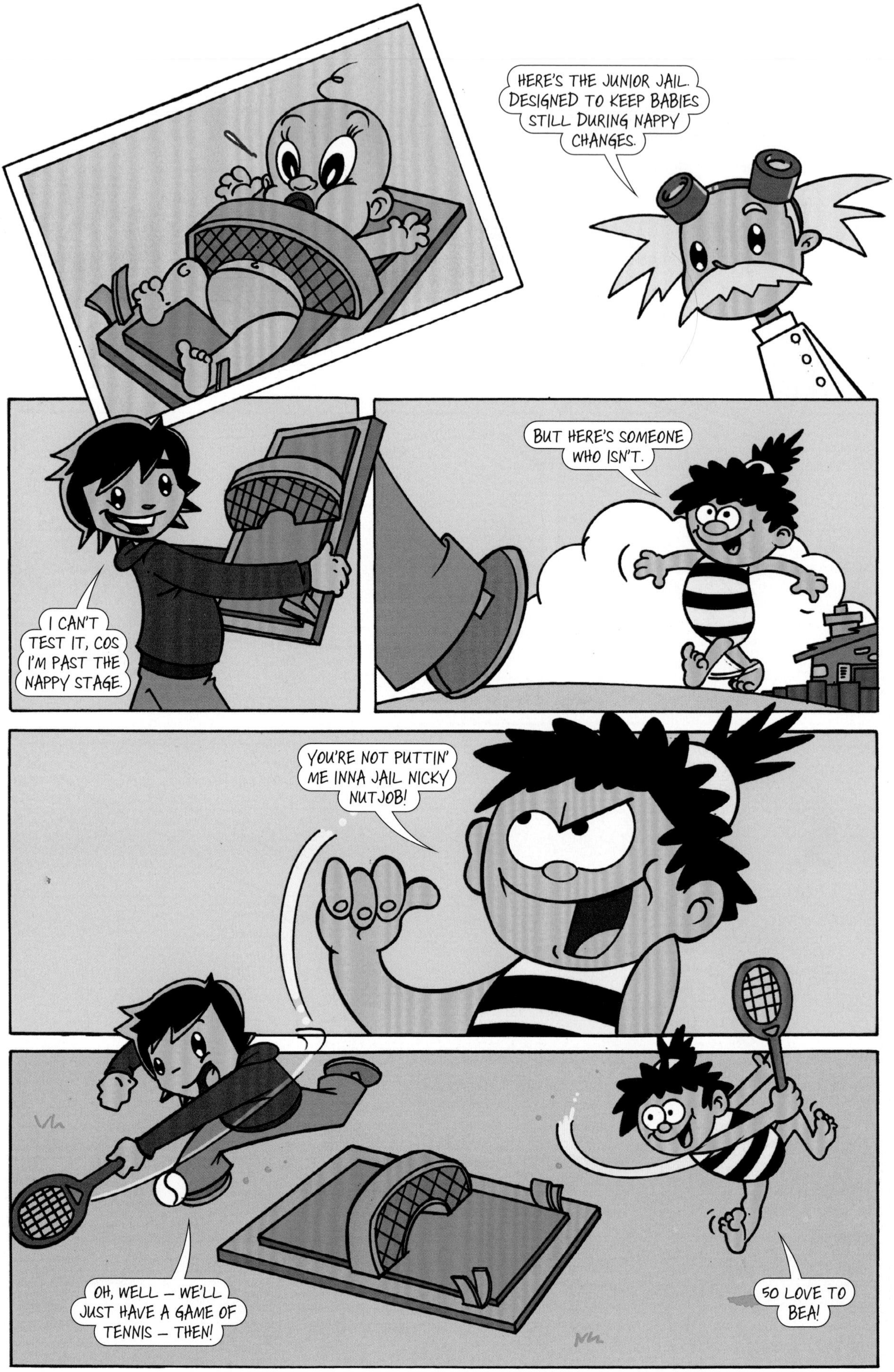
HERE'S THE JUNIOR JAIL. DESIGNED TO KEEP BABIES STILL DURING NAPPY CHANGES.
I CAN'T TEST IT, COS I'M PAST THE NAPPY STAGE.
BUT HERE'S SOMEONE WHO ISN'T.
YOU'RE NOT PUTTIN' ME INNA JAIL NICKY NUTJOB!
OH, WELL – WE'LL JUST HAVE A GAME OF TENNIS – THEN!
50 LOVE TO BEA!

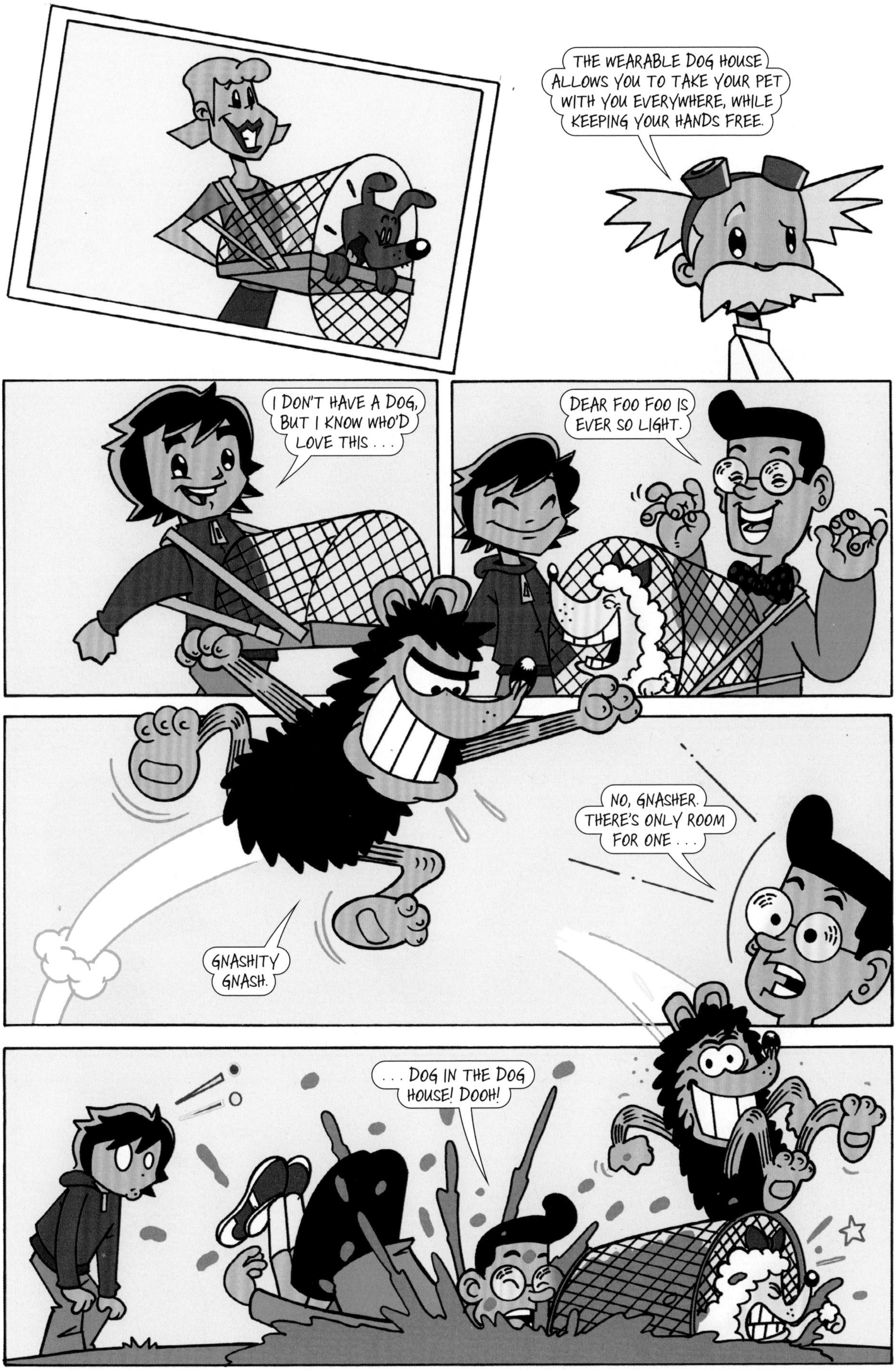
THE WEARABLE DOG HOUSE ALLOWS YOU TO TAKE YOUR PET WITH YOU EVERYWHERE, WHILE KEEPING YOUR HANDS FREE.
I DON'T HAVE A DOG, BUT I KNOW WHO'D LOVE THIS . . .
DEAR FOO FOO IS EVER SO LIGHT.
NO, GNASHER. THERE'S ONLY ROOM FOR ONE . . .
GNASHITY GNASH.
. . . DOG IN THE DOG HOUSE! DOOH!

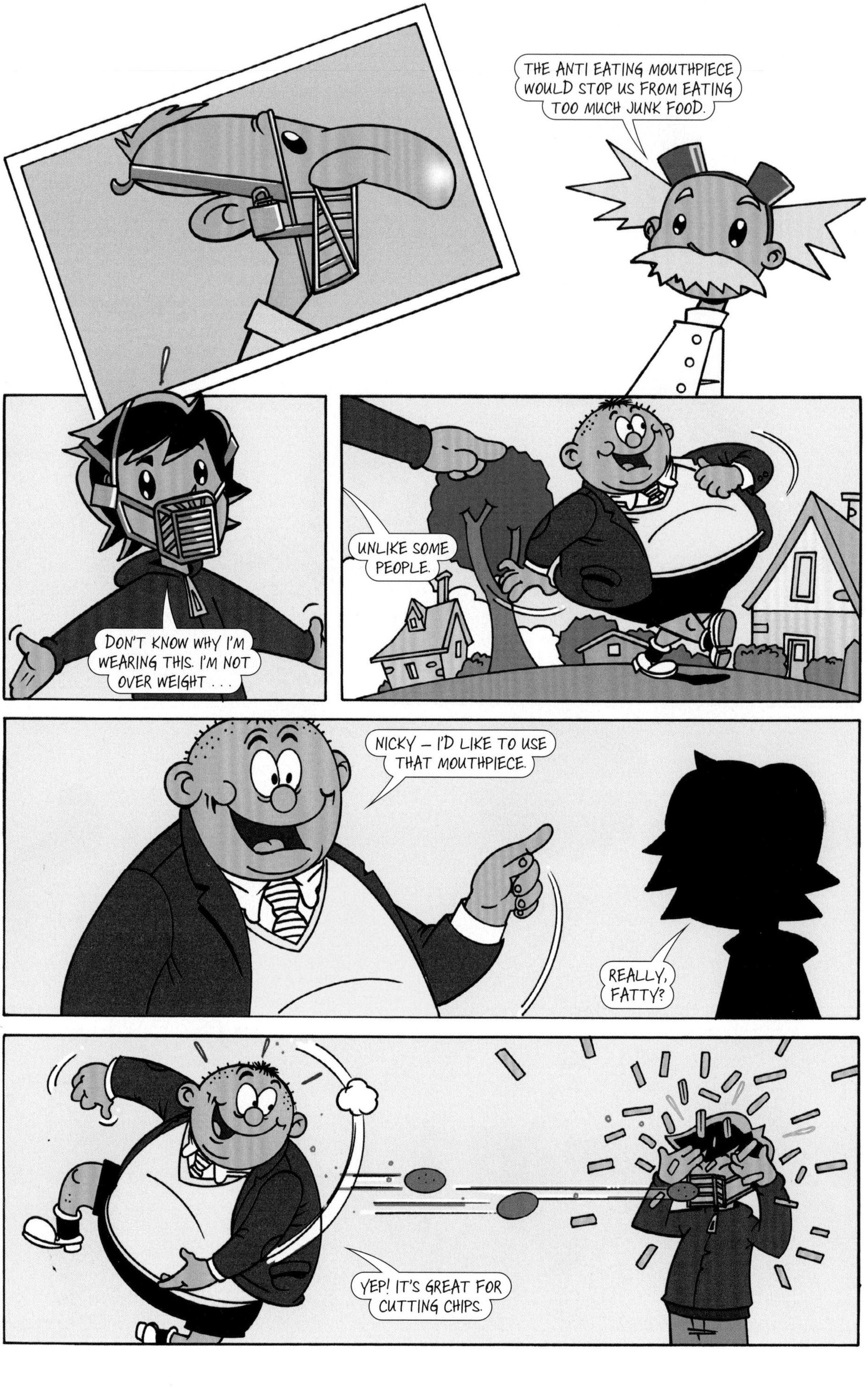
THE ANTI EATING MOUTHPIECE WOULD STOP US FROM EATING TOO MUCH JUNK FOOD.
!
DON'T KNOW WHY I'M WEARING THIS. I'M NOT OVER WEIGHT . . .
UNLIKE SOME PEOPLE.
NICKY – I'D LIKE TO USE THAT MOUTHPIECE.
REALLY, FATTY?
YEP! IT'S GREAT FOR CUTTING CHIPS.

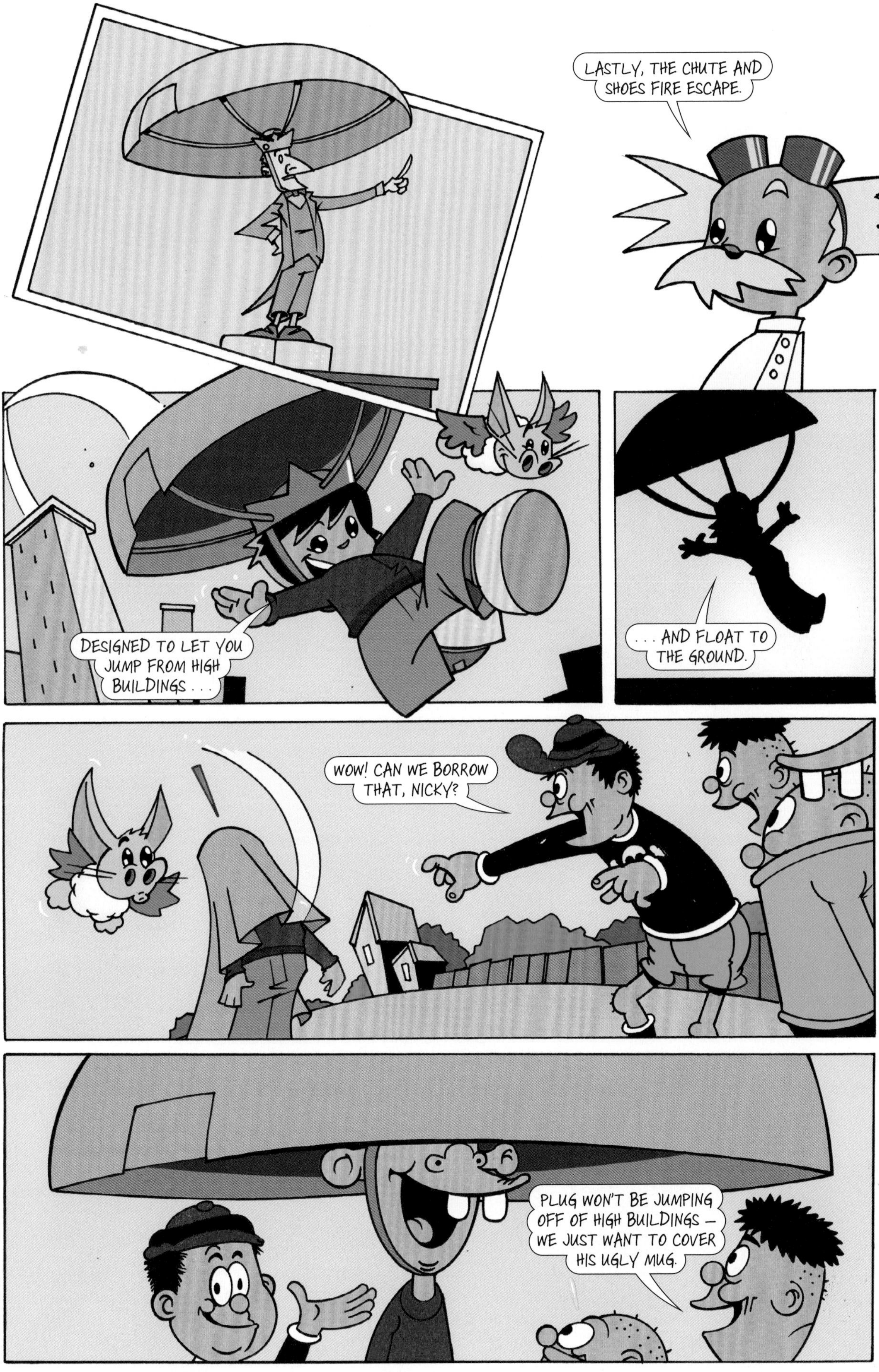
LASTLY, THE CHUTE AND SHOES FIRE ESCAPE.
DESIGNED TO LET YOU JUMP FROM HIGH BUILDINGS . . .
. . . AND FLOAT TO THE GROUND.
WOW! CAN WE BORROW THAT, NICKY?
PLUG WON'T BE JUMPING OFF OF HIGH BUILDINGS — WE JUST WANT TO COVER HIS UGLY MUG.

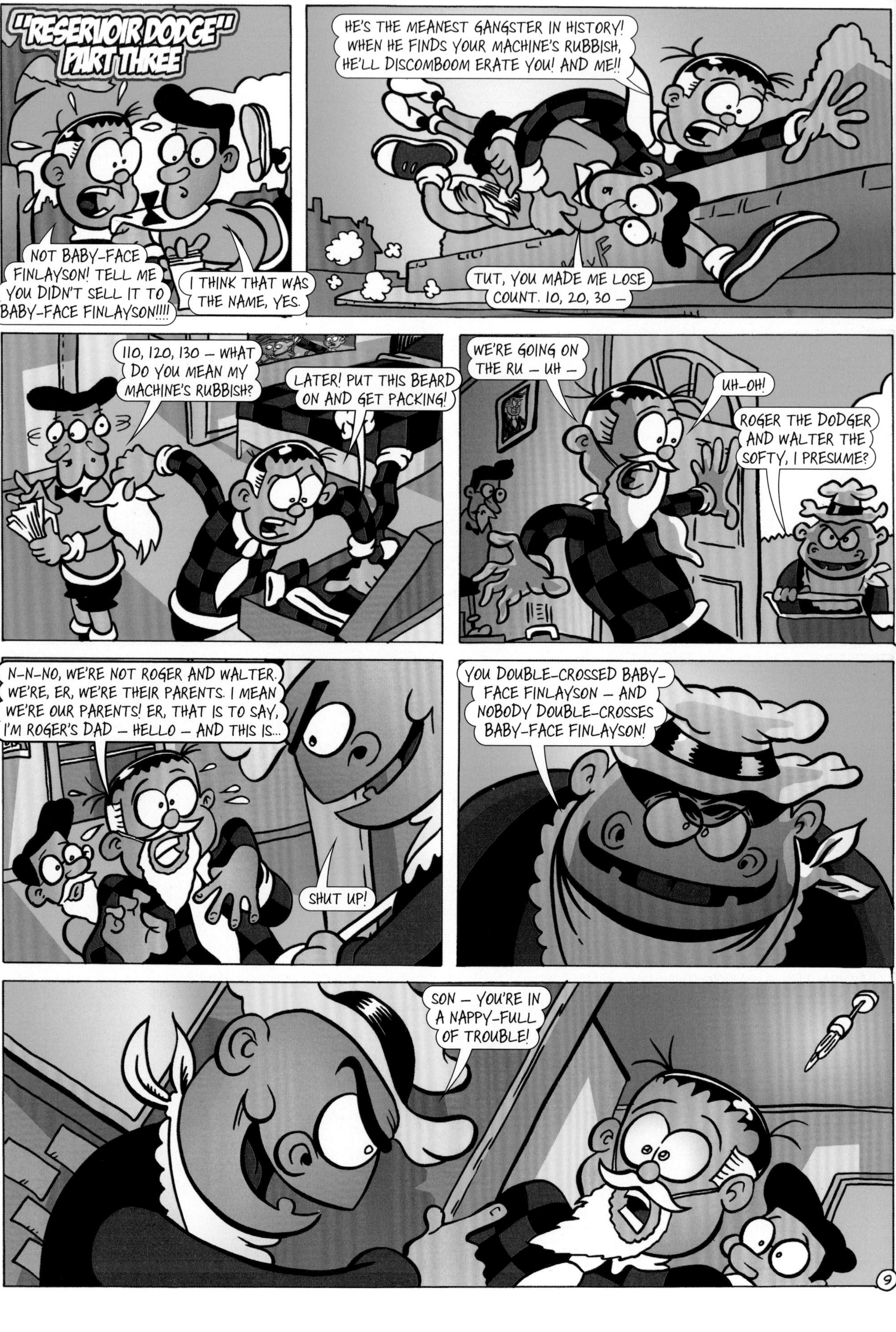

"RESERVOIR DODGE" PART THREE
NOT BABY-FACE FINLAYSON! TELL ME YOU DIDN'T SELL IT TO BABY-FACE FINLAYSON!!!!
I THINK THAT WAS THE NAME, YES.
HE'S THE MEANEST GANGSTER IN HISTORY! WHEN HE FINDS YOUR MACHINE'S RUBBISH, HE'LL DISCOMBOOM ERATE YOU! AND ME!!
TUT, YOU MADE ME LOSE COUNT. 10, 20, 30 –
110, 120, 130 – WHAT DO YOU MEAN MY MACHINE'S RUBBISH?
LATER! PUT THIS BEARD ON AND GET PACKING!
WE'RE GOING ON THE RU – UH –
UH-OH!
ROGER THE DODGER AND WALTER THE SOFTY, I PRESUME?
N-N-NO, WE'RE NOT ROGER AND WALTER. WE'RE, ER, WE'RE THEIR PARENTS. I MEAN WE'RE OUR PARENTS! ER, THAT IS TO SAY, I'M ROGER'S DAD – HELLO – AND THIS IS...
SHUT UP!
YOU DOUBLE-CROSSED BABY-FACE FINLAYSON – AND NOBODY DOUBLE-CROSSES BABY-FACE FINLAYSON!
SON – YOU'RE IN A NAPPY-FULL OF TROUBLE!

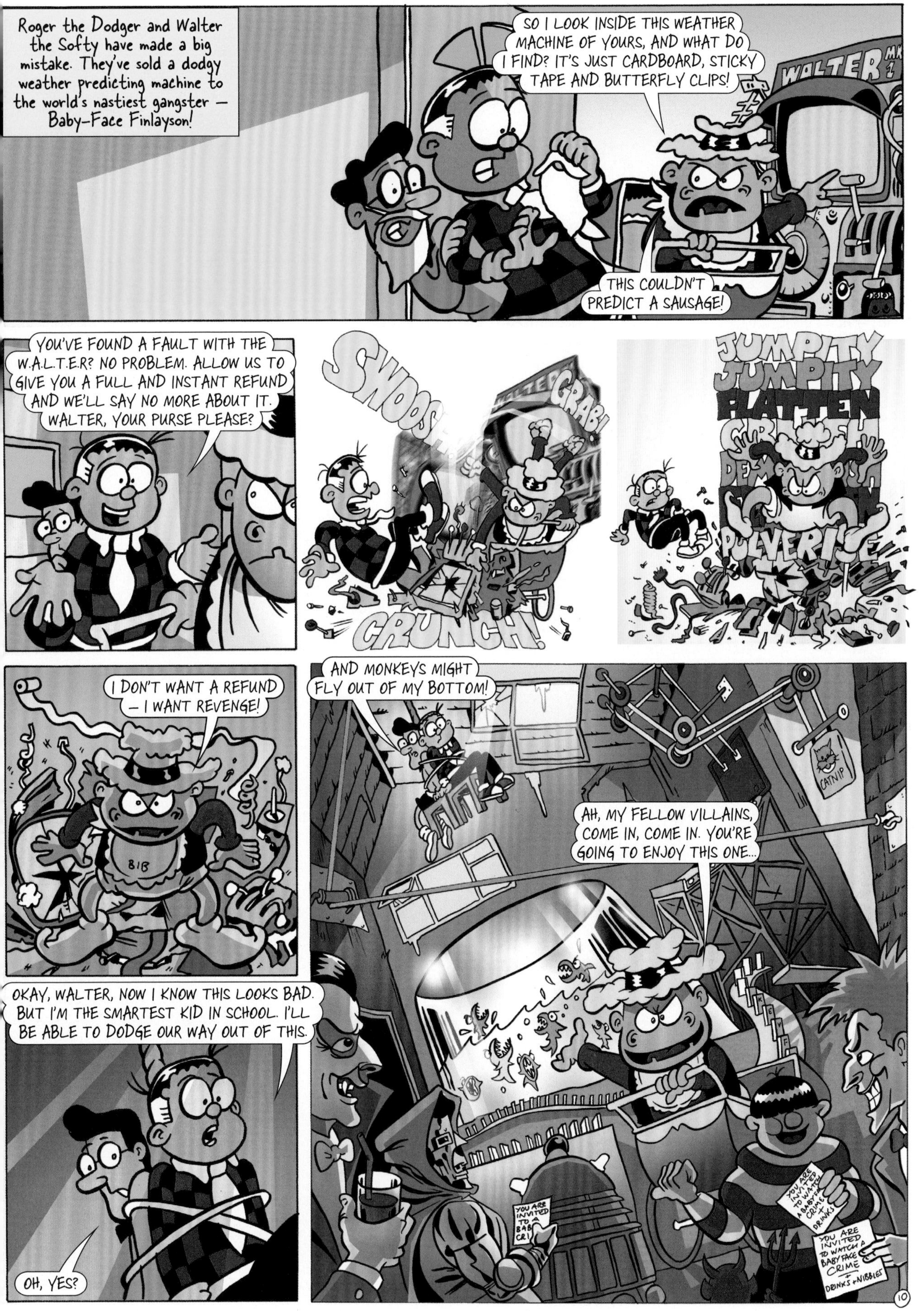
Roger the Dodger and Walter the Softy have made a big mistake. They've sold a dodgy weather predicting machine to the world's nastiest gangster — Baby-Face Finlayson!
SO I LOOK INSIDE THIS WEATHER MACHINE OF YOURS, AND WHAT DO I FIND? IT'S JUST CARDBOARD, STICKY TAPE AND BUTTERFLY CLIPS!
WALTER MK 1
THIS COULDN'T PREDICT A SAUSAGE!
YOU'VE FOUND A FAULT WITH THE W.A.L.T.E.R.? NO PROBLEM. ALLOW US TO GIVE YOU A FULL AND INSTANT REFUND AND WE'LL SAY NO MORE ABOUT IT. WALTER, YOUR PURSE PLEASE?
GRAB!
CRUNCH!
JUMPITY
JUMPITY
FLATTEN
I DON'T WANT A REFUND — I WANT REVENGE!
BIB
AND MONKEYS MIGHT FLY OUT OF MY BOTTOM!
CATNIP
AH, MY FELLOW VILLAINS, COME IN, COME IN. YOU'RE GOING TO ENJOY THIS ONE...
OKAY, WALTER, NOW I KNOW THIS LOOKS BAD. BUT I'M THE SMARTEST KID IN SCHOOL. I'LL BE ABLE TO DODGE OUR WAY OUT OF THIS.
OH, YES?
YOU ARE INVITED TO WATCH A BABYFACE CRIME + DRINKS + NIBBLES

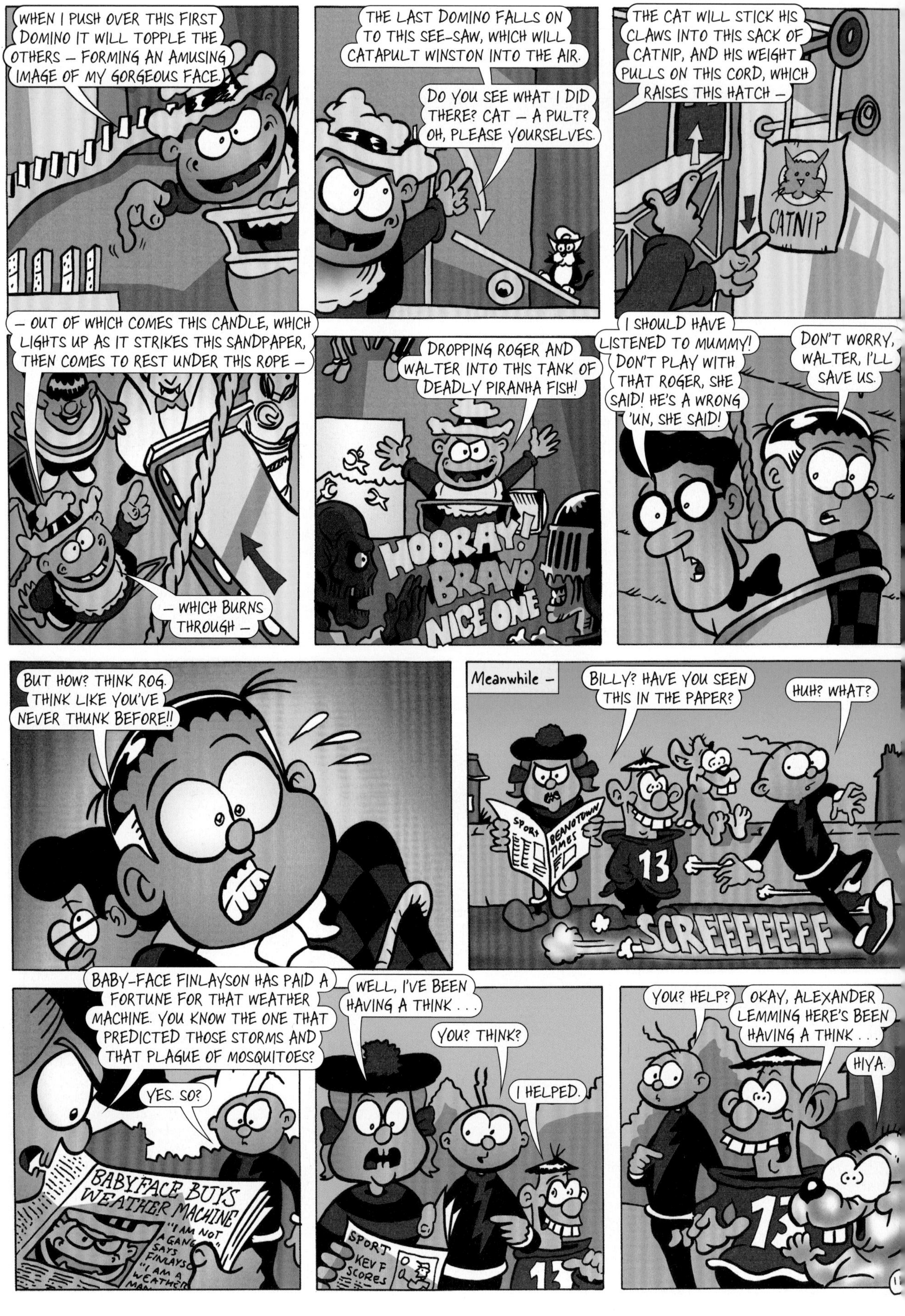
WHEN I PUSH OVER THIS FIRST DOMINO IT WILL TOPPLE THE OTHERS – FORMING AN AMUSING IMAGE OF MY GORGEOUS FACE.
THE LAST DOMINO FALLS ON TO THIS SEE-SAW, WHICH WILL CATAPULT WINSTON INTO THE AIR.
DO YOU SEE WHAT I DID THERE? CAT – A PULT? OH, PLEASE YOURSELVES.
THE CAT WILL STICK HIS CLAWS INTO THIS SACK OF CATNIP, AND HIS WEIGHT PULLS ON THIS CORD, WHICH RAISES THIS HATCH –
CATNIP
– OUT OF WHICH COMES THIS CANDLE, WHICH LIGHTS UP AS IT STRIKES THIS SANDPAPER, THEN COMES TO REST UNDER THIS ROPE –
– WHICH BURNS THROUGH –
DROPPING ROGER AND WALTER INTO THIS TANK OF DEADLY PIRANHA FISH!
HOORAY! BRAVO NICE ONE
I SHOULD HAVE LISTENED TO MUMMY! DON'T PLAY WITH THAT ROGER, SHE SAID! HE'S A WRONG 'UN, SHE SAID!
DON'T WORRY, WALTER, I'LL SAVE US.
BUT HOW? THINK ROG. THINK LIKE YOU'VE NEVER THUNK BEFORE!!
Meanwhile –
BILLY? HAVE YOU SEEN THIS IN THE PAPER?
HUH? WHAT?
SPORT
BEANOTOWN TIMES
13
SCREEEEEEEF
BABY-FACE FINLAYSON HAS PAID A FORTUNE FOR THAT WEATHER MACHINE. YOU KNOW THE ONE THAT PREDICTED THOSE STORMS AND THAT PLAGUE OF MOSQUITOES?
YES. SO?
BABYFACE BUYS WEATHER MACHINE
"I AM NOT A GANG... SAYS FINLAYSO... "I AM A WEATHER MAN
WELL, I'VE BEEN HAVING A THINK . . .
YOU? THINK?
I HELPED.
SPORT
KEV F SCORES
YOU? HELP?
OKAY, ALEXANDER LEMMING HERE'S BEEN HAVING A THINK . . .
HIYA.

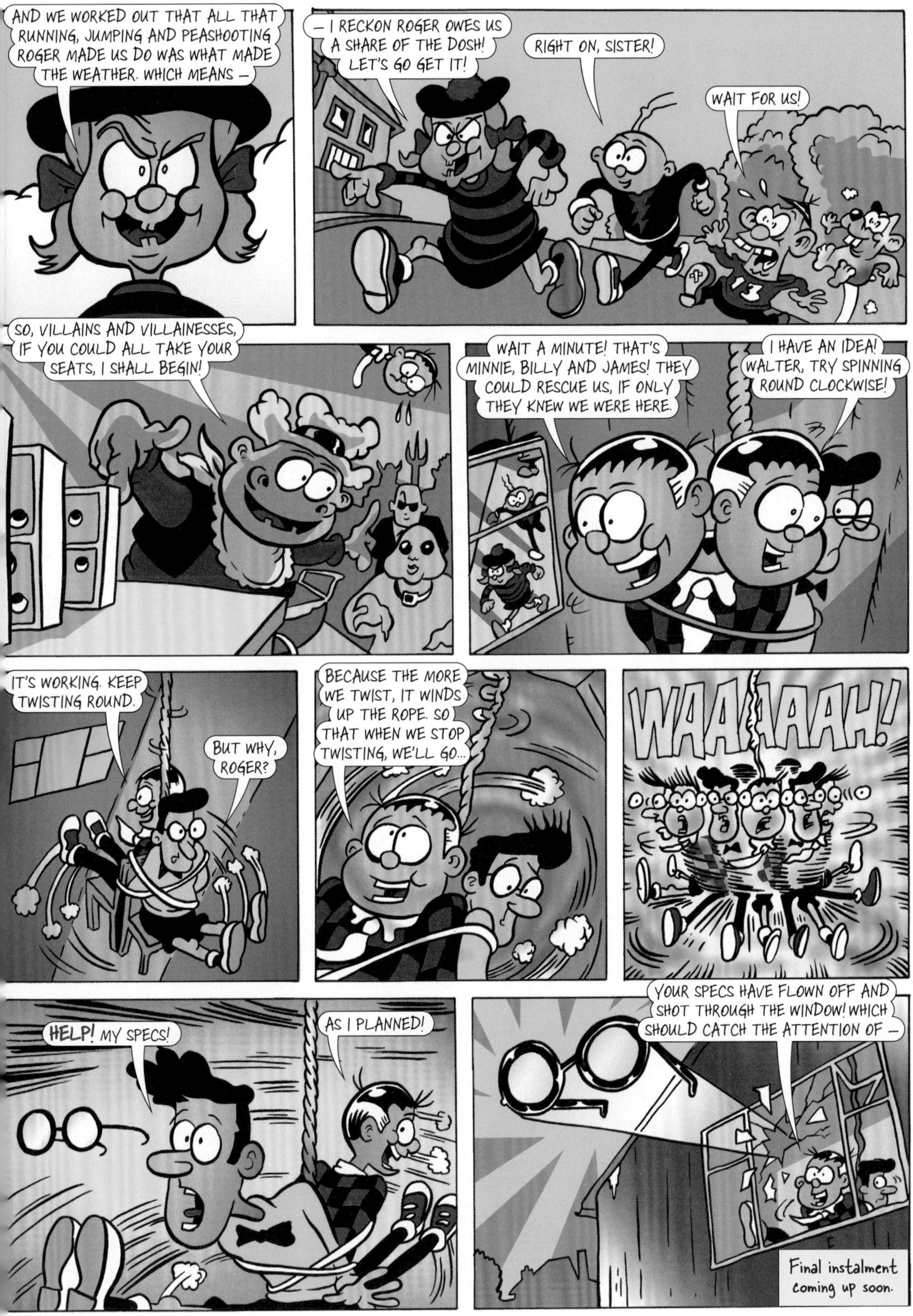
AND WE WORKED OUT THAT ALL THAT RUNNING, JUMPING AND PEASHOOTING ROGER MADE US DO WAS WHAT MADE THE WEATHER. WHICH MEANS –
– I RECKON ROGER OWES US A SHARE OF THE DOSH! LET'S GO GET IT!
RIGHT ON, SISTER!
WAIT FOR US!
SO, VILLAINS AND VILLAINESSES, IF YOU COULD ALL TAKE YOUR SEATS, I SHALL BEGIN!
WAIT A MINUTE! THAT'S MINNIE, BILLY AND JAMES! THEY COULD RESCUE US, IF ONLY THEY KNEW WE WERE HERE.
I HAVE AN IDEA! WALTER, TRY SPINNING ROUND CLOCKWISE!
IT'S WORKING. KEEP TWISTING ROUND.
BUT WHY, ROGER?
BECAUSE THE MORE WE TWIST, IT WINDS UP THE ROPE. SO THAT WHEN WE STOP TWISTING, WE'LL GO...
WAAAAAAH!
HELP! MY SPECS!
AS I PLANNED!
YOUR SPECS HAVE FLOWN OFF AND SHOT THROUGH THE WINDOW! WHICH SHOULD CATCH THE ATTENTION OF –
Final instalment coming up soon.

WALTER AND HIS AMAZING

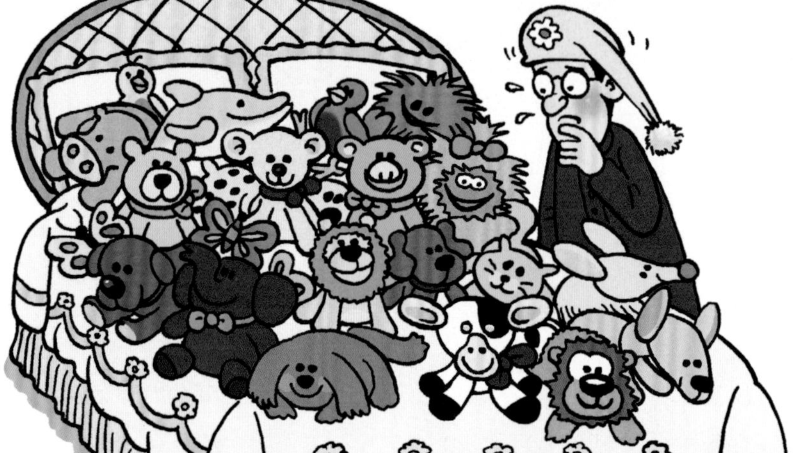

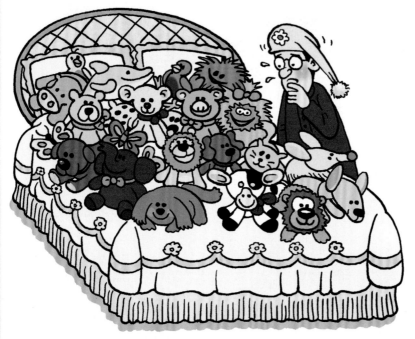

ONCE upon a time there was a little soft boy named Walter with a BIG problem. No, not the BIG problem he'd had for years with that ruffian neighbour of his, Dennis The Menace — this was a new BIG problem! His problem was cuddly toys — he owned so many of the brightly — coloured, fluffy darlings that there was no longer enough room in his little bed for him to sleep there too.

As usual, Mummy had the answer.

"What to do is, once you've given your toys their goodnight cuddle, pop into the spare room and snuggle down in that bed there."

So that's just what the little soft boy did.

"Night-night, Mrs Tickletum!" he said to his pink hippo.

"Sweet dreams, Squidger!" he trilled to his primrose aardvark.

"Sleep tight, Flump!" he cooed to his crimson elephant.

"See you in the morning, Tiggle-Wiggle, Pussums, Splosh, Flutter and the rest of you," he whispered to an assortment of colourful lambs, butterflies, dicky birds, dolphins and gonks.

Carrying his favourite lilac hyena, Martina, to the window, he made the grinning toy wave her paw as he simpered.

"Goodnight, butterflies! Goodnight, birdies! Goodnight, pretty flowers!"

From below, Gnasher, the fierce dog next door, looked up at the sickly sweet scene and issued a low growl. Then he clambered up on to the top of his kennel and issued a not-quite-so-low growl.

"Oo! That horrid, smelly hound!" squealed Walter. "Shall we teach him a

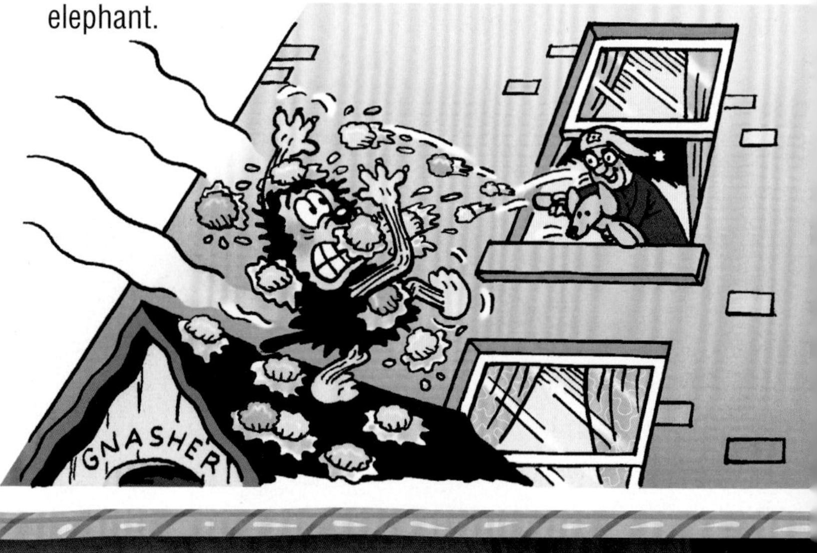
GNASHER

TECHNICOLOUR HOUSECOAT

lesson, Martina?" giggled the soft boy. "Yes, let's!"

Making Martina pick up some coloured cotton-wool balls in her paws, Walter helped the cuddly toy dip them in lavender water and toss them out of the open window.

SPLIT! SPLAT! SPLOT! The soggy cotton balls rained down on the shocked Gnasher, who soon looked and smelled like a polka-dot powder-puff.

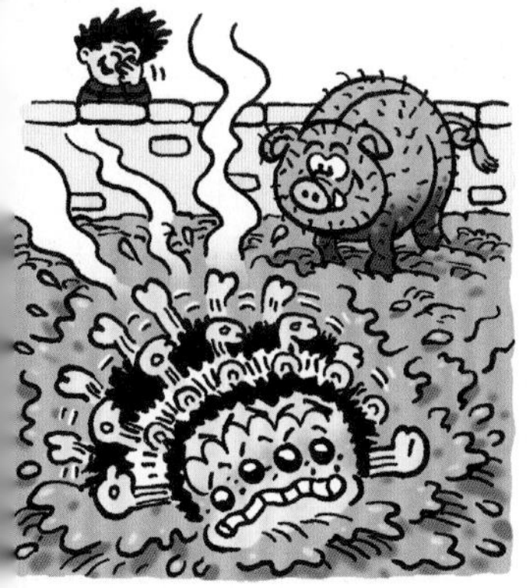

Walter clapped his hands with glee and giggled.

"Well done, Martina! Well done! Hee-hee-hee-hee!"

The Menace Hound was horrified. He had to roll around in his pal Rasher's pigsty and get his master, Dennis, to tip a particularly niffy dustbin over him so that he could get rid of the sickeningly sweet smell.

With REVENGE in his eyes, Gnasher barked out an

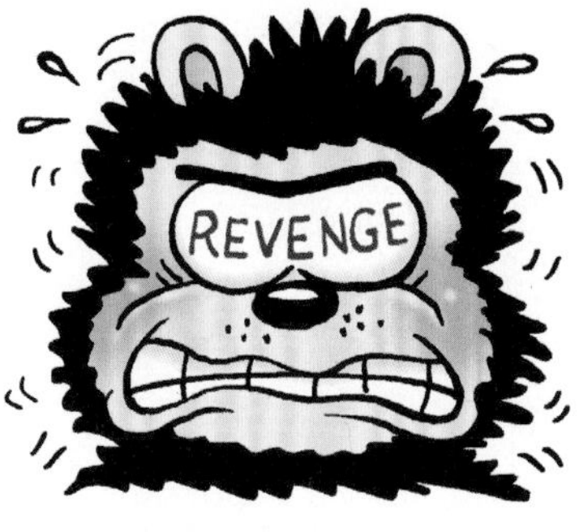
REVENGE

order to Dennis.

"GNETCH GNEEGNAW GNOW!"

Dennis understood perfectly and soon dragged his little sister, Bea's small see-saw over to where Gnasher stood.

Carefully positioning himself on the "down" side of the see-saw, Gnasher waited for Dennis to bring a large, stone, garden gnome from beside Dad's ornamental pond.

"Ready, Gnasher?" asked Dennis, lifting the unsuspecting gnome high in the air before dropping him — WHUMP! — on the "up" end of the see-saw.

With a loud "GNASH!" and the glint of flashing fangs, the toothy terror sped through the night sky before dropping neatly through Walter's bedroom window.

By this time, Walter was in his new beddy-byes, dreaming of Sugar Plum Fairies. It was just as well, as, in the next room a scene of devastation was taking place.

Unnerved by dozens of staring, beady eyes, Gnasher went into a gnashing frenzy. He looked over Walter's music-box and as "Old MacDonald Had A Farm" played, Gnasher set to work with a GNASH-GNASH! here and a GNASH-GNASH! there. Here a GNASH! there a GNASH!

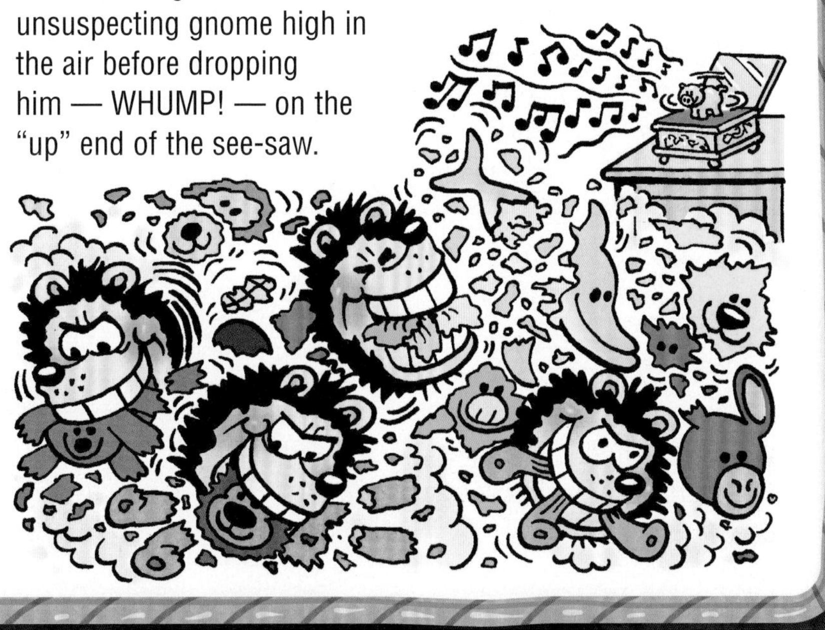

everywhere a GNASH-GNASH! The fluffy creatures didn't stand a chance!

Gripping the four corners of a sheet between his impressive teeth, a satisfied Gnasher leapt from the window and parachuted back to his garden.

Meanwhile, in the next room, Walter was dreaming of taking part in a skipping race — READY, STEADY, GO! Walter woke with a START! (Oh, suit yourself!).

"AACHOO!" he sneezed as some floating fibres tickled his nose. Just a minute — these were no ordinary fibres. They were soft toy innards!

All of a flutter, he entered his bedroom to find a scene of utter horror within — beady eyes rolled on the floor, white stuffing floated around like snowflakes and pieces of coloured fur littered the carpet.

"BOO-HOO-HOO! Even my gold lamé dressing gown has been torn to bits!" wailed the devastated Softy.

Suddenly, a bright light lit up the doorway and a sweet voice trilled.

"There — there, little one! Dry those tears!"

OK — hands up all of you who think it's going to be a Fairy Godmother coming to the rescue? WRONG! That's Cinderella you're thinking

of. Forget the Fairy parts and keep the Mother bit. Yes, it's was Walter's Mummy holding a candle in one hand and a large darning needle and thread in the other.

"C-Can y-you MAKE m-my f-furry ch-chums b-better again?" stuttered Walter.

"Hmm! Even I can't manage that, Waltey-Poo. But I'll do what I can," said Mummy sending her little one out of the room.

It was a long and delicate operation worthy of Casualty or Holby City but

eventually Mumsy emerged from the scene of destruction to be met by her trembling son.

"I've got one piece of bad news and two pieces of good news," announced Mum.

"Bad news first, please," quaked Walter.

"I'm afraid I wasn't able to save any of your toys — their injuries were just too serious."

"Can there be good news after that?" wailed the Softy.

"Yes! I've managed to make one extra-special Supersoft Patchwork Toy!" she announced producing a

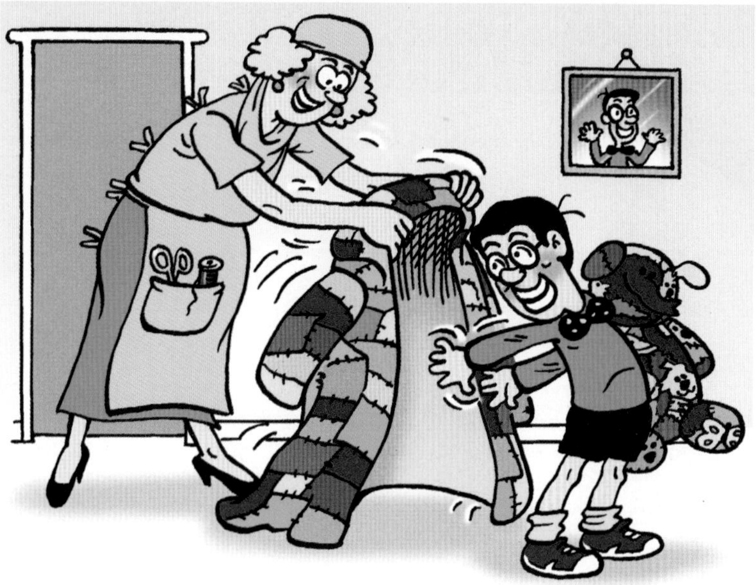

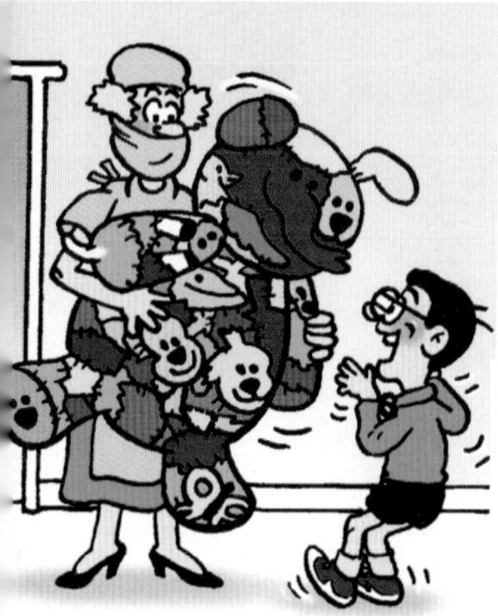

weird but charming creature made from the remains of Walter's army of soft toys.

"WOW! It's wonderful!" said Walter, hugging and kissing the huge soft toy.

"Now tell me the other piece of good news!" he begged.

"Look what else I've made from the wreckage, my little angel!" said Mummy, producing something from behind her back.

"WAHOO! AN AMAZING TECHNICOLOUR HOUSECOAT!" gasped Walter. "How fab!"

. . . And so, Walter lived happily ever after . . . but what of naughty Gnasher?

Well, he certainly wasn't happy. He eventually had to shove two rubber bones in his ears to drown out the sound of Walter as he trilled "Any Dream Will Do" to his new soft chum for the 393rd time that day.

I wore my coat (I wore my coat) with golden lining,
Bright colours shining,
wonderful and new . . .

How much punishment can one dog take?

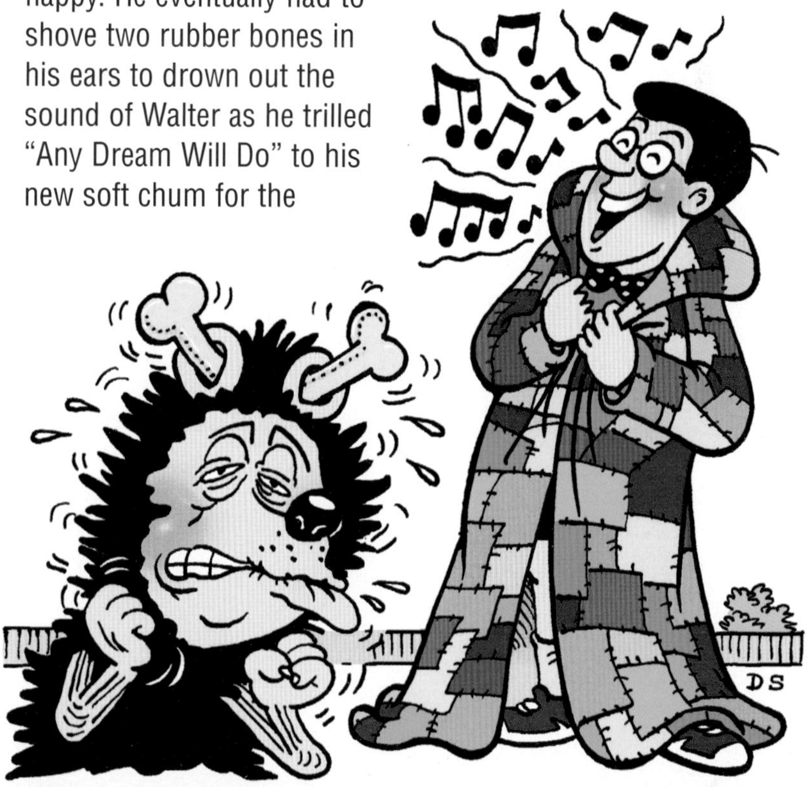
DS

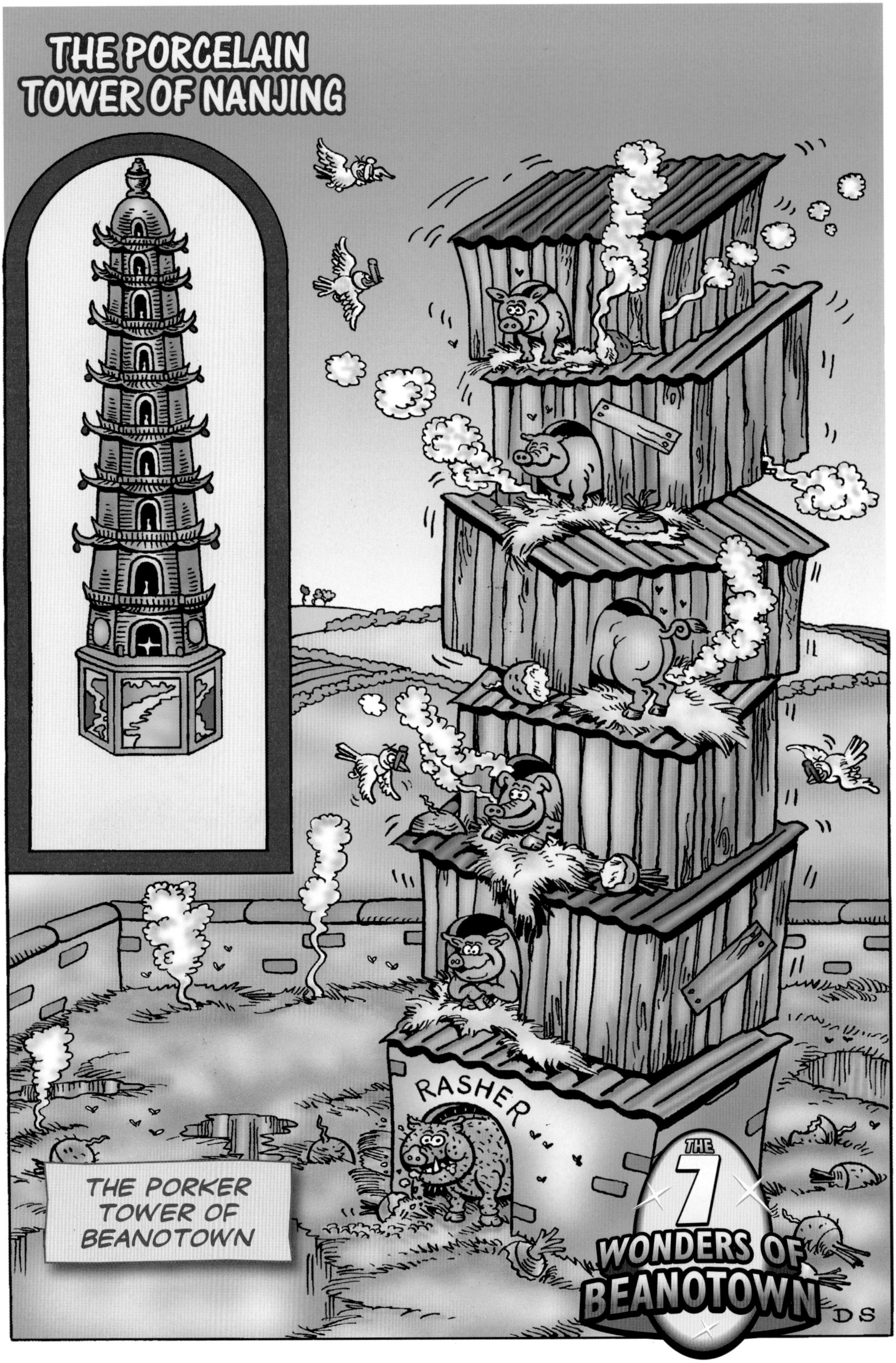
THE PORCELAIN TOWER OF NANJING
RASHER
THE PORKER TOWER OF BEANOTOWN
THE 7 WONDERS OF BEANOTOWN
DS

DENNIS the MENACE and GNASHER

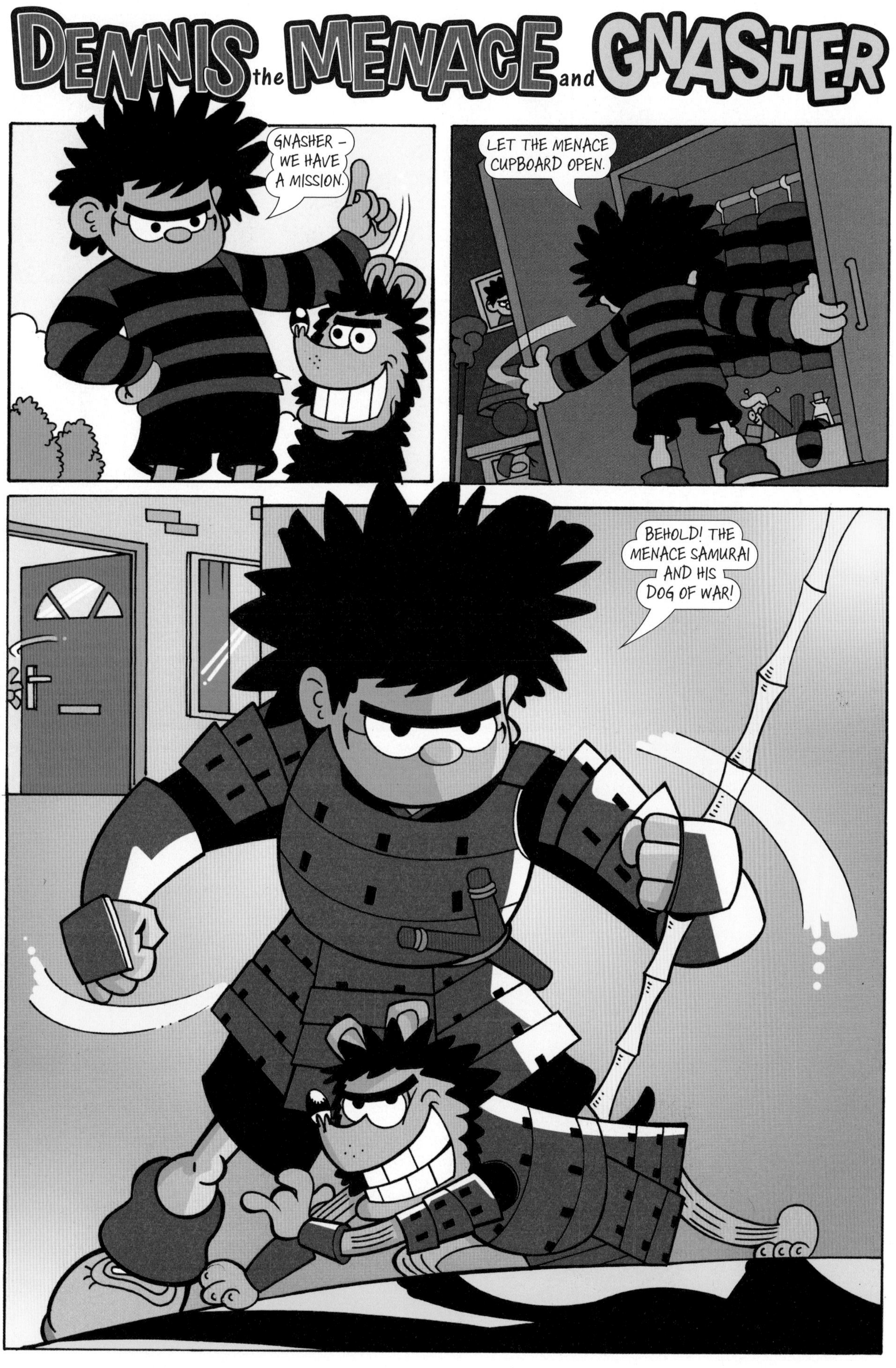
GNASHER – WE HAVE A MISSION.
LET THE MENACE CUPBOARD OPEN.
BEHOLD! THE MENACE SAMURAI AND HIS DOG OF WAR!

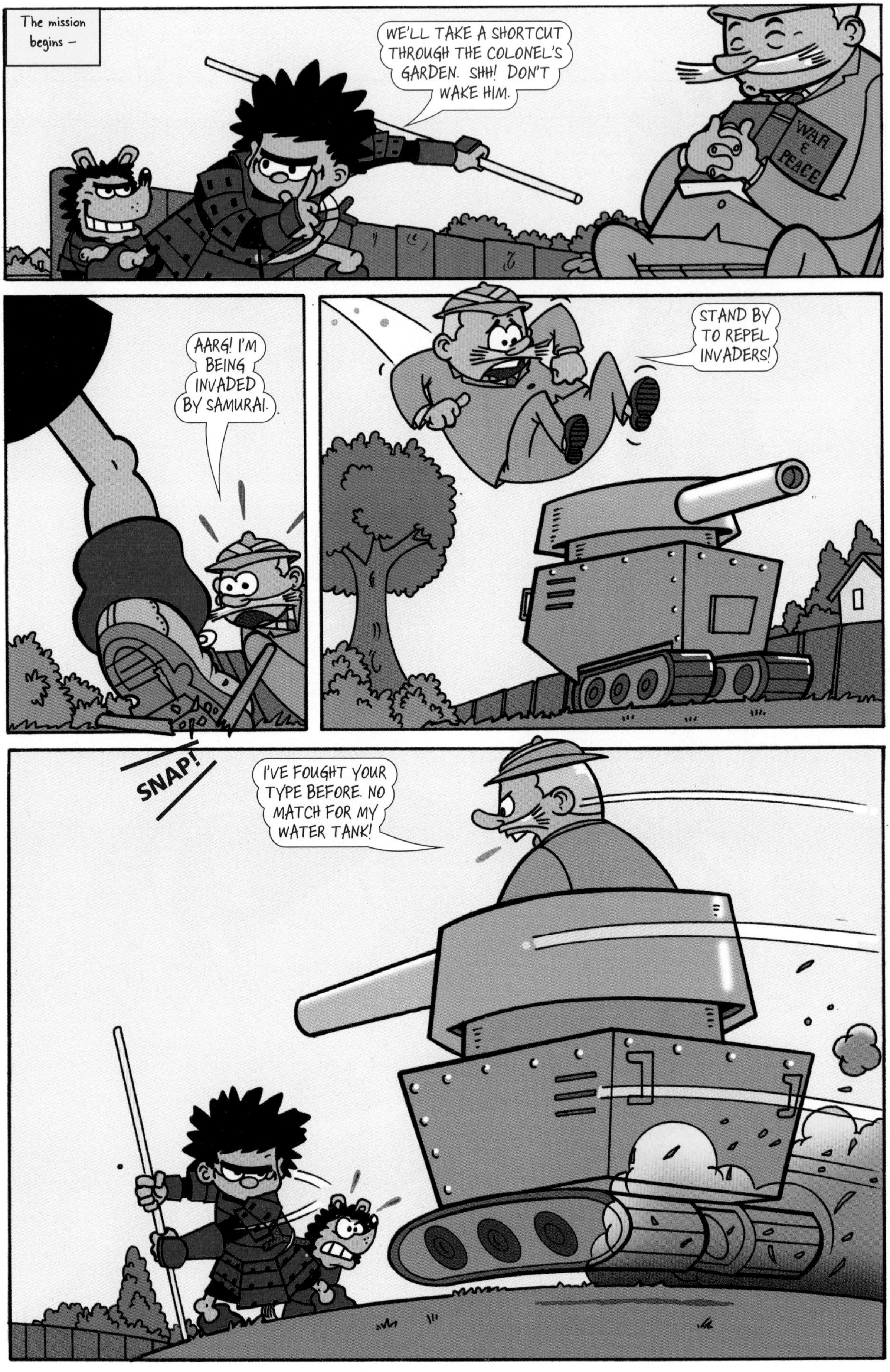
The mission begins –
WE'LL TAKE A SHORTCUT THROUGH THE COLONEL'S GARDEN. SHH! DON'T WAKE HIM.
WAR & PEACE
AARG! I'M BEING INVADED BY SAMURAI.
STAND BY TO REPEL INVADERS!
SNAP!
I'VE FOUGHT YOUR TYPE BEFORE. NO MATCH FOR MY WATER TANK!

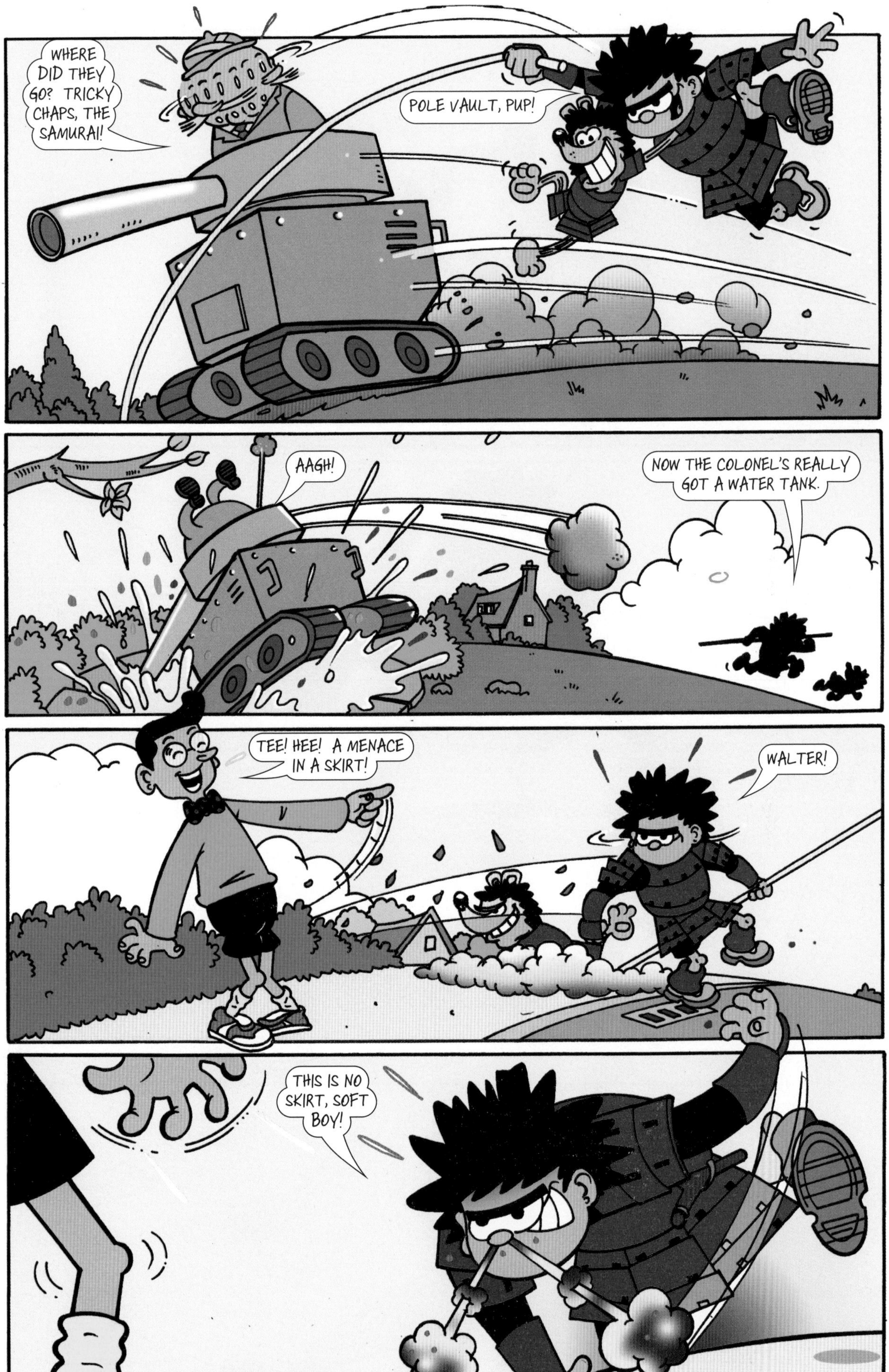
WHERE DID THEY GO? TRICKY CHAPS, THE SAMURAI!
POLE VAULT, PUP!
AAGH!
NOW THE COLONEL'S REALLY GOT A WATER TANK.
TEE! HEE! A MENACE IN A SKIRT!
WALTER!
THIS IS NO SKIRT, SOFT BOY!

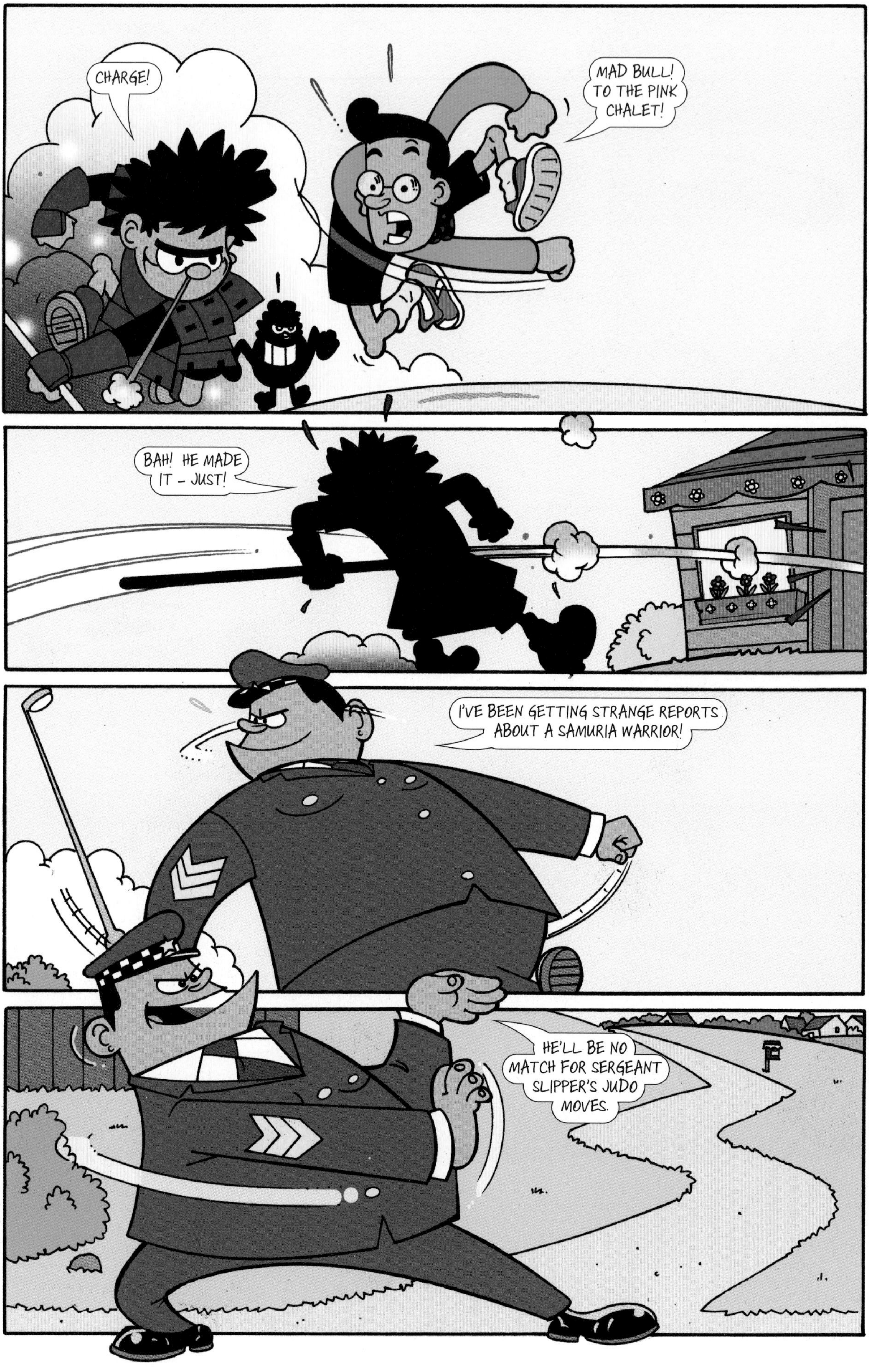
CHARGE!
MAD BULL! TO THE PINK CHALET!
BAH! HE MADE IT – JUST!
I'VE BEEN GETTING STRANGE REPORTS ABOUT A SAMURIA WARRIOR!
HE'LL BE NO MATCH FOR SERGEANT SLIPPER'S JUDO MOVES.

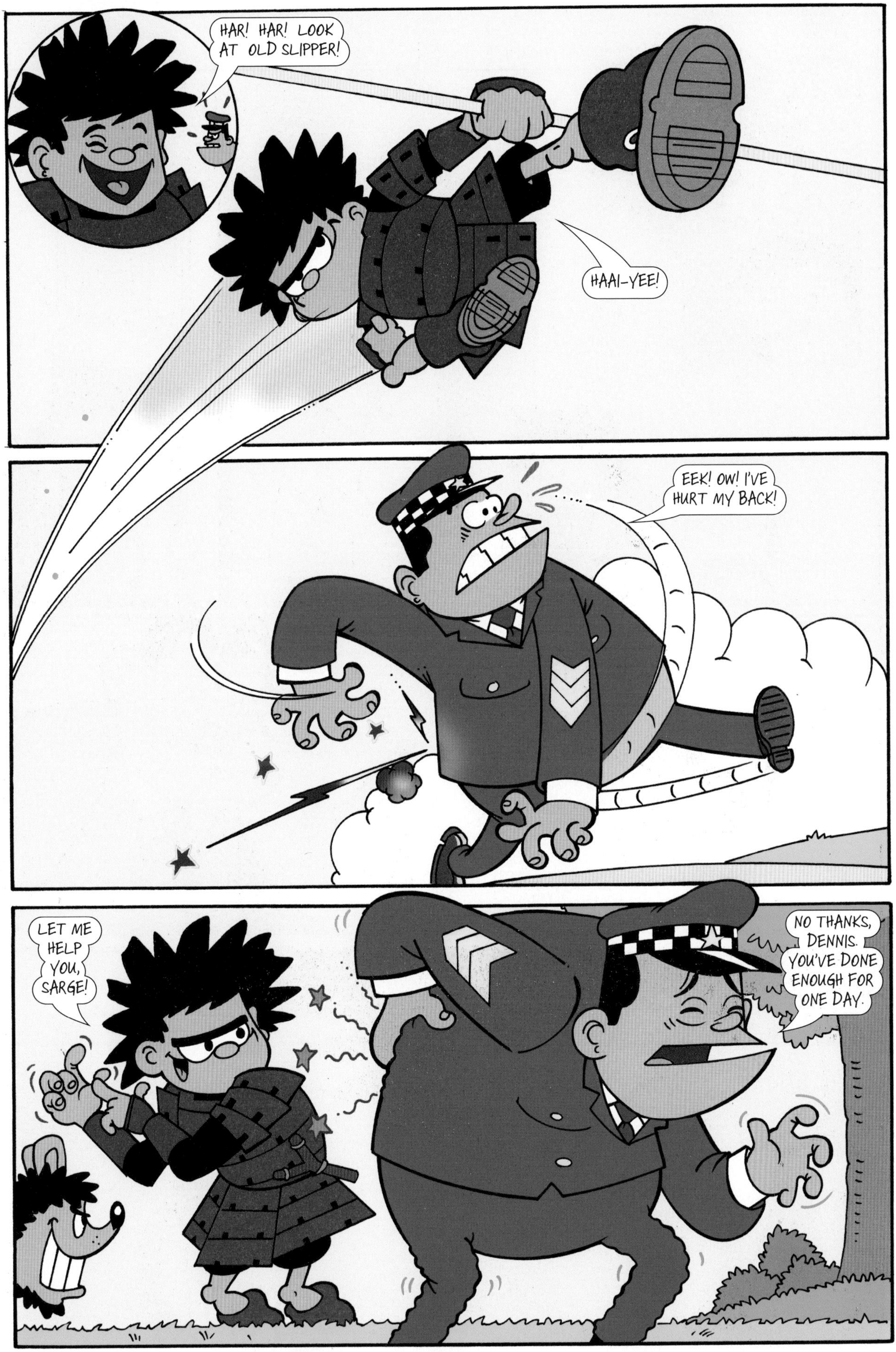
HAR! HAR! LOOK AT OLD SLIPPER!
HAAI-YEE!
EEK! OW! I'VE HURT MY BACK!
LET ME HELP YOU, SARGE!
NO THANKS, DENNIS. YOU'VE DONE ENOUGH FOR ONE DAY.

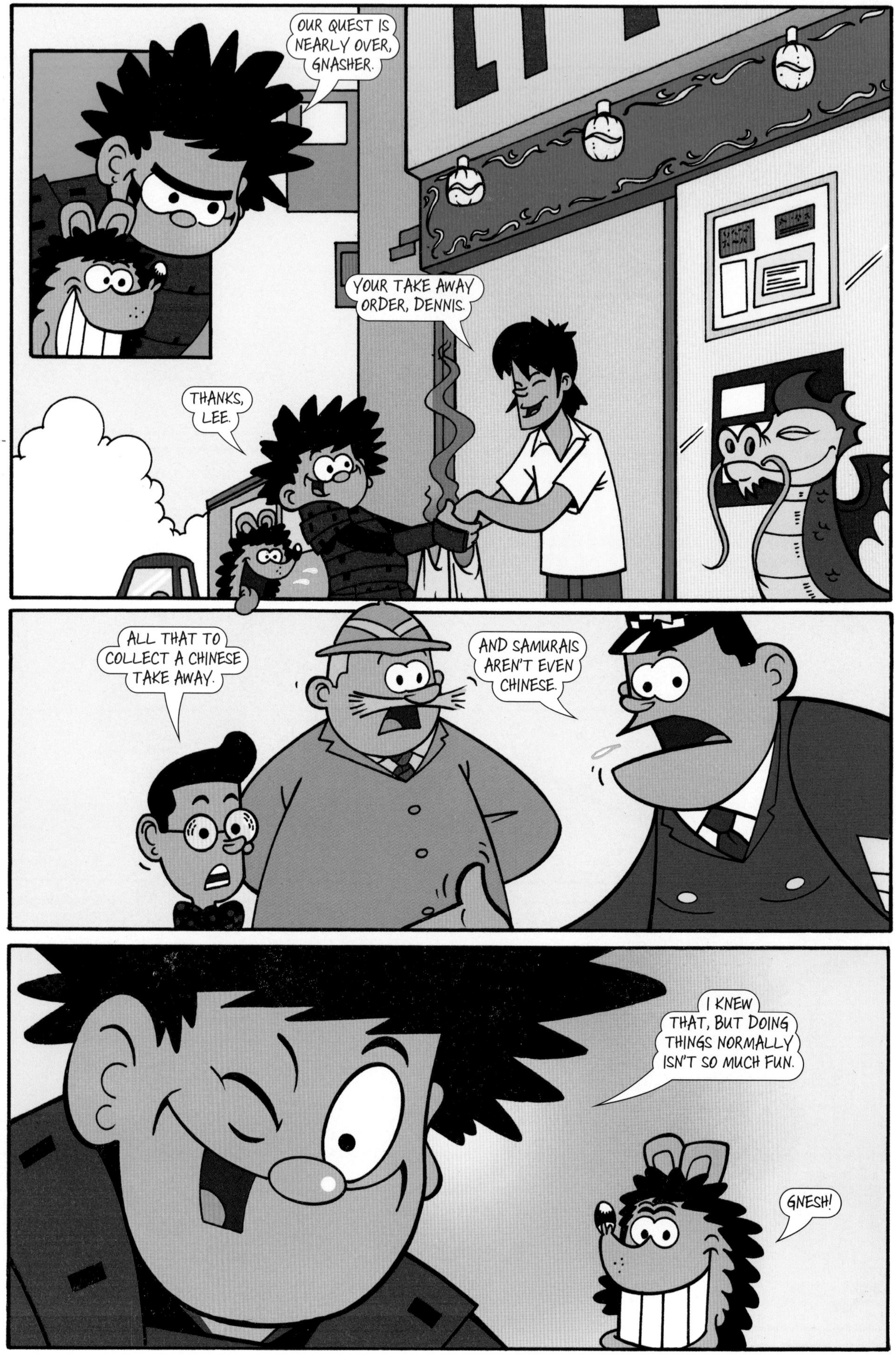
OUR QUEST IS NEARLY OVER, GNASHER.
YOUR TAKE AWAY ORDER, DENNIS.
THANKS, LEE.
ALL THAT TO COLLECT A CHINESE TAKE AWAY.
AND SAMURAIS AREN'T EVEN CHINESE.
I KNEW THAT, BUT DOING THINGS NORMALLY ISN'T SO MUCH FUN.
GNESH!

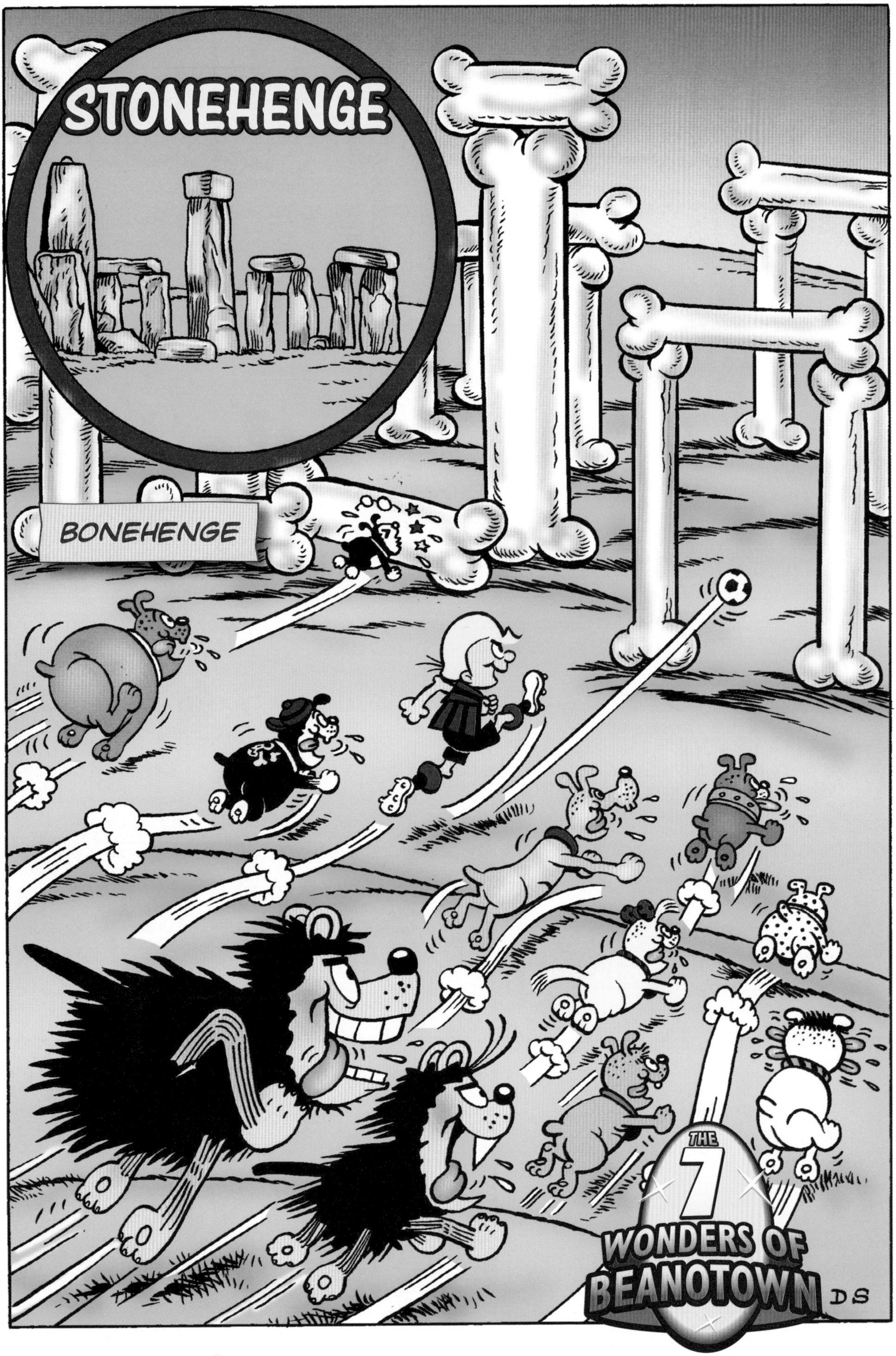
STONEHENGE
BONEHENGE
THE 7 WONDERS OF BEANOTOWN
DS

LITTLE PLUM

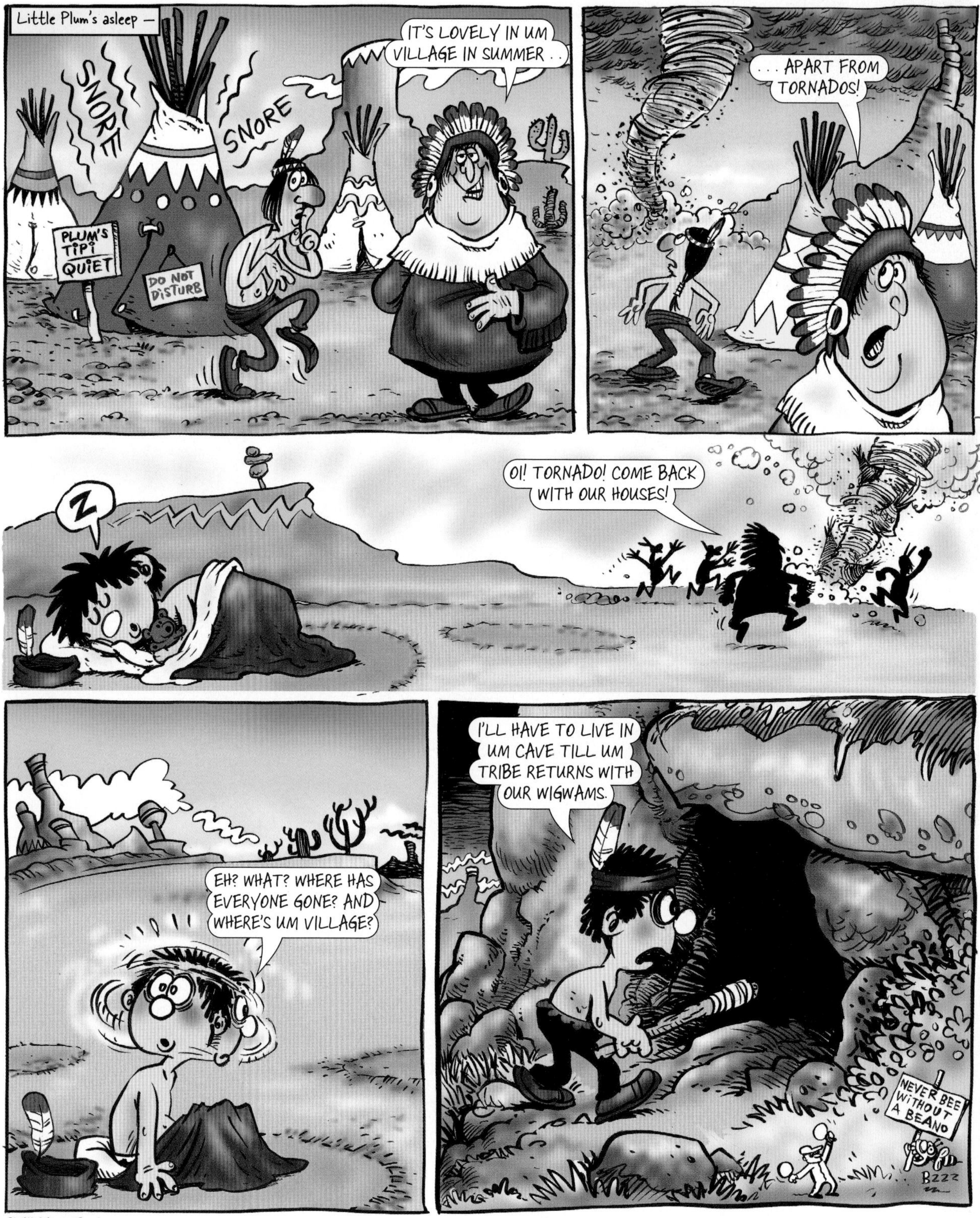

Little Plum's asleep —
SNORE
SNORE
PLUM'S TIPI QUIET
DO NOT DISTURB
IT'S LOVELY IN UM VILLAGE IN SUMMER . .
. . . APART FROM TORNADOS!
Z
OI! TORNADO! COME BACK WITH OUR HOUSES!
EH? WHAT? WHERE HAS EVERYONE GONE? AND WHERE'S UM VILLAGE?
I'LL HAVE TO LIVE IN UM CAVE TILL UM TRIBE RETURNS WITH OUR WIGWAMS.
NEVER BEE WITHOUT A BEANO
Bzzz

PLUM MAX 002-A

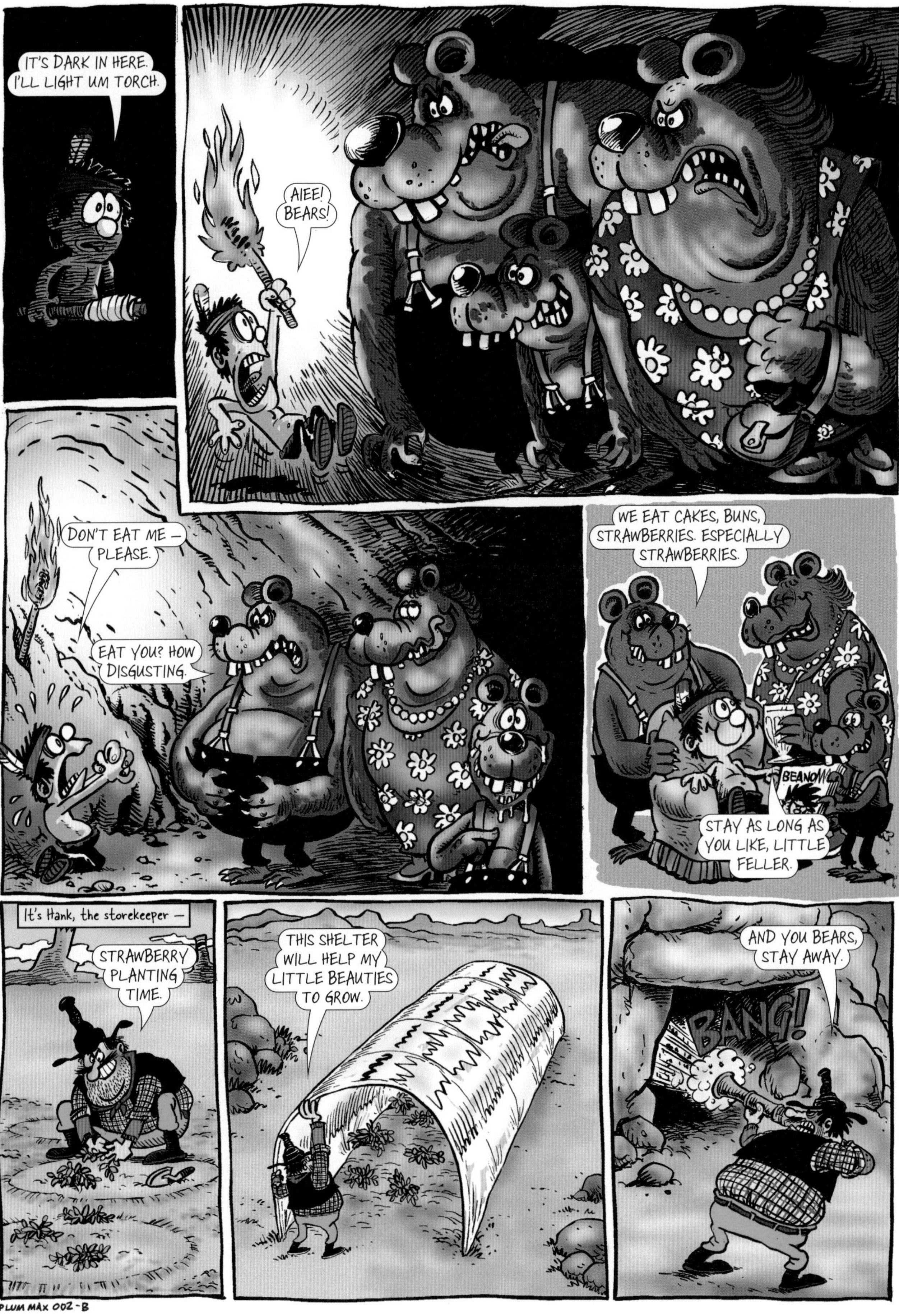
IT'S DARK IN HERE. I'LL LIGHT UM TORCH.
AIEE! BEARS!
DON'T EAT ME — PLEASE.
EAT YOU? HOW DISGUSTING.
WE EAT CAKES, BUNS, STRAWBERRIES. ESPECIALLY STRAWBERRIES.
BEANO
STAY AS LONG AS YOU LIKE, LITTLE FELLER.
It's Hank, the storekeeper —
STRAWBERRY PLANTING TIME.
THIS SHELTER WILL HELP MY LITTLE BEAUTIES TO GROW.
AND YOU BEARS, STAY AWAY.
BANG!

PLUM MAX 002-B

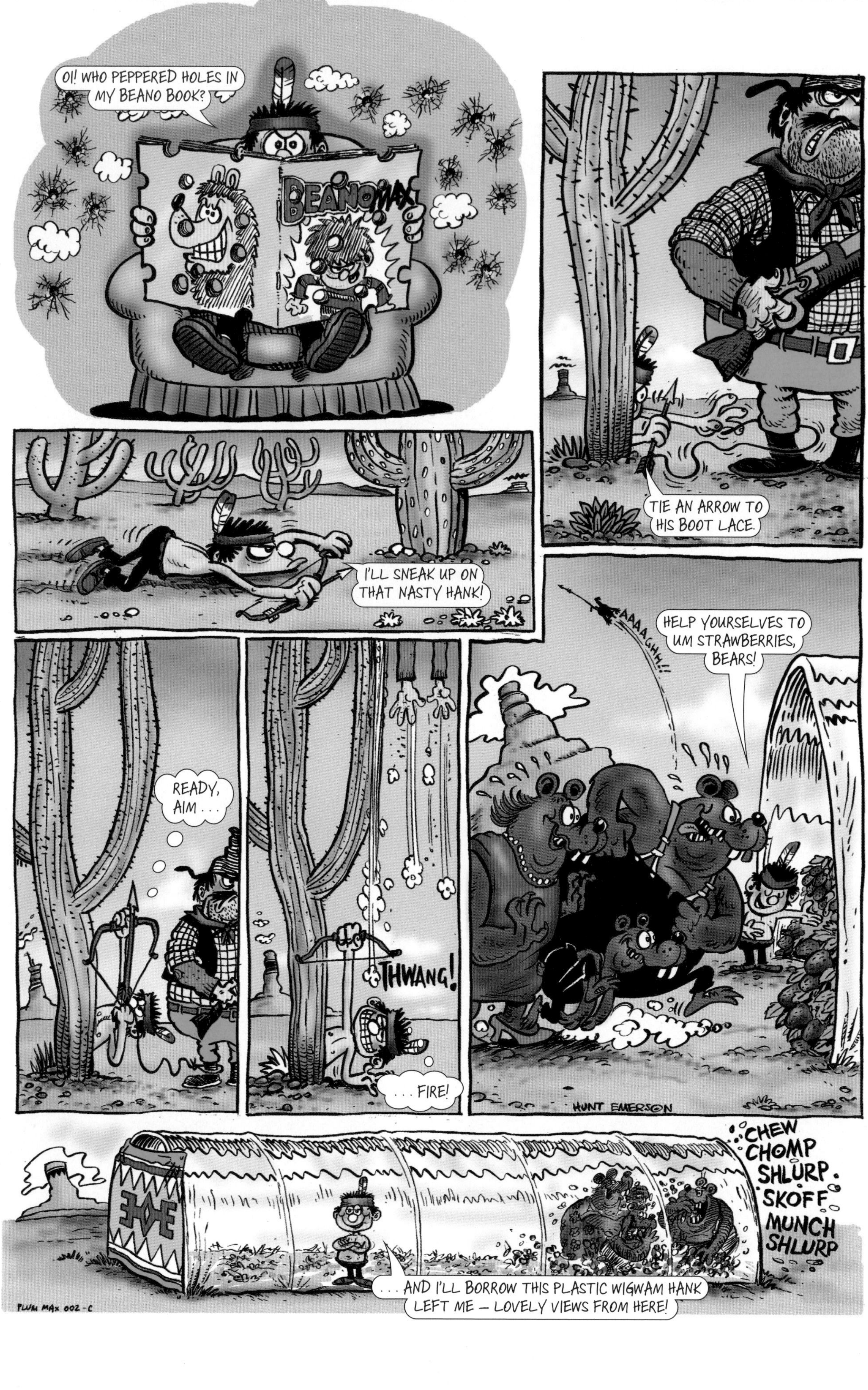
OI! WHO PEPPERED HOLES IN MY BEANO BOOK?
BEANOMAX
I'LL SNEAK UP ON THAT NASTY HANK!
TIE AN ARROW TO HIS BOOT LACE.
READY, AIM . . .
THWANG!
. . . FIRE!
AAAAGHH!!
HELP YOURSELVES TO UM STRAWBERRIES, BEARS!
HUNT EMERSON
CHEW
CHOMP
SHLURP
SKOFF
MUNCH
SHLURP
. . . AND I'LL BORROW THIS PLASTIC WIGWAM HANK LEFT ME – LOVELY VIEWS FROM HERE!
PLUM MAX 002-C

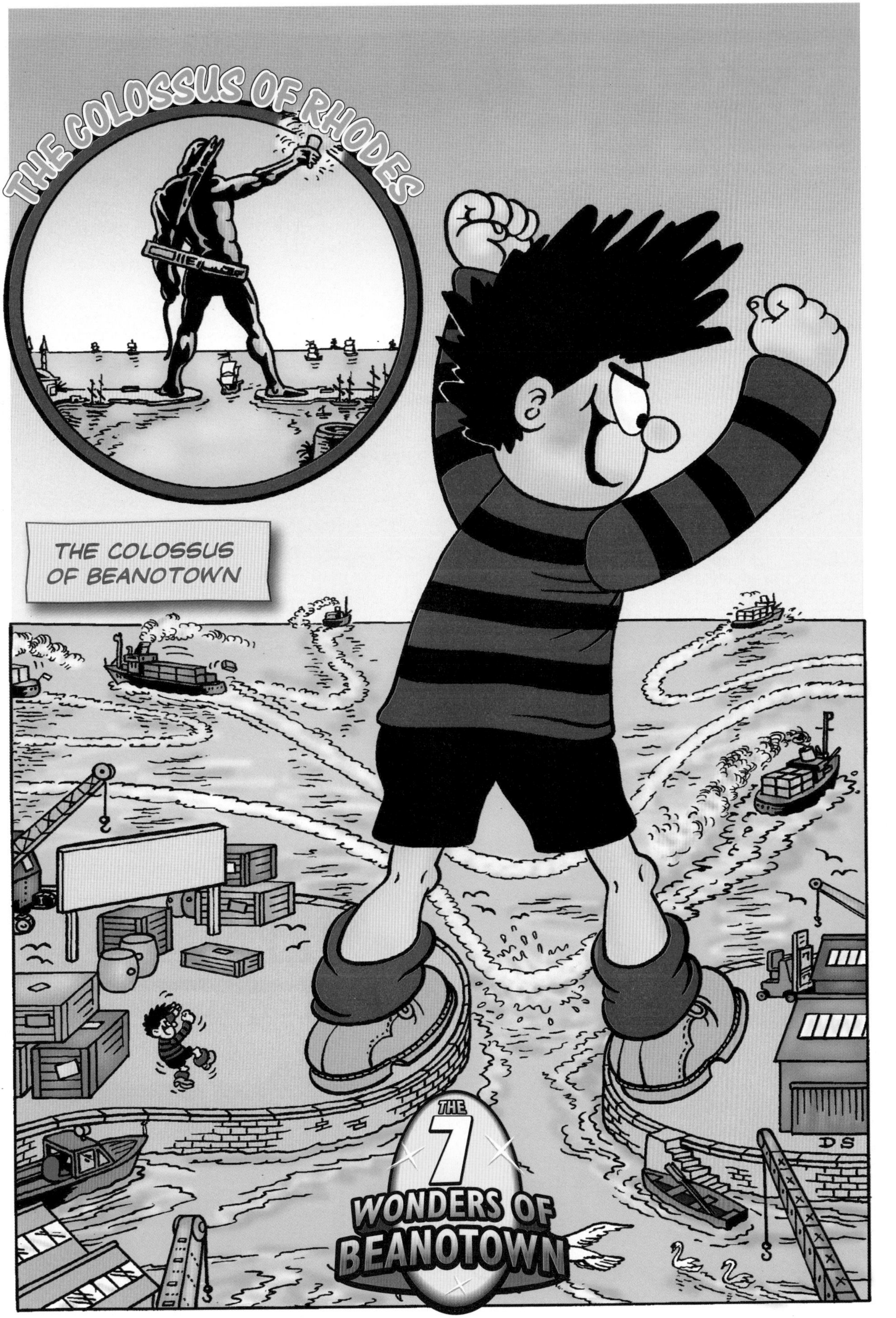
THE COLOSSUS OF RHODES
THE COLOSSUS
OF BEANOTOWN
DS
THE
7
WONDERS OF
BEANOTOWN

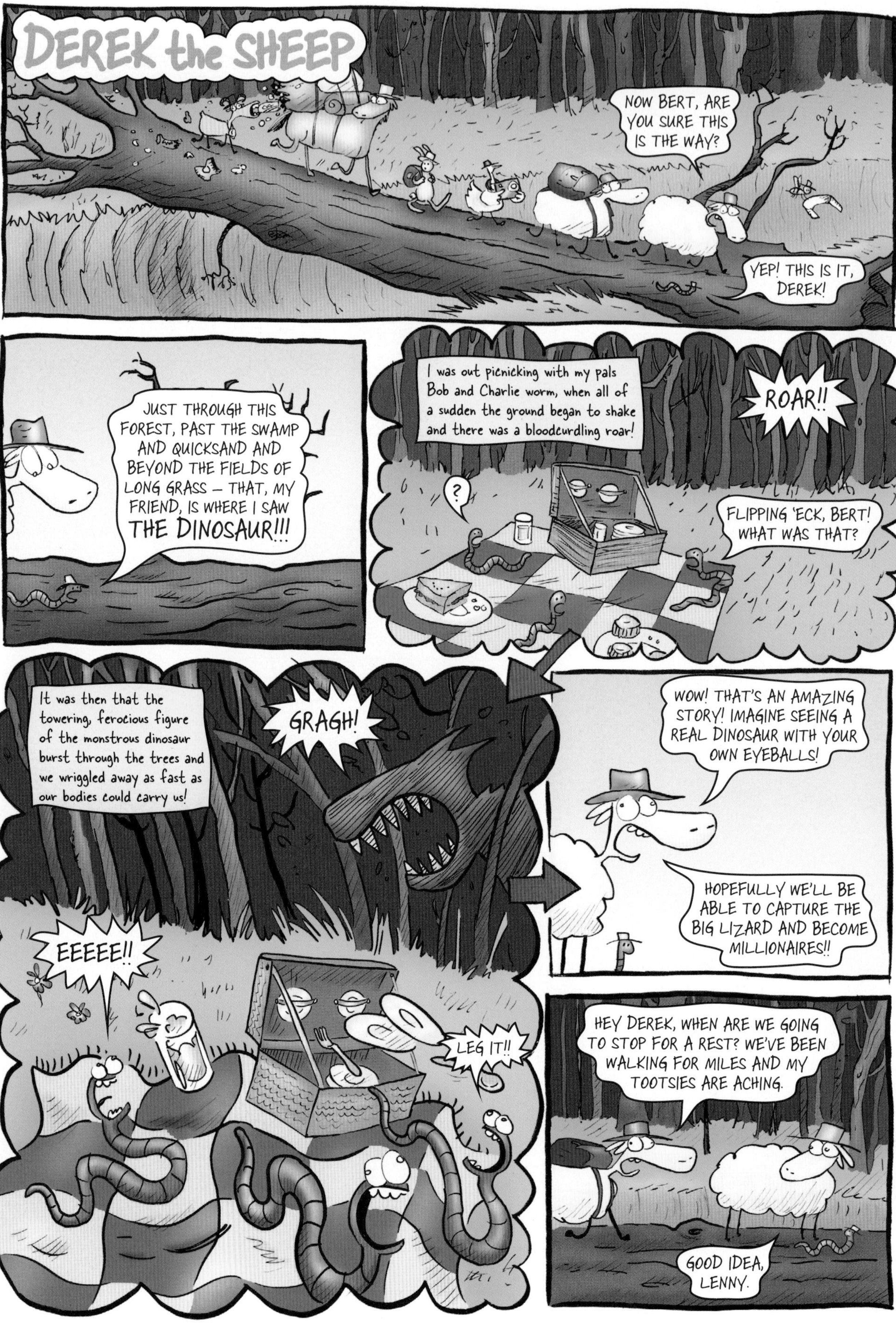

DEREK the SHEEP
NOW BERT, ARE YOU SURE THIS IS THE WAY?
YEP! THIS IS IT, DEREK!
JUST THROUGH THIS FOREST, PAST THE SWAMP AND QUICKSAND AND BEYOND THE FIELDS OF LONG GRASS – THAT, MY FRIEND, IS WHERE I SAW THE DINOSAUR!!!
I was out picnicking with my pals Bob and Charlie worm, when all of a sudden the ground began to shake and there was a bloodcurdling roar!
ROAR!!
?
FLIPPING 'ECK, BERT! WHAT WAS THAT?
It was then that the towering, ferocious figure of the monstrous dinosaur burst through the trees and we wriggled away as fast as our bodies could carry us!
GRAGH!
EEEEE!!
LEG IT!!
WOW! THAT'S AN AMAZING STORY! IMAGINE SEEING A REAL DINOSAUR WITH YOUR OWN EYEBALLS!
HOPEFULLY WE'LL BE ABLE TO CAPTURE THE BIG LIZARD AND BECOME MILLIONAIRES!!
HEY DEREK, WHEN ARE WE GOING TO STOP FOR A REST? WE'VE BEEN WALKING FOR MILES AND MY TOOTSIES ARE ACHING.
GOOD IDEA, LENNY.

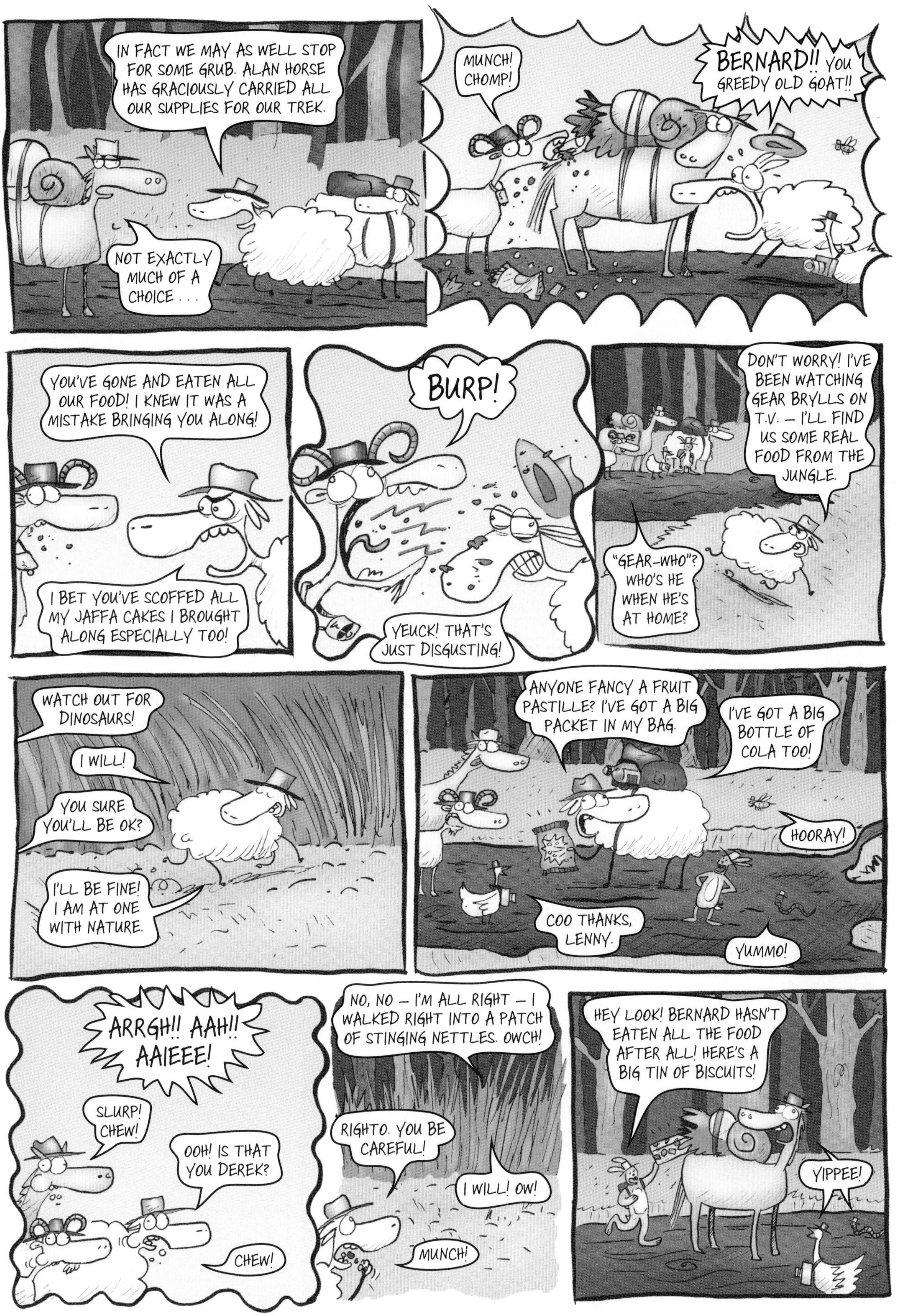
IN FACT WE MAY AS WELL STOP FOR SOME GRUB. ALAN HORSE HAS GRACIOUSLY CARRIED ALL OUR SUPPLIES FOR OUR TREK.
NOT EXACTLY MUCH OF A CHOICE . . .
MUNCH! CHOMP!
BERNARD!! YOU GREEDY OLD GOAT!!
YOU'VE GONE AND EATEN ALL OUR FOOD! I KNEW IT WAS A MISTAKE BRINGING YOU ALONG!
I BET YOU'VE SCOFFED ALL MY JAFFA CAKES I BROUGHT ALONG ESPECIALLY TOO!
BURP!
YEUCK! THAT'S JUST DISGUSTING!
DON'T WORRY! I'VE BEEN WATCHING GEAR BRYLLS ON T.V. – I'LL FIND US SOME REAL FOOD FROM THE JUNGLE.
"GEAR–WHO"? WHO'S HE WHEN HE'S AT HOME?
WATCH OUT FOR DINOSAURS!
I WILL!
YOU SURE YOU'LL BE OK?
I'LL BE FINE! I AM AT ONE WITH NATURE.
ANYONE FANCY A FRUIT PASTILLE? I'VE GOT A BIG PACKET IN MY BAG.
I'VE GOT A BIG BOTTLE OF COLA TOO!
HOORAY!
COO THANKS, LENNY.
YUMMO!
ARRGH!! AAH!! AAIEEE!
SLURP! CHEW!
OOH! IS THAT YOU DEREK?
CHEW!
NO, NO – I'M ALL RIGHT – I WALKED RIGHT INTO A PATCH OF STINGING NETTLES. OWCH!
RIGHTO. YOU BE CAREFUL!
I WILL! OW!
MUNCH!
HEY LOOK! BERNARD HASN'T EATEN ALL THE FOOD AFTER ALL! HERE'S A BIG TIN OF BISCUITS!
YIPPEE!

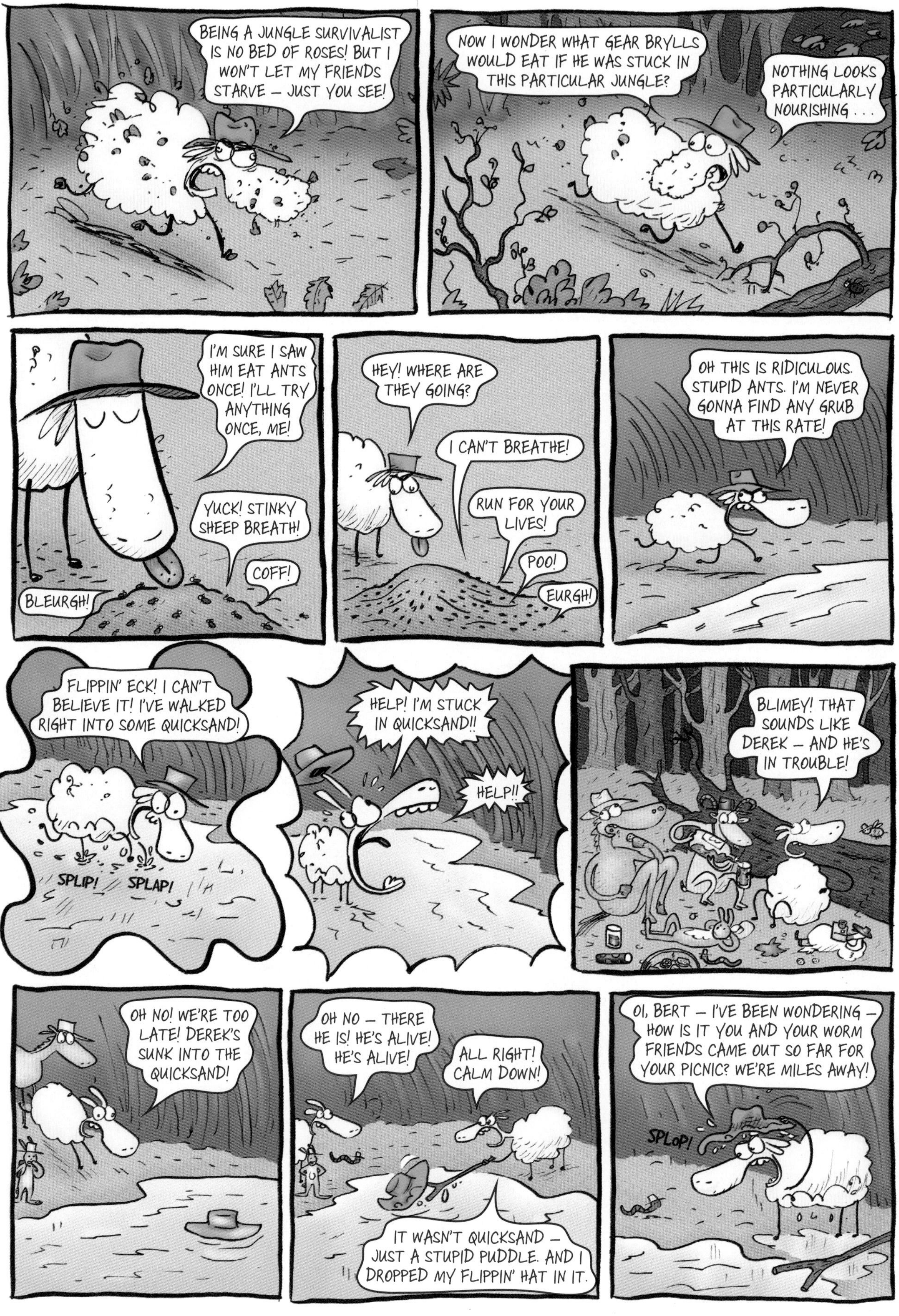
BEING A JUNGLE SURVIVALIST IS NO BED OF ROSES! BUT I WON'T LET MY FRIENDS STARVE – JUST YOU SEE!
NOW I WONDER WHAT GEAR BRYLLS WOULD EAT IF HE WAS STUCK IN THIS PARTICULAR JUNGLE?
NOTHING LOOKS PARTICULARLY NOURISHING . . .
I'M SURE I SAW HIM EAT ANTS ONCE! I'LL TRY ANYTHING ONCE, ME!
YUCK! STINKY SHEEP BREATH!
COFF!
BLEURGH!
HEY! WHERE ARE THEY GOING?
I CAN'T BREATHE!
RUN FOR YOUR LIVES!
POO!
EURGH!
OH THIS IS RIDICULOUS. STUPID ANTS. I'M NEVER GONNA FIND ANY GRUB AT THIS RATE!
FLIPPIN' ECK! I CAN'T BELIEVE IT! I'VE WALKED RIGHT INTO SOME QUICKSAND!
SPLIP!
SPLAP!
HELP! I'M STUCK IN QUICKSAND!!
HELP!!
BLIMEY! THAT SOUNDS LIKE DEREK – AND HE'S IN TROUBLE!
OH NO! WE'RE TOO LATE! DEREK'S SUNK INTO THE QUICKSAND!
OH NO – THERE HE IS! HE'S ALIVE! HE'S ALIVE!
ALL RIGHT! CALM DOWN!
IT WASN'T QUICKSAND – JUST A STUPID PUDDLE. AND I DROPPED MY FLIPPIN' HAT IN IT.
OI, BERT – I'VE BEEN WONDERING – HOW IS IT YOU AND YOUR WORM FRIENDS CAME OUT SO FAR FOR YOUR PICNIC? WE'RE MILES AWAY!
SPLOP!

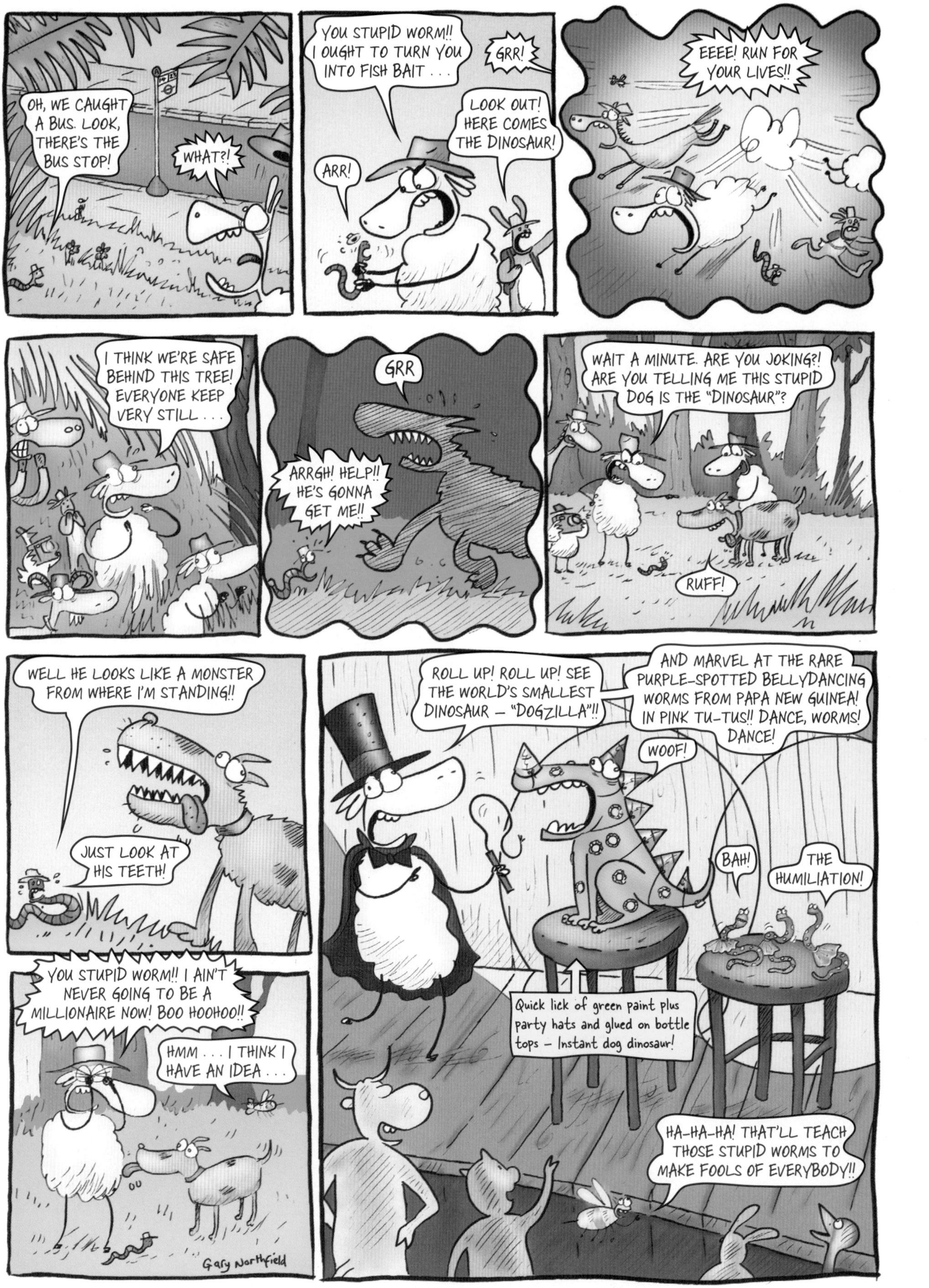

OH, WE CAUGHT A BUS. LOOK, THERE'S THE BUS STOP!
WHAT?!
YOU STUPID WORM!! I OUGHT TO TURN YOU INTO FISH BAIT . . .
GRR!
ARR!
LOOK OUT! HERE COMES THE DINOSAUR!
EEEE! RUN FOR YOUR LIVES!!
I THINK WE'RE SAFE BEHIND THIS TREE! EVERYONE KEEP VERY STILL . . .
GRR
ARRGH! HELP!! HE'S GONNA GET ME!!
WAIT A MINUTE. ARE YOU JOKING?! ARE YOU TELLING ME THIS STUPID DOG IS THE "DINOSAUR"?
RUFF!
WELL HE LOOKS LIKE A MONSTER FROM WHERE I'M STANDING!!
JUST LOOK AT HIS TEETH!
YOU STUPID WORM!! I AIN'T NEVER GOING TO BE A MILLIONAIRE NOW! BOO HOOHOO!!
HMM . . . I THINK I HAVE AN IDEA . . .
Gary Northfield
ROLL UP! ROLL UP! SEE THE WORLD'S SMALLEST DINOSAUR – "DOGZILLA"!!
AND MARVEL AT THE RARE PURPLE-SPOTTED BELLYDANCING WORMS FROM PAPA NEW GUINEA! IN PINK TU-TUS!! DANCE, WORMS! DANCE!
WOOF!
BAH!
THE HUMILIATION!
Quick lick of green paint plus party hats and glued on bottle tops – Instant dog dinosaur!
HA-HA-HA! THAT'LL TEACH THOSE STUPID WORMS TO MAKE FOOLS OF EVERYBODY!!

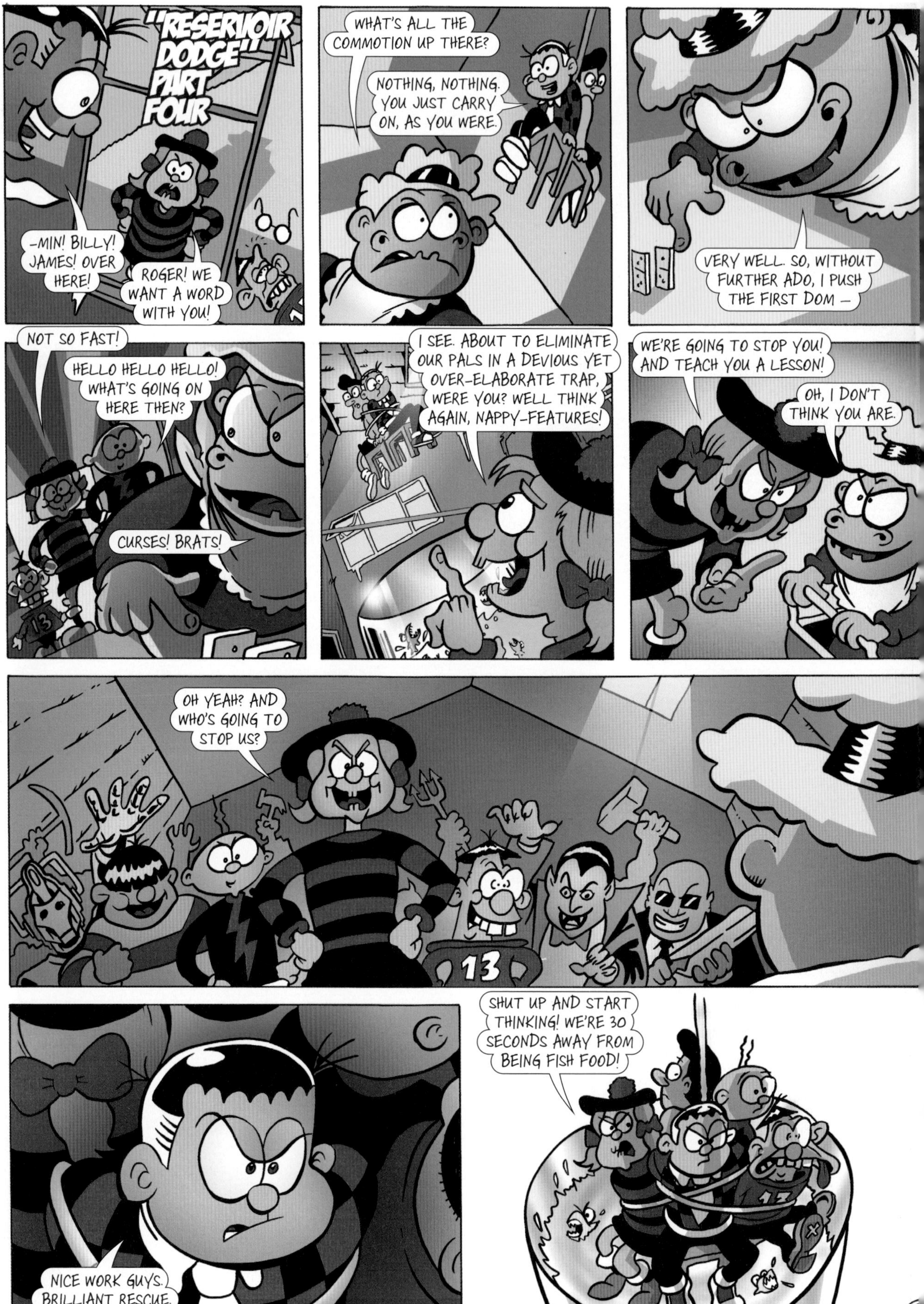
"RESERVOIR DODGE" PART FOUR
-MIN! BILLY! JAMES! OVER HERE!
ROGER! WE WANT A WORD WITH YOU!
WHAT'S ALL THE COMMOTION UP THERE?
NOTHING, NOTHING. YOU JUST CARRY ON, AS YOU WERE.
VERY WELL. SO, WITHOUT FURTHER ADO, I PUSH THE FIRST DOM –
NOT SO FAST!
HELLO HELLO HELLO! WHAT'S GOING ON HERE THEN?
CURSES! BRATS!
I SEE. ABOUT TO ELIMINATE OUR PALS IN A DEVIOUS YET OVER-ELABORATE TRAP, WERE YOU? WELL THINK AGAIN, NAPPY-FEATURES!
WE'RE GOING TO STOP YOU! AND TEACH YOU A LESSON!
OH, I DON'T THINK YOU ARE.
OH YEAH? AND WHO'S GOING TO STOP US?
NICE WORK GUYS. BRILLIANT RESCUE.
SHUT UP AND START THINKING! WE'RE 30 SECONDS AWAY FROM BEING FISH FOOD!

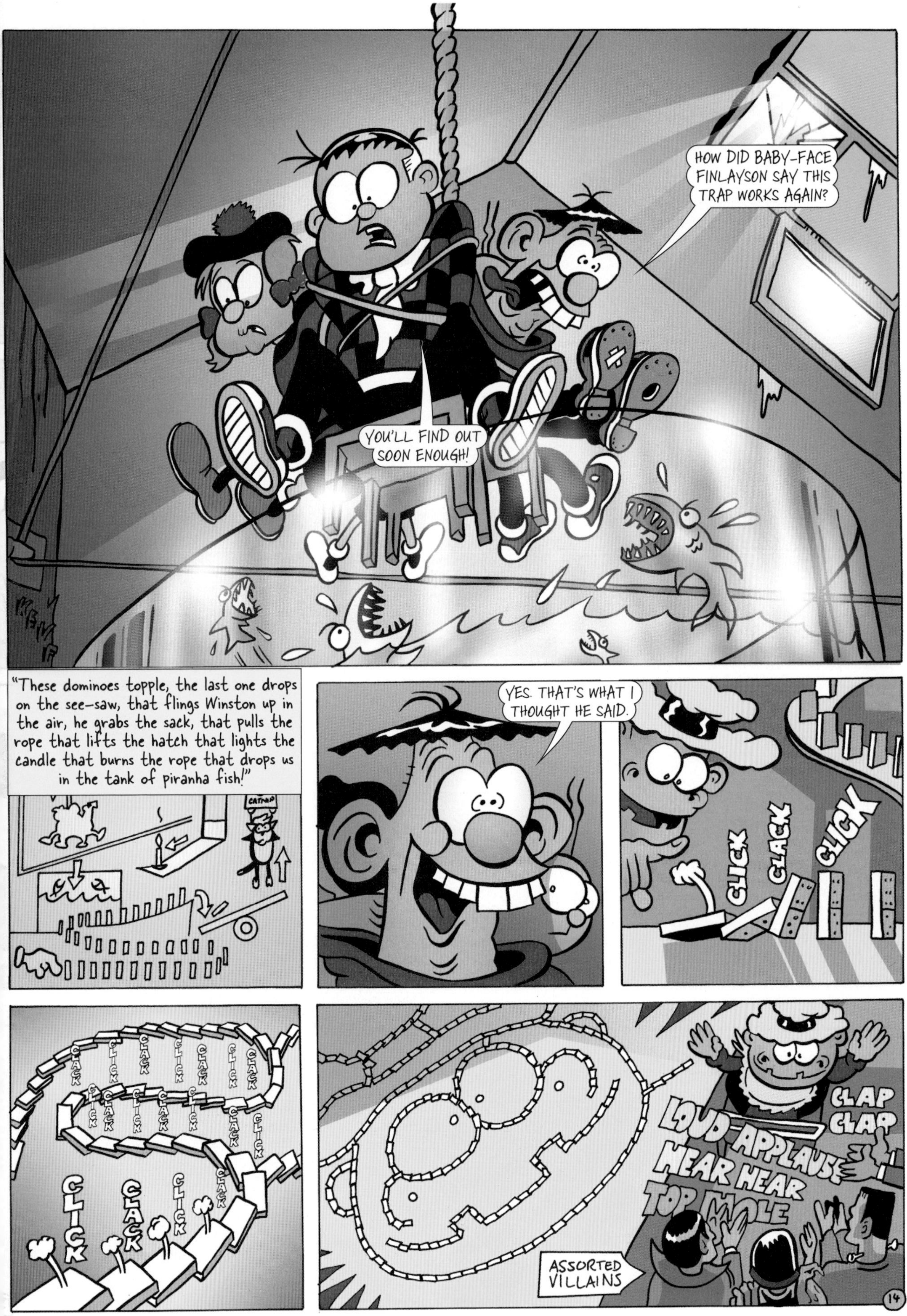

HOW DID BABY-FACE FINLAYSON SAY THIS TRAP WORKS AGAIN?
YOU'LL FIND OUT SOON ENOUGH!
"These dominoes topple, the last one drops on the see-saw, that flings Winston up in the air, he grabs the sack, that pulls the rope that lifts the hatch that lights the candle that burns the rope that drops us in the tank of piranha fish!"
CATNIP
YES. THAT'S WHAT I THOUGHT HE SAID.
CLICK CLACK CLICK
CLICK CLACK CLICK CLACK CLICK CLACK
CLICK CLACK CLICK CLACK CLICK CLACK CLICK
CLICK CLACK CLICK CLACK
CLAP CLAP
LOUD APPLAUSE
HEAR HEAR
TOP HOLE
ASSORTED VILLAINS

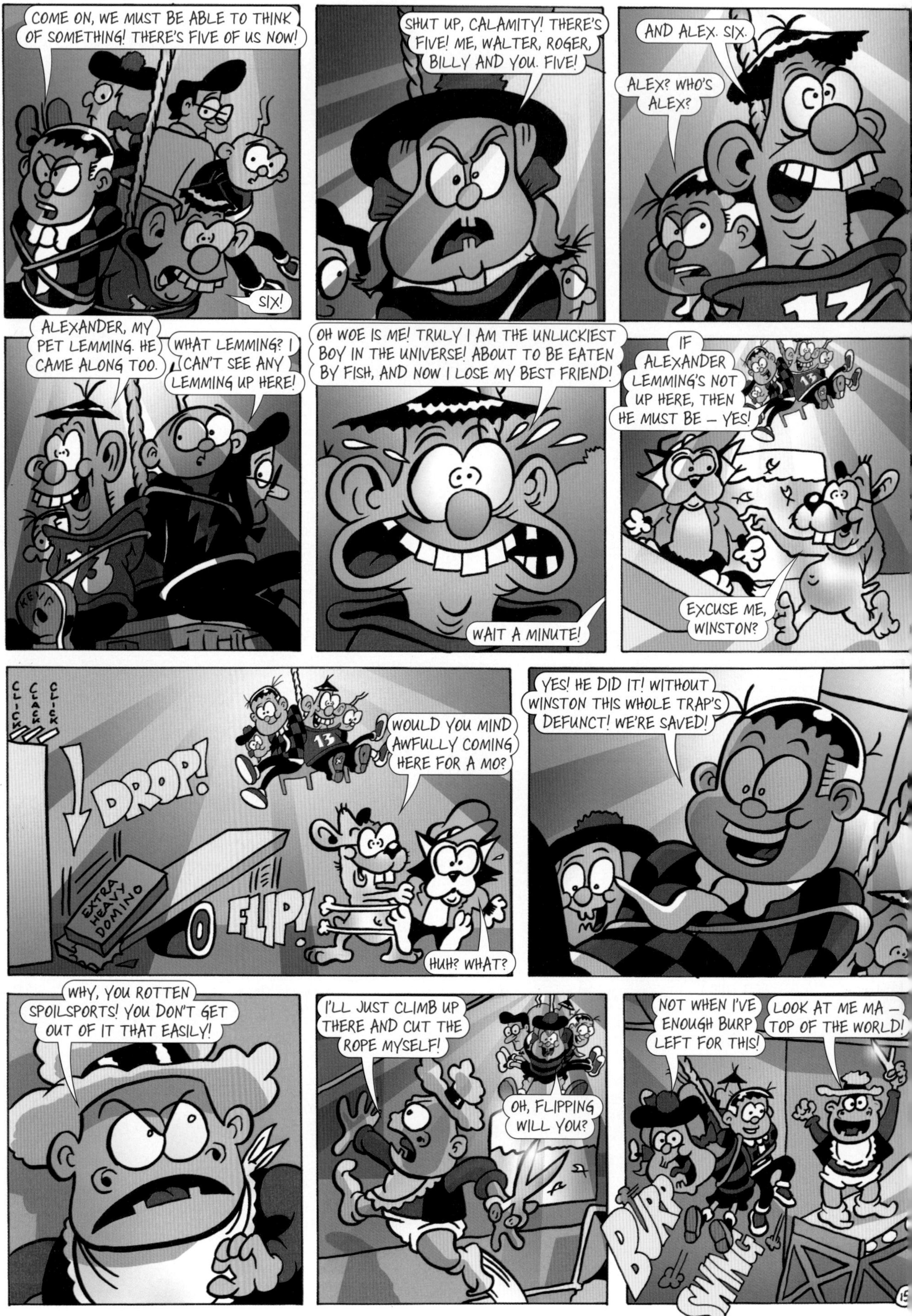
COME ON, WE MUST BE ABLE TO THINK OF SOMETHING! THERE'S FIVE OF US NOW!
SIX!
SHUT UP, CALAMITY! THERE'S FIVE! ME, WALTER, ROGER, BILLY AND YOU. FIVE!
AND ALEX. SIX.
ALEX? WHO'S ALEX?
ALEXANDER, MY PET LEMMING. HE CAME ALONG TOO.
WHAT LEMMING? I CAN'T SEE ANY LEMMING UP HERE!
OH WOE IS ME! TRULY I AM THE UNLUCKIEST BOY IN THE UNIVERSE! ABOUT TO BE EATEN BY FISH, AND NOW I LOSE MY BEST FRIEND!
WAIT A MINUTE!
IF ALEXANDER LEMMING'S NOT UP HERE, THEN HE MUST BE — YES!
EXCUSE ME, WINSTON?
CLICK CLACK CLICK
DROP!
WOULD YOU MIND AWFULLY COMING HERE FOR A MO?
EXTRA HEAVY DOMINO
FLIP!
HUH? WHAT?
YES! HE DID IT! WITHOUT WINSTON THIS WHOLE TRAP'S DEFUNCT! WE'RE SAVED!
WHY, YOU ROTTEN SPOILSPORTS! YOU DON'T GET OUT OF IT THAT EASILY!
I'LL JUST CLIMB UP THERE AND CUT THE ROPE MYSELF!
OH, FLIPPING WILL YOU?
NOT WHEN I'VE ENOUGH BURP LEFT FOR THIS!
LOOK AT ME MA — TOP OF THE WORLD!
BURP
SWING

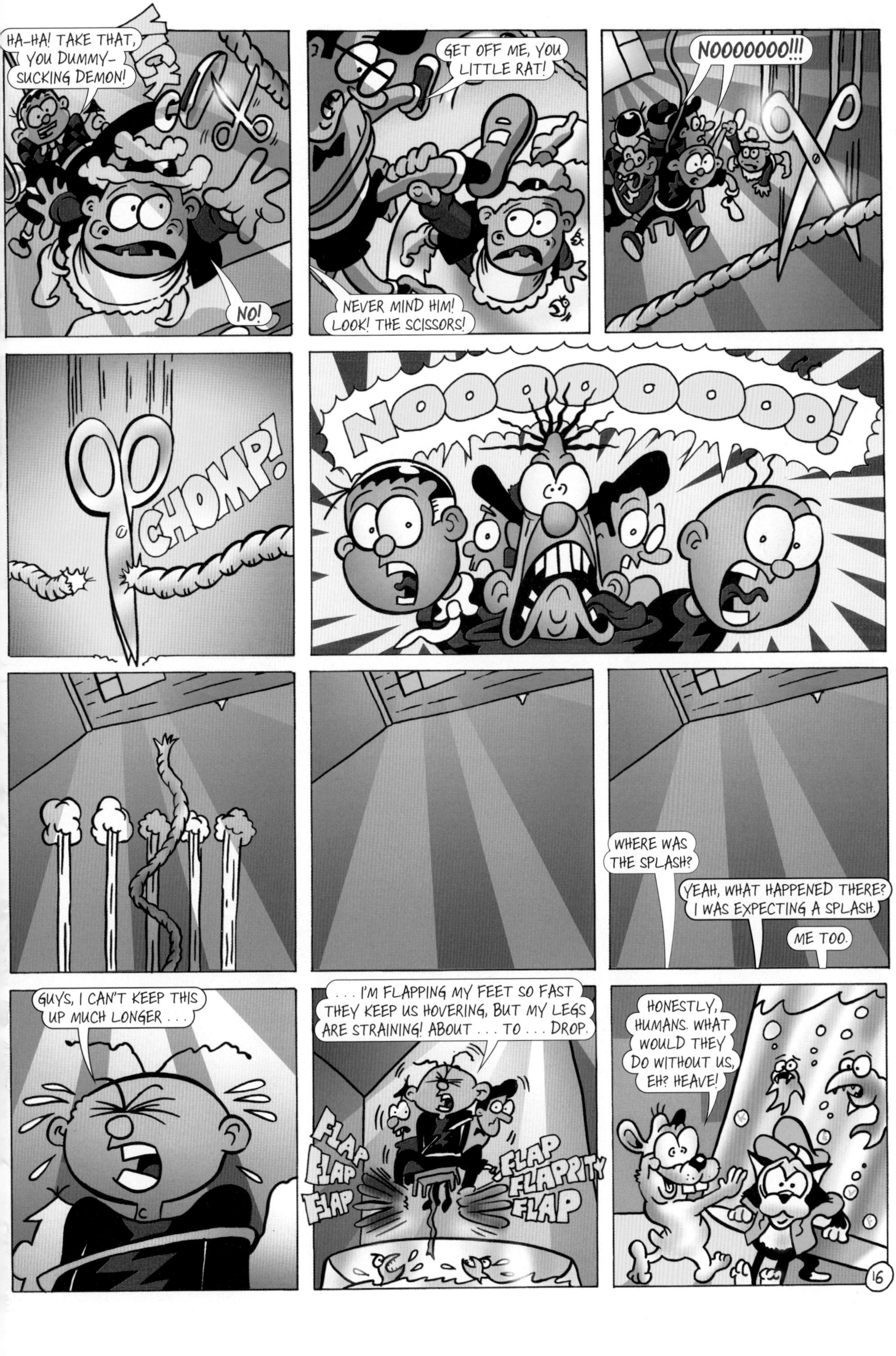
HA-HA! TAKE THAT, YOU DUMMY-SUCKING DEMON!
NO!
GET OFF ME, YOU LITTLE RAT!
NEVER MIND HIM! LOOK! THE SCISSORS!
NOOOOOOO!!!
CHOMP!
NOOOOOOOOO!
WHERE WAS THE SPLASH?
YEAH, WHAT HAPPENED THERE? I WAS EXPECTING A SPLASH.
ME TOO.
GUYS, I CAN'T KEEP THIS UP MUCH LONGER . . .
. . . I'M FLAPPING MY FEET SO FAST THEY KEEP US HOVERING, BUT MY LEGS ARE STRAINING! ABOUT . . . TO . . . DROP.
FLAP FLAP FLAP
FLAP FLAPPITY FLAP
HONESTLY, HUMANS. WHAT WOULD THEY DO WITHOUT US, EH? HEAVE!

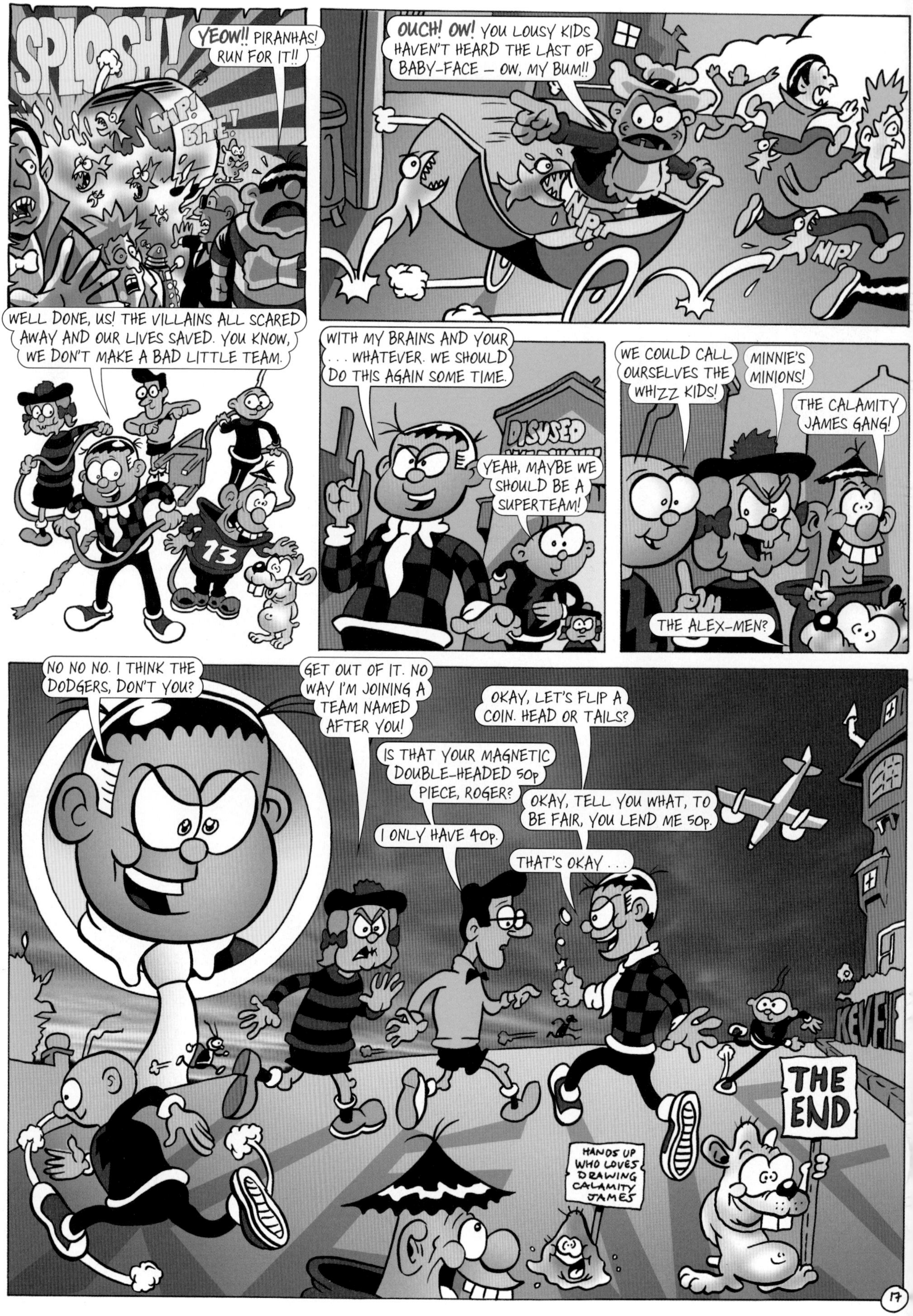
SPLOSH!
YEOW!! PIRANHAS! RUN FOR IT!!
NIP! BITE!
OUCH! OW! YOU LOUSY KIDS HAVEN'T HEARD THE LAST OF BABY-FACE – OW, MY BUM!!
NIP!
NIP!
WELL DONE, US! THE VILLAINS ALL SCARED AWAY AND OUR LIVES SAVED. YOU KNOW, WE DON'T MAKE A BAD LITTLE TEAM.
13
WITH MY BRAINS AND YOUR . . . WHATEVER. WE SHOULD DO THIS AGAIN SOME TIME.
DISUSED
YEAH, MAYBE WE SHOULD BE A SUPERTEAM!
WE COULD CALL OURSELVES THE WHIZZ KIDS!
MINNIE'S MINIONS!
THE CALAMITY JAMES GANG!
THE ALEX-MEN?
NO NO NO. I THINK THE DODGERS, DON'T YOU?
GET OUT OF IT. NO WAY I'M JOINING A TEAM NAMED AFTER YOU!
OKAY, LET'S FLIP A COIN. HEAD OR TAILS?
IS THAT YOUR MAGNETIC DOUBLE-HEADED 50p PIECE, ROGER?
OKAY, TELL YOU WHAT, TO BE FAIR, YOU LEND ME 50p.
I ONLY HAVE 40p.
THAT'S OKAY . . .
KEVF
THE END
HANDS UP WHO LOVES DRAWING CALAMITY JAMES

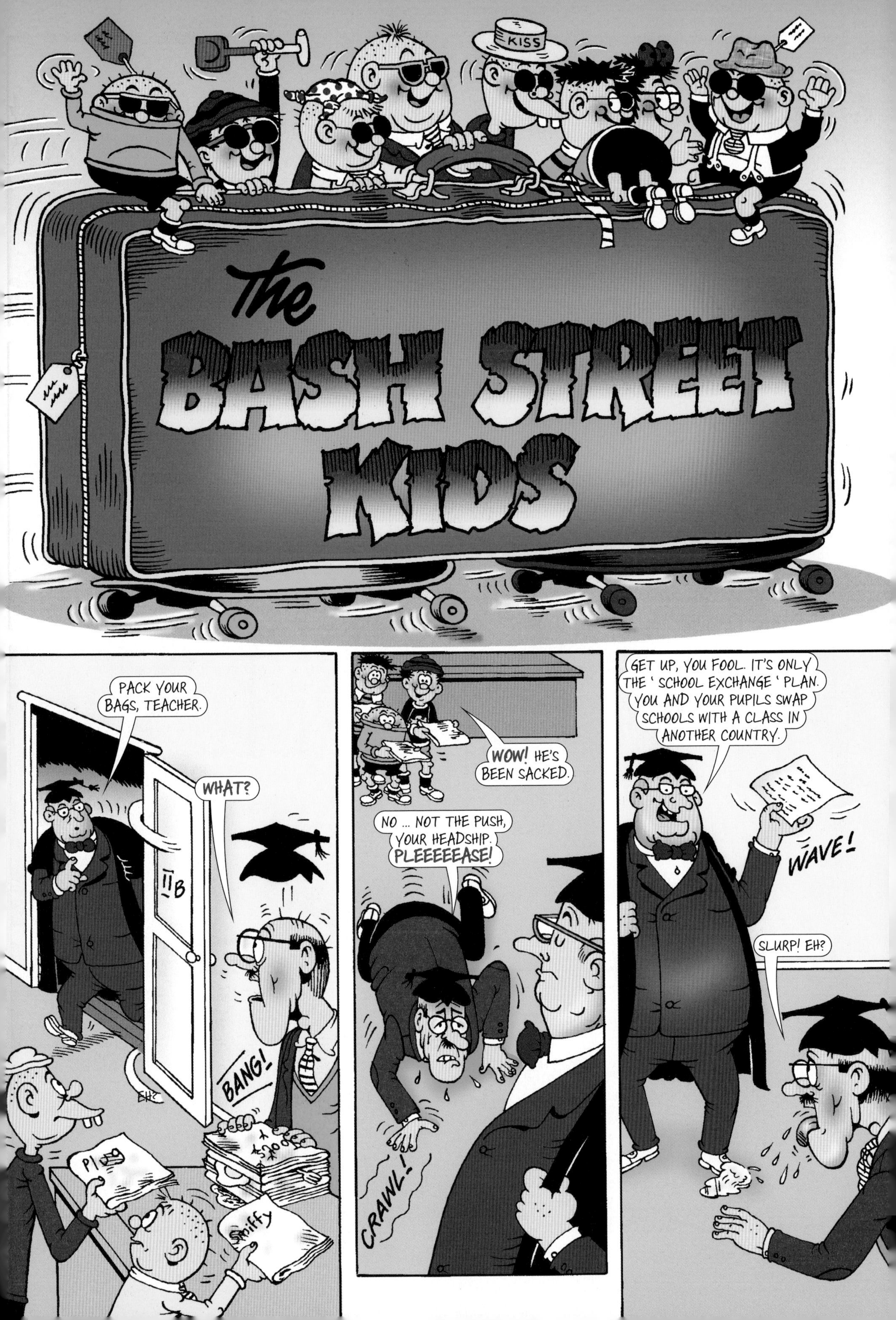
KISS
the BASH STREET KIDS
PACK YOUR BAGS, TEACHER.
WHAT?
!!B
BANG!
EH?
WOW! HE'S BEEN SACKED.
NO ... NOT THE PUSH, YOUR HEADSHIP. PLEEEEEASE!
CRAWL!
GET UP, YOU FOOL. IT'S ONLY THE ' SCHOOL EXCHANGE ' PLAN. YOU AND YOUR PUPILS SWAP SCHOOLS WITH A CLASS IN ANOTHER COUNTRY.
WAVE!
SLURP! EH?
Smiffy

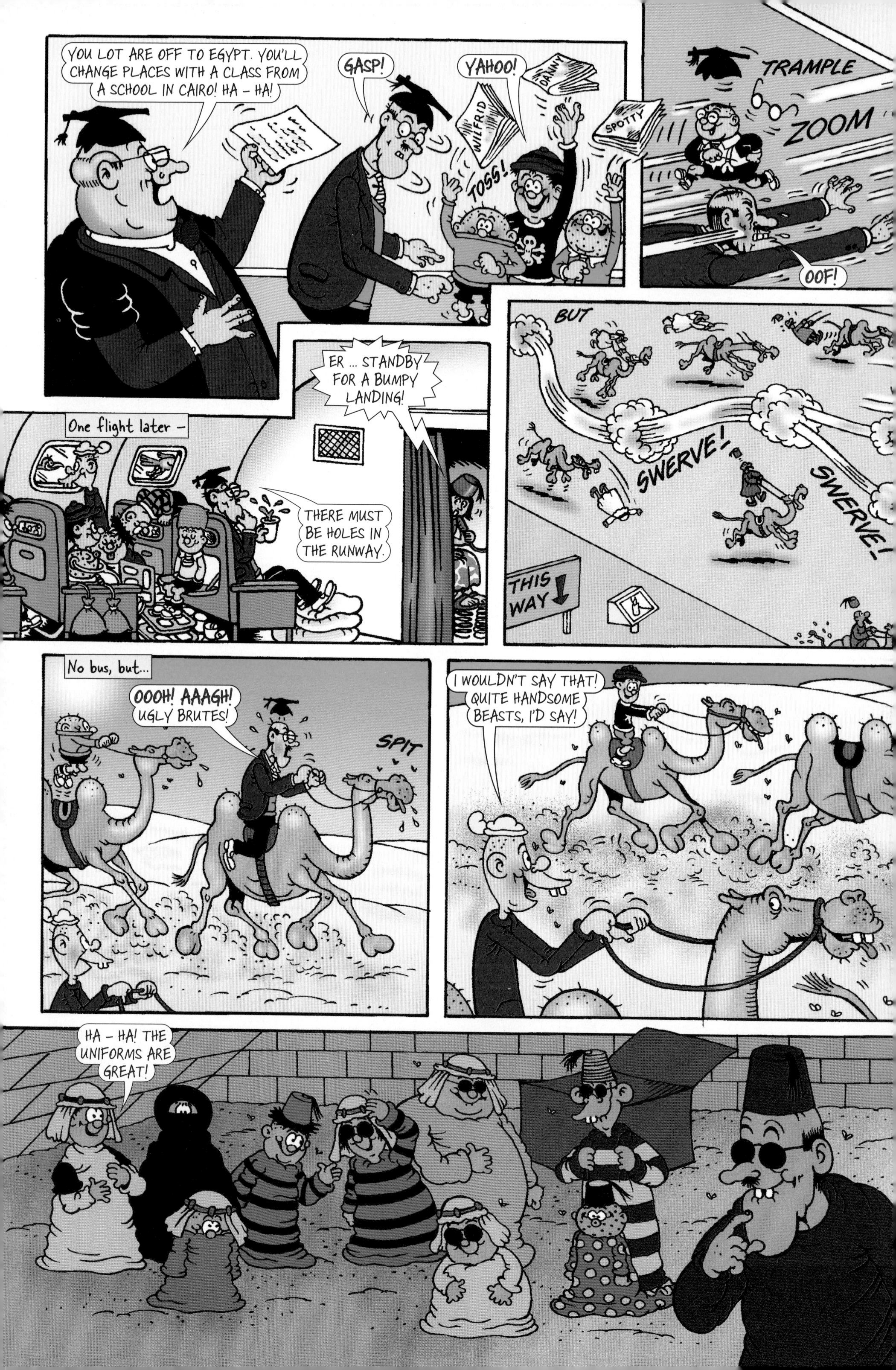
YOU LOT ARE OFF TO EGYPT. YOU'LL CHANGE PLACES WITH A CLASS FROM A SCHOOL IN CAIRO! HA – HA!
GASP!
YAHOO!
DANNY
WILFRID
SPOTTY
TOSS!
TRAMPLE
ZOOM
OOF!
One flight later –
ER ... STANDBY FOR A BUMPY LANDING!
THERE MUST BE HOLES IN THE RUNWAY.
BUT
SWERVE!
SWERVE!
THIS WAY
No bus, but...
OOOH! AAAGH! UGLY BRUTES!
SPIT
I WOULDN'T SAY THAT! QUITE HANDSOME BEASTS, I'D SAY!
HA – HA! THE UNIFORMS ARE GREAT!

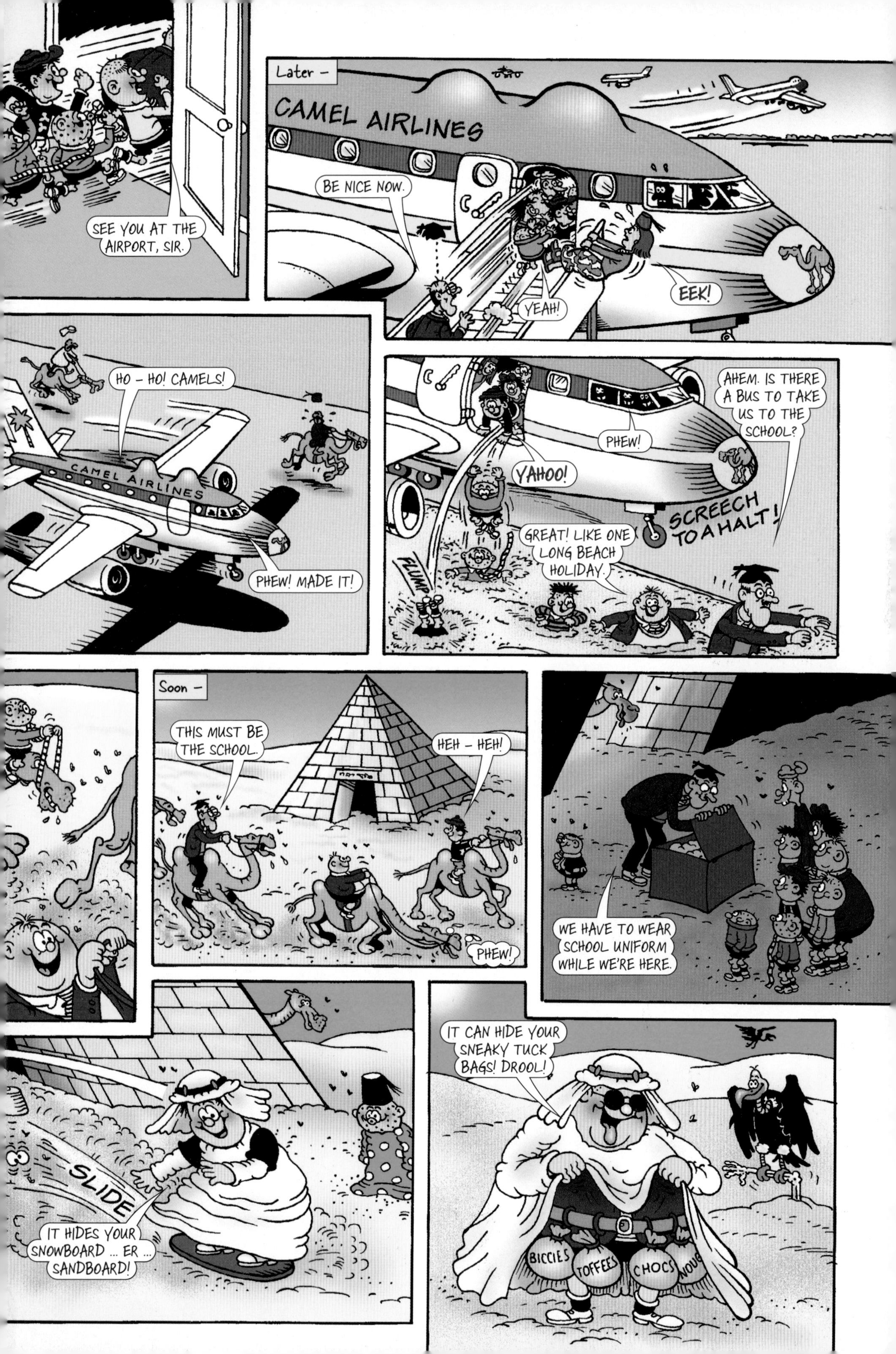
SEE YOU AT THE AIRPORT, SIR.
Later –
CAMEL AIRLINES
BE NICE NOW.
YEAH!
EEK!
HO – HO! CAMELS!
CAMEL AIRLINES
PHEW! MADE IT!
YAHOO!
PHEW!
AHEM. IS THERE A BUS TO TAKE US TO THE SCHOOL?
SCREECH TO A HALT!
GREAT! LIKE ONE LONG BEACH HOLIDAY.
FLUMP
Soon –
THIS MUST BE THE SCHOOL.
HEH – HEH!
PHEW!
WE HAVE TO WEAR SCHOOL UNIFORM WHILE WE'RE HERE.
SLIDE
IT HIDES YOUR SNOWBOARD ... ER ... SANDBOARD!
IT CAN HIDE YOUR SNEAKY TUCK BAGS! DROOL!
BICCIES
TOFFEES
CHOCS

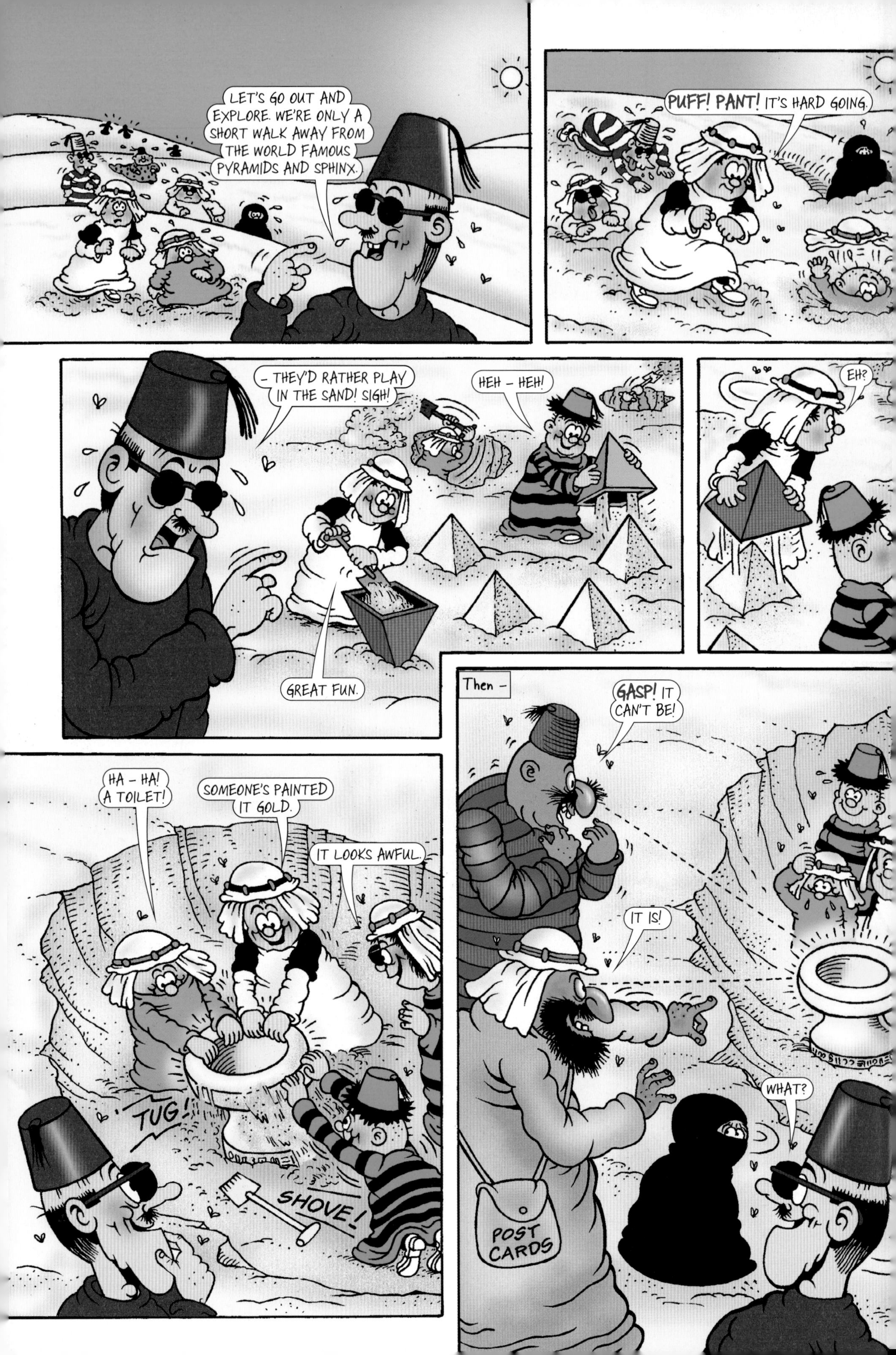
LET'S GO OUT AND EXPLORE. WE'RE ONLY A SHORT WALK AWAY FROM THE WORLD FAMOUS PYRAMIDS AND SPHINX.
PUFF! PANT! IT'S HARD GOING.
– THEY'D RATHER PLAY IN THE SAND! SIGH!
HEH – HEH!
GREAT FUN.
EH?
Then –
GASP! IT CAN'T BE!
IT IS!
WHAT?
HA – HA! A TOILET!
SOMEONE'S PAINTED IT GOLD.
IT LOOKS AWFUL.
TUG!
SHOVE!
POST CARDS

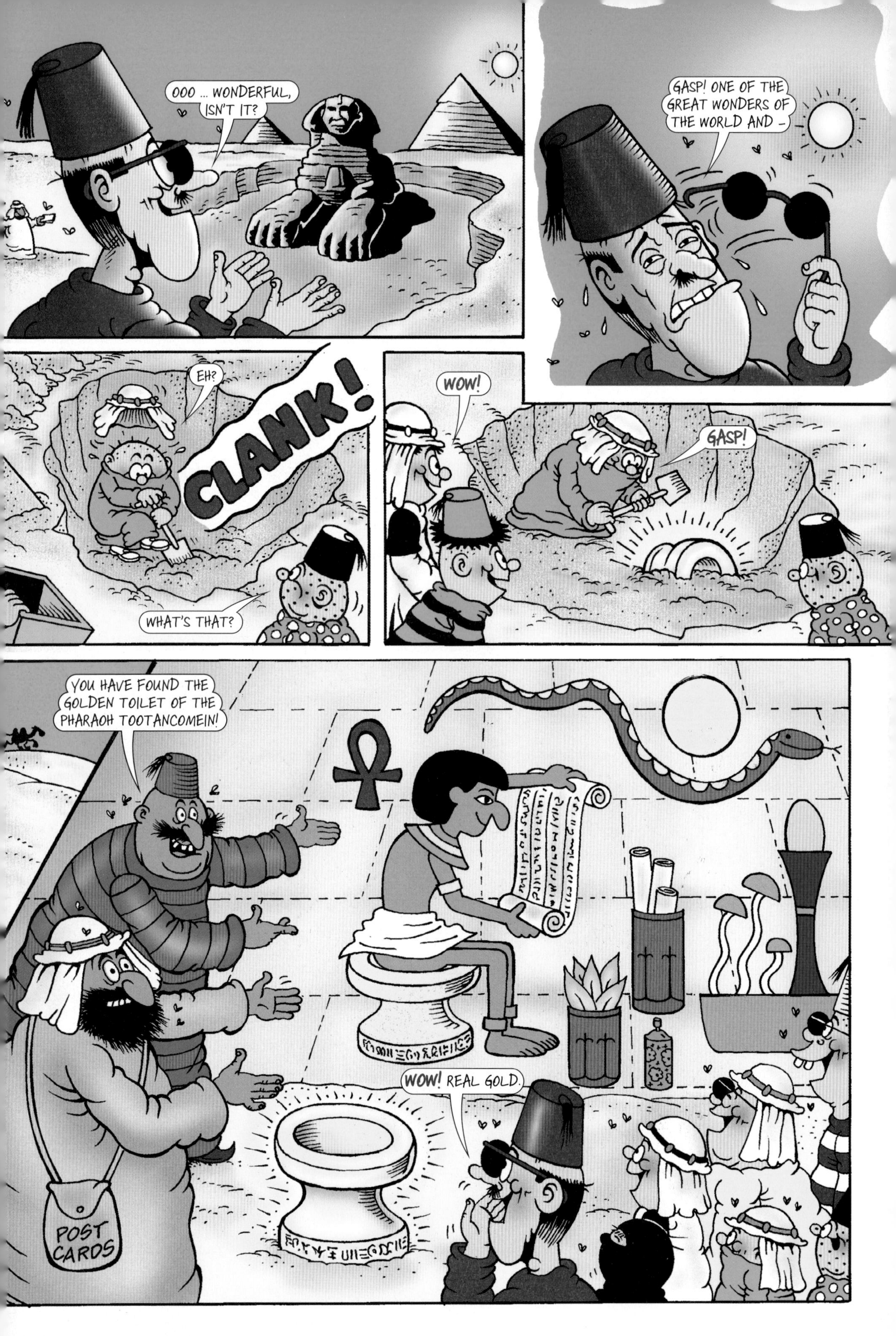
OOO ... WONDERFUL, ISN'T IT?
GASP! ONE OF THE GREAT WONDERS OF THE WORLD AND –
EH?
CLANK!
WHAT'S THAT?
WOW!
GASP!
YOU HAVE FOUND THE GOLDEN TOILET OF THE PHARAOH TOOTANCOMEIN!
WOW! REAL GOLD.
POST CARDS

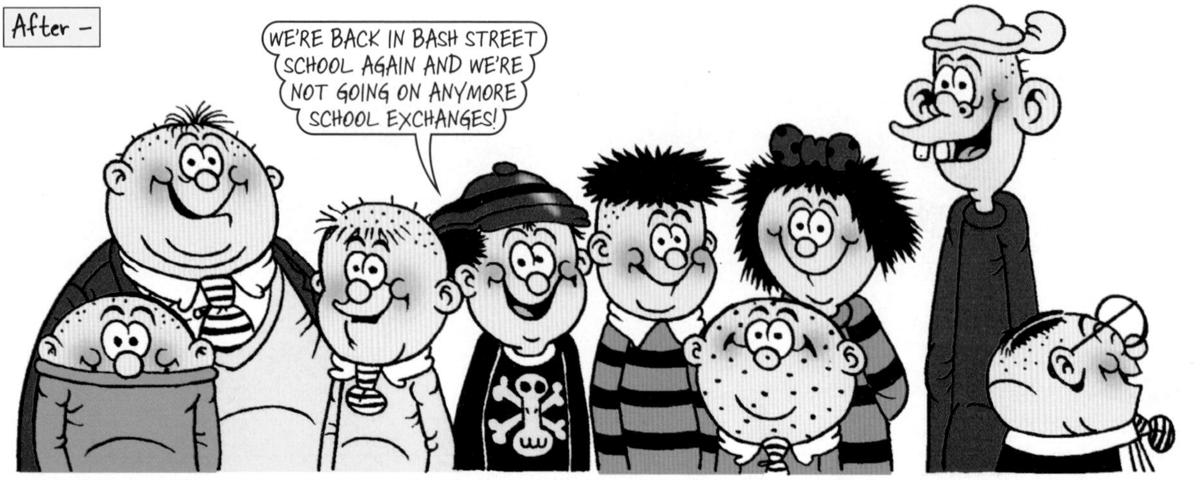
After -
WE'RE BACK IN BASH STREET SCHOOL AGAIN AND WE'RE NOT GOING ON ANYMORE SCHOOL EXCHANGES!

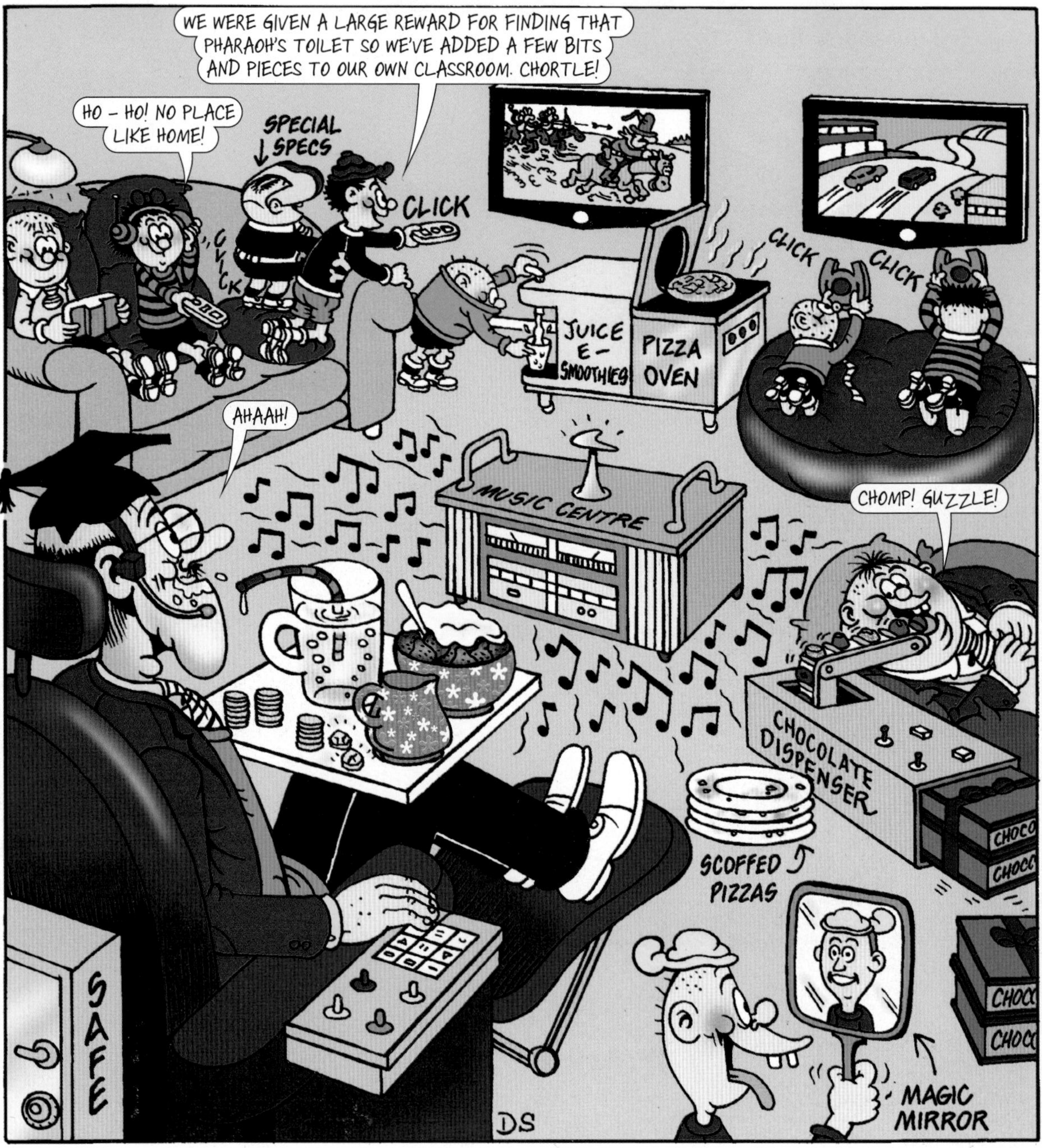
WE WERE GIVEN A LARGE REWARD FOR FINDING THAT PHARAOH'S TOILET SO WE'VE ADDED A FEW BITS AND PIECES TO OUR OWN CLASSROOM. CHORTLE!
HO – HO! NO PLACE LIKE HOME!
SPECIAL SPECS
CLICK
CLICK
CLICK
CLICK
JUICE E-SMOOTHIES
PIZZA OVEN
AHAAH!
MUSIC CENTRE
CHOMP! GUZZLE!
CHOCOLATE DISPENSER
CHOCO
CHOCO
SCOFFED PIZZAS
SAFE
CHOCO
CHOCO
MAGIC MIRROR
DS

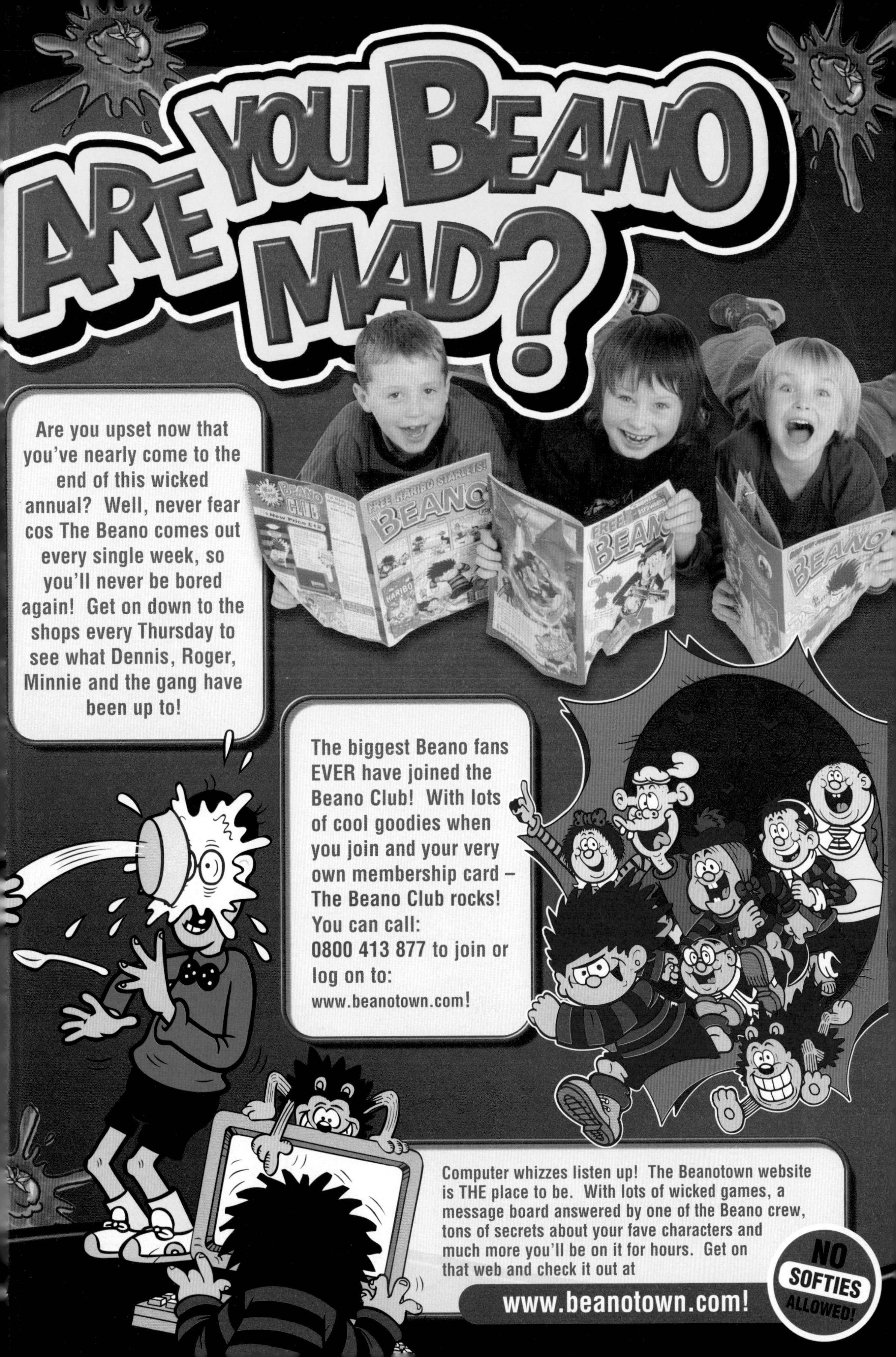

ARE YOU BEANO MAD?
Are you upset now that you've nearly come to the end of this wicked annual? Well, never fear cos The Beano comes out every single week, so you'll never be bored again! Get on down to the shops every Thursday to see what Dennis, Roger, Minnie and the gang have been up to!
The biggest Beano fans EVER have joined the Beano Club! With lots of cool goodies when you join and your very own membership card – The Beano Club rocks! You can call: 0800 413 877 to join or log on to: www.beanotown.com!
Computer whizzes listen up! The Beanotown website is THE place to be. With lots of wicked games, a message board answered by one of the Beano crew, tons of secrets about your fave characters and much more you'll be on it for hours. Get on that web and check it out at
www.beanotown.com!
NO SOFTIES ALLOWED!

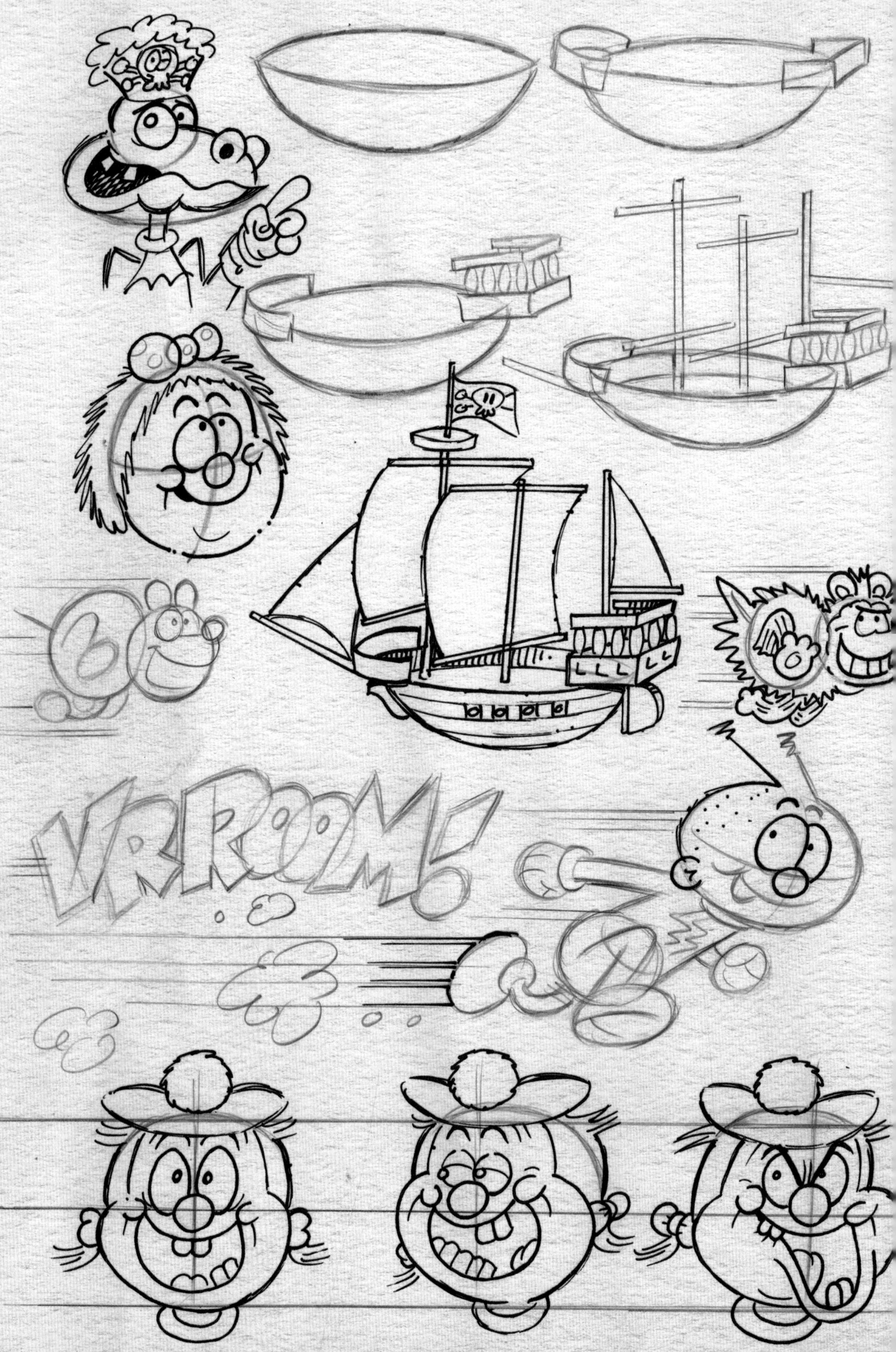
VROOM!